THE SAGE FROM GALILEE

THE SAGE FROM GALILEE

Rediscovering Jesus' Genius

David Flusser

with

R. Steven Notley

With an Introduction by

James H. Charlesworth

WILLIAM B. EERDMANS PUBLISHING COMPANY
GRAND RAPIDS, MICHIGAN / CAMBRIDGE, U.K.

First published in German as
Jesus in Selbstzeugnissen und Bilddokumenten
© 1968 Rowohlt, Hamburg

First English edition, under the title *Jesus,* © 1997 Magnes Press, Jerusalem
Second English edition © 1998 Magnes Press, Jerusalem
Third English edition © 2001 Magnes Press, Jerusalem
Fourth English edition, under the title *The Sage from Galilee,*
© 2007 Wm. B. Eerdmans Publishing Company

Published 2007 by
Wm. B. Eerdmans Publishing Co.
2140 Oak Industrial Drive N.E., Grand Rapids, Michigan 49505 /
P.O. Box 163, Cambridge CB3 9PU U.K.

Printed in the United States of America

12 11 10 09 08 07   7 6 5 4 3 2 1

Library of Congress Cataloging-in-Publication Data

Flusser, David, 1917-2000.
The sage from Galilee: rediscovering Jesus' genius / David Flusser with R. Steven Notley;
with an introduction by James H. Charlesworth. — 4th expanded ed.
p.   cm.
Includes bibliographical references and indexes.
ISBN 978-0-8028-2587-2 (pbk.: alk. paper)
1. Jesus Christ — Biography.   I. Notley, R. Steven.
II. Flusser, David, 1917-2000. Jesus in Selbstzeugnissen
und Bilddokumenten. English.   III. Title.

BT301.3.F58   2007
232.9'01 — dc22
[B]

2007012410

www.eerdmans.com

Dedicated to my Mennonite friends

Contents

Foreword

This newly revised edition of David Flusser's historical biography marks the tenth anniversary of the initiative by Magnes Press to publish in English Flusser's important German work by the same title. It also comes six years after Flusser's unwelcome death on his 83rd birthday, September 15, 2000. Wm. B. Eerdmans Publishing Company's decision to republish the work should surprise few. In spite of the difficulty and expense for readers outside of Israel to obtain the book, it has remained one of the best-selling volumes offered by Magnes Press.

When Flusser first asked me to assist in the republication of the 1968 English edition of *Jesus,* I assumed that it would merely be a task of improving and correcting the language problems that plagued that uneventful English version. However, I quickly realized that with the passage of almost 30 years, it would be necessary to rewrite the book, in effect creating an entirely new work. Not only had there been a wealth of new discoveries, Flusser's own thinking had evolved in light of this information. An early misstep fortunately has been corrected by Eerdmans in this newly revised edition. Because the title and author remained the same, readers were given the mistaken impression that the content was likewise the same. Yet, those familiar with the 1968 English version or its German counterpart recognized the vast differences between the two works. The 1968 English translation, long out of print, represented the beginnings of Flusser's investigation into the historical Jesus, whereas the present volume is its culmination. Rightly, Eerdmans has decided to publish this new edition under a new title. They have also fulfilled one of Flusser's oft-stated desires that the work appear in paperback, so as to be accessible to a wider audience.

In addition to the new title and paperback format, readers familiar with the previous editions in hardback will recognize other changes. The structure of the book has returned to its original twelve chapters. It was felt that the cumbersome supplementary studies disrupted the structure of the earlier work that has proved so widely popular in German. Most of the supplementary articles have appeared elsewhere in print. Only two of the studies were published solely in this work. Desiring not to lose the content of those studies, I have integrated them into the structure of the existing chapters.

The first study, "Jesus Weeps Over Jerusalem," examined the varying traditions in the Synoptic Gospels of Jesus' statements concerning Jerusalem's future. Scholars have given little notice to Mark's omission of Jesus' laments over Jerusalem. The Evangelist also removes any note of hope for the future redemption of the holy city. When read together with other trends in the Second Gospel, Flusser presents the reader with some unanticipated conclusions. I have integrated the contents of this study into the chapter "Jerusalem," which aptly deals with Jesus' final approach to Jerusalem and statements made by Jesus about the city during the days leading up to his arrest.

Flusser reckoned his other study, "The Stages of Redemption History according to John the Baptist and Jesus," to be the most important chapter in the book. As he related to me on more than one occasion, "If I had had this insight earlier, I would have written the book differently. Not that what I have written is mistaken, but I would have stated it differently." The study is not simply an investigation of Jesus and John's eschatology. Instead, it explores Jesus' place within the varying and competing streams of Jewish thought in the first century and highlights his own creative genius. It also contributes to our understanding of Jesus' high self-awareness. Since a central element in the study is Jesus' innovative use of the phrase, "the kingdom of heaven," I have integrated much of the study's content into the preexisting Chapter 7 on "the kingdom of heaven."

Interest in Flusser's prodigious scholarship has not abated with time. In the winter of 2005, John G. Gager of Princeton University devoted an article entirely to Flusser's investigation of Christian origins, lamenting that in "the English-speaking world of scholars who deal with the origins of Christianity" his work has not received the attention it deserves.[1]

---

1. J. G. Gager, "Scholarship as Moral Vision: David Flusser on Jesus, Paul, and the Birth of Christianity," *JQR* 95/1 (2005), 60-73.

Magnes published posthumously a two-volume collection of Flusser's Hebrew studies, *Judaism of the Second Temple Period* (2 vols.; ed. S. Ruzer; Jerusalem: Magnes Press, 2002). These volumes are currently being translated and will be jointly published by Magnes Press, Jerusalem Perspective, and Eerdmans in the near future. In 2006, the Jerusalem School of Synoptic Research, which includes colleagues and students of Flusser, published a collection of articles in honor of him and his two friends and research companions — Shmuel Safrai and Robert L. Lindsey — *Jesus' Last Week: Jerusalem Studies in the Synoptic Gospels — Volume One* (ed. R. S. Notley, M. Turnage, and B. Becker; Leiden: Brill, 2006). This collection also included an important unpublished article by Flusser, "The Synagogue and the Church in the Synoptic Gospels."

Like other students of Flusser, my own research continues to be shaped by my years with him. Seldom is the day when I do not lament my inability to pick up the phone and speak with him about some troubling text or fresh insight. I traveled in 1983 to study with Flusser at the Hebrew University, motivated by the notion that the issues of language, culture, history, and physical setting should make a difference in how we read the Gospels. My years with him did not disappoint. Too often, we Christians read the stories and sayings of Jesus with little knowledge of contemporary issues, personages, or nuances of language that provide such an important element in molding our understanding of his life and teachings.

Few scholars achieve Flusser's mastery of the classical sources and his ability to use them in such a way that the person and message of Jesus find fresh and simple clarity. It is even more rare to find an individual with such a passion for his scholarly pursuits. My wife can attest to the times when we were awakened by the telephone late at night, only to hear in the darkness Flusser's unmistakable voice on the other end, "Do you have your synopsis?" Sound asleep, the answer was obvious. He would wait as I climbed out of bed, retrieved my edition of the *Synopsis Quattuor Evangeliorum,* and then I would listen as he excitedly shared a new insight he had gained retracing a familiar passage. Any thoughts I had of inconvenience were soon overwhelmed by his excitement and desire to share his new discoveries in a late-night lecture by telephone.

Flusser's philological-historical approach calls for a reconsideration of how we read the literary sources. He has brought to bear the wealth of new information concerning the first-century setting in the light of the Dead Sea Scrolls, historical inquiry, and recent archaeological discoveries. What results from this biographical study is a portrait of Jesus that gains additional depth, because Flusser viewed Jesus within the context of contemporary Jewish thought and life.

Jesus was comfortable with the warp and woof of Jewish dialectic. Flusser demonstrates that Jesus was familiar with — and even remarkably skilled at — the sometimes intricate nature of Jewish hermeneutic. Yet, while Jesus echoes many of the sentiments of his contemporaries, it would be a distortion to ignore his distinctive contributions to the landscape of first-century Jewish ideas. Even so, what Flusser advances in this volume is a claim that even Jesus' most radical conclusions would have been unthinkable without the innovations of those in the generations before him and the nurturing environment of evolving Jewish thought.

Much has been written in recent years about the reclamation of Jesus by Jewish scholarship. It is difficult, however, to explain to those who did not know Flusser, what it was that made Flusser so distinctive. One feature that set him apart was that while he understood Jesus to belong fully to the diverse and competing streams of Jewish thinking in the first century, Flusser felt no need to deny Jesus his high self-awareness. In his understanding, the historical Jesus was both identified with his people and the cornerstone of the faith of the early Christian community.

Flusser did not hesitate to question the assumptions that are foundational to many contemporary New Testament scholars. He was an original thinker who was willing to consider afresh the evidence — even if it meant challenging long-held opinions, sometimes his own.

I am often asked why I traveled to Israel to study with Flusser. In answer I usually relate the following episode. In January of 1983 I spent a month in Jerusalem considering whether I should move my family there to pursue my doctorate at the Hebrew University. I had the opportunity to attend one of Flusser's evening classes, which regularly took place around his dining table. At one point as he was explaining a particular saying of Jesus, a student objected: "I studied with you two years ago and you explained this verse in an entirely different way." Flusser responded, "I hope that a man my age is still permitted to learn." Those who have studied with teachers who long-since ceased to engage actively their discipline will understand what motivated me to study with a man who opened texts each day with an unencumbered, fresh sense of discovery.

In the sixteen years that we studied and worked together, Flusser's appetite for learning was never satiated. Recently, another of Flusser's students, Hanan Eshel, related to me that one of the studies from his posthumous two volumes was written from his hospital bed days before his death. It reminded me of my own experience a few months prior. Flusser and I had been working on the revisions and additions for the third edition of *Jesus*. He was excited about new insights he had gained into Jesus' statement in Matthew 23:34-35. The day before he was to go into the hospital for routine tests, we met to begin work on a footnote for the book, but we were unable to finish for lack of time. Unfortunately, complications developed during the tests and Flusser slipped into a coma for several weeks.

When he awoke from his coma, the family allowed a few visitors. Upon entering the room, I saw him with an array of tubes that prevented him from speaking. He had a Hebrew spell-board, and with the help of his son Yohanan, Flusser pointed to letters to communicate with his visitors. When he saw me, he began to spell in Hebrew, "I have. . . ." We could not make out the next word. Then with his hands he drew a square in the air. For a few moments we were puzzled. Then it struck me that he was depicting a book. I ventured, "You have . . . a footnote for the book." He nodded. Flusser had apparently been mulling over in his conscious (and perhaps unconscious!) mind our discussion weeks prior about a new footnote regarding Jesus' words in Matthew 23.

Another characteristic of Flusser was his appreciation for "the historical Jesus." As Israel's foremost scholar on Jesus and nascent Christianity, he was often asked to give comment on "the Jewishness of Jesus" or to provide "the Jewish perspective." Few requests irritated him more. Flusser's close attention to philology and textual analysis cut against the grain of New Testament scholarship's penchant for "trendiness," in which Jesus is re-created in the mold of whichever psychological or political trend is in vogue. He reminded his students that his was not the study of "the Jewish Jesus" but the Jesus of history. That Jesus was Jewish is a matter of historical record. His optimism that careful philological-historical research could produce fruitful results in the study of the historical Jesus will surprise some skeptics.

Finally, whether reading Greek philosophers, medieval theologians, or the words of Jesus, Flusser did not work as a detached historian. He worked as a man of faith who believed his scholarship had relevance for the complex challenges of the present age. This facet of Flusser's character was illustrated by an incident that was related to me by Brad Young, who studied with Flusser for a number of years in Jerusalem.

Flusser had a student who went to study at the University of Zürich. When a professor there discovered that he was Flusser's student, he failed him without warrant. The failing mark ruined the student's academic career. A few years later, a student of that same professor was studying in Flusser's class. He turned in a paper, the content of which was mediocre. Flusser instructed Young, who was his teaching assistant at the time, to give the student an "A." When Young inquired why, he related the story of his own student and then repeated his instruction, "Give the student an 'A.' This I have learned from Jesus."

During my years of study and work with Flusser, I observed his desire not only to understand the teachings of Jesus, but to see their relevancy in difficult circumstances. On the eve of the Gulf War, January 15, 1991, the streets of Jerusalem were virtually empty in anticipation of the outbreak of war and the Iraqi reprisals, launching scud missiles on the civilian Israeli population. I went to Flusser's home needing to discuss my dissertation. Upon opening the door, he pondered aloud, "Interesting days we are living in. What would Jesus say? Let's go look and find out." Without further explanation we proceeded to his study and he invited me to open the New Testament to the passage of the "Two Swords" (Luke 22:35-38). He began to explain the words of Jesus, as if by understanding the relevant texts we could gain some glimpse into what Jesus might have thought — and by extension what we should think — about the current crisis. Flusser explained Jesus' delicate balance between pacifism — the avoidance of conflict — and the right to defend oneself. His exposition was concise, original, and pertinent to the current situation.

What struck me about Flusser then and still was not simply his insights into Jesus' teaching, but his assumption that the study of the words of Jesus should make a difference in how we conduct our lives. Of course, most Christians will find nothing remarkable in that notion, but many students will testify how exceptional it is to find a scholar whose research has relevance for life. I hope that my own contribution to this book has made it more accessible to its readers and strengthened Professor Flusser's desire that his biography "serve as a mouthpiece for Jesus' message today."

R. Steven Notley

Introducing David Flusser's Jesus

I am pleased that Bill Eerdmans has chosen to make available for a wider audience David Flusser's *Jesus* [the previous title]. I am also honored that he has asked me to write a new introduction to the book. I do so, remembering the many years David Flusser and I would sit in his home, not far from where his colleague, Martin Buber, lived, influencing all, including David and me, that we should see others in an "I-Thou" relationship of reverence. What do I remember most about Flusser? Ah, let me tell you.

The Man Called David Flusser

David Flusser was a featured speaker at many symposia in Jerusalem and elsewhere, including two I chaired: one on "Hillel and Jesus," and one on "Jesus and Archaeology — The Millennium Celebration in Jerusalem." The proceedings of the first was published by Fortress, the second by Eerdmans and titled *Jesus and Archaeology* (2006).

Flusser was engaging and often attractively emotional. He had a flair for the theatrical and dramatic. When he mentioned the Romans, who crucified Jesus in 30, he would often thrust a bent finger into his mouth and bite down. By this gesture he denounced the prefects (esp. Pontius Pilate) and procurators, and condemned Titus and the Roman troops who burned the Temple in 70, and Hadrian who turned the Holy City into *Aelia Capitolina*. Along with Flusser, I often feel disgust for the ways Romans massacred Jews, including hundreds of crucifixions, notably of the Jewish leader called Yeshua ben Yosef.

On January 7, 1993, David told me that he was bothered yet intrigued by the account of the woman accused of adultery (John 7:53–8:11). What should be done with this woman? Jesus is told that no one remained to condemn her. Jesus then admitted he could not condemn her. Why? The latter normative *halakot* demanded two witnesses. According to Flusser, Jesus sides with normative *halakot*. He lived when the process of defining *halakot* was developing. Jesus' life and decisions disclose the transitional stage toward normative *halakot*. He stated, "As a scholar I was pleased to open the window and see this insight." We agreed that the pericope of the woman caught in adultery warned about setting too clear a barrier between canon and other "scriptural" passages, since this section of John is where the so-called apocryphal New Testament appears in the canonical New Testament. We also agreed that this pericope has a very good chance of reflecting a historical event. Thus, we should be leery about assuming traditions recorded later (according to extant sources) must be devoid of historical insights.

Flusser's *Jesus*

What aspect of Flusser's *Jesus* is the most unique and important? I am convinced the answer is as follows: Flusser's perception of Jesus' concept of "love." On the one hand, he recognizes that Jesus' elevated concept of love rides on the crest of a wave in Jewish recognition of the importance of love, often based on an exegetical expansion on Leviticus 19. On the other hand, he applauds Jesus' exhortation to love our enemies, which represents the best morality found in pre-70 Judaism.

Jesus' injunction was placarded as absurd by Jewish exegetes at the beginning of the twentieth century. Montefiore rightly reported that Jews have been harshly critical of Jesus' exhortation to love our enemies. Most of us would agree that Jesus' charge to love our enemies sounds impossible and impractical. One can sympathize with those who castigate a teacher who would exhort his followers to be so defenseless in our hostile world. How can one do that? In light of our retina retention of towers burning on 9/11, and the promise to annihilate us from some in Afghanistan, Iran, and Iraq, just how can we really "love our enemies"? Could we have been able to do that in Nazi Germany?

For Israelis, who remember the Shoah (or Holocaust) and vividly recall suicide bombers who have killed their loved ones, the injunction to love one's enemies seems idiotic and suicidal. For Palestinians, who believe Israelis have robbed them of their land and oppress them, it seems absurd.

One episode may indicate that in our time some have sought to love their enemies. Israelis have tried to love their enemies and have been successful. During the 1972 Olympics in Munich the Israeli athletes were murdered, two in the Olympic Village and the rest in Furstenfeldbruck Airport. Why? They were slaughtered because of Palestinian terrorists — led by a man named Issa (or Jesus). They were demanding that two hundred Palestinians be released from jail. The sports broadcaster, eventually after confusion and the announcement that all were safe, had to tell the attentive world, "They're all gone."

The Olympic flag hung at half mast. The civilized world mourned. How could anyone go on? Surely, it would be a lack of Wisdom to exhort us to love our enemies.

Peter Jennings who covered the event was asked how he was able to keep his wits during the terrorists' bombings known as 9/11. He replied, "I was at Munich in 1972." I also heard Peter Jennings say, "It was all so new in 1972. How we have changed!"

The Israelis had every reason to jeer when Palestinian athletes walked into the Olympic Stadium for the first time. It was in 1996 in Atlanta. What did the Israelis do? They stood and cheered.

Surely, we can go on, striving to love our enemies, remembering not only the vision and action of Israeli athletes but also the early Christian martyrs, especially Peter and Paul, Jews, who died trying to live out the message of Jesus from Nazareth — the Yeshua who brought out of the genius of Early Judaism a new, challenging, message.

His early disciples never imagined that what was happening in and through them would become one of the most powerful religions in the world. Maybe, just maybe, David Flusser was right to stress that Jesus' exhortation to love our enemies contains a power that might change the world. It is based, after all, on Leviticus 19.

JAMES H. CHARLESWORTH
Princeton
Christmas, Hanukkah 2006

Preface

The present volume not only reflects the truism that Jesus was a Jew and wanted to remain within the Jewish faith, but it argues that, without the long preparatory work of contemporaneous Jewish faith, the teaching of Jesus would be unthinkable. This biography of Jesus has grown out of my earlier work entitled *Jesus,* written in German and first published in May of 1968 by Rowohlt Taschenbuch Verlag. When writing the German edition of *Jesus,* I stood more or less at the threshold of my research into the origins of Christianity. Since that time I have learned a great deal and have written extensively on the New Testament, especially on Jesus. Thus, the present biography is far from being identical with the German work. I believe that *The Sage from Galilee* is not merely longer, but also significantly better than its German forerunner.

Herder and Herder published an English translation of the German edition of *Jesus* in 1969. Not being widely read, this translation was never reprinted and is no longer available. The German book, however, was reprinted repeatedly and translated into dozens of other languages. The uneventfulness of the English translation in comparison to the success of the original German edition and its translation into other languages led me to conclude that a new, improved English version of my work about Jesus was badly needed. I have not only corrected the numerous inaccuracies in the previous English translation, but I have found it necessary to include fresh insights drawn from both rabbinic literature and the Dead Sea Scrolls. Although thoroughly revised and augmented, the structure of the German original remains largely intact.

The illustrations are not identical with those which appeared in the earlier editions of *Jesus*. I have updated them to reflect the wealth of recent archeological discoveries in Israel and other places. Quotations from Josephus are taken from the bilingual edition of the Loeb Classical Library. The English translation of the Bible is taken mostly from the New International Version.

The German edition of my work was very well received in Europe, and encountered only slight opposition from some excessively conservative Christian circles. Their American counterparts should understand that, because of my Jewish background, I cannot be more Christian than the majority of believers in Jesus. My interpretation of the Gospels, however, is more conservative than that of many New Testament scholars today. I attribute my conservative approach to my training, which was neither that of a Jewish nor a Christian theologian, but of a classicist. My method is rooted in the discipline of classical studies whose interest is Greek and Latin texts. I am confident that the first three Gospels reliably reflect the reality of the "historical" Jesus. Moreover, I do not like the dichotomy made between the "historical" Jesus and "kerygmatic" Christ. I am not suggesting in any way that the texts should be read uncritically. This should become clear after reading the first chapter, where I briefly discuss my critical method.

My conservative approach to the Gospels also stems from my Jewish identity. As a Jew I have studied, as far as possible, the various trends within ancient Judaism. This course of study is very helpful for interpreting the Jewish aspects of the Gospels, particularly the words and deeds of Jesus.

I know that some readers will open this book in order to inquire what the prevailing Jewish opinion is about Jesus. I have not written this book to describe Jesus from the "Jewish standpoint." The truth of the matter is that I am motivated by scholarly interest to learn as much as I can about Jesus, but at the same time being a practicing Jew and not a Christian, I am independent of any church. I readily admit, however, that I personally identify myself with Jesus' Jewish worldview, both moral and political, and I believe that the content of his teachings and the approach he embraced have always had the potential to change our world and prevent the greatest part of evil and suffering.

Here a short explanation will not be out of place. As a boy I grew up in the strongly Catholic, Bohemian town of Příbram. The town was one of the great centers of pilgrimage in Central Europe. Because of the humane atmosphere in Czechoslovakia at that time, I did not experience any sort of

Christian aversion to my Jewish background. In particular, I never heard any accusation of deicide directed against my people. As a student at the University of Prague, I became acquainted with Josef Perl, a pastor and member of the Unity of Bohemian Brethren, and I spent many evenings conversing with him at the local YMCA in Prague. The strong emphasis which this pastor and his fellow brethren placed on the teaching of Jesus and on the early, believing community in Jerusalem, stirred in me a healthy, positive interest in Jesus, and influenced the very understanding of my own Jewish faith as well. Interacting with these Bohemian Brethren played a decisive role in the cultivation of my scholarly interests; their influence was one of the foremost reasons that I decided to occupy myself with the person and message of Jesus.

Later in life I became interested in the history of the Bohemian Brethren, and I discovered links between this group and other similar movements in the past and present. I have since had the honor to become acquainted with members of one such movement having spiritual links to the Bohemian Brethren — the Mennonites in Canada and the United States. When my German book on Jesus was first published, a leading Mennonite asked me if the book were Christian or Jewish. I replied, "If the Christians would be Mennonites, then my work would be a Christian book." What I have set out to do here is to illuminate and interpret, at least in part, Jesus' person and opinions within the framework of his time and people. My ambition is simply to serve as a mouthpiece for Jesus' message today.

This new study on Jesus would not have seen the light of day without the invaluable assistance of my former student, Dr. R. Steven Notley, professor of biblical studies at the New York City campus of Nyack College. He collaborated with me in correcting, revising, and augmenting the earlier English study, and he has added new essential contributions throughout the work. I also appreciate the initiative of Professor William Klassen of St. Paul's United College in Waterloo, Ontario, and a guest lecturer at the Ecole Biblique, Jerusalem, and Professor Brad H. Young of Oral Roberts University in Tulsa, Oklahoma. Nor can I forget the practical assistance of my student and friend Joseph Frankovic. I express special thanks to Dan Benovici of The Magnes Press, Jerusalem for his efforts. In matters of rabbinics, as always, I am obliged to my colleague and long-time friend Professor Shmuel Safrai.

DAVID FLUSSER

CHAPTER 1

The Sources

The main purpose of this book is to show that it is possible to write the story of Jesus' life. True, we have fuller records about the lives of contemporaneous emperors and some of the Roman poets. With the exception of the historian Josephus Flavius and possibly St. Paul, however, Jesus is the one Jew of post–Old Testament times about whom we know most.

Every biography has its own peculiar problems. We can hardly expect to find information about Jesus in non-Christian documents. He shares this fate with Moses, Buddha, and Mohammed, who likewise received no mention in the reports of non-believers. The only important Christian sources concerning Jesus are the four Gospels: Matthew, Mark, Luke, and John. The rest of the New Testament tells us almost nothing about his life.

The first three Gospels are primarily based upon common historical material, while the fourth Gospel, John, is correctly regarded as more concerned with presenting a theological perspective. The parallels between Matthew, Mark, and Luke are such that they can be printed in three columns to form a synopsis — hence the name "Synoptic Gospels" given to the first three books of the New Testament.

Is the absence of non-Christian documents an insuperable obstacle to learning about the life of Christ? When a religious genius appears within an environment that allows the precise documentation of his development and the circumstances of his life, there is always a temptation to try to uncover the psychological background leading to this religious phenomenon. However, such psychological studies are often unsatisfactory, because the Spirit blows where it wills. This is especially true of personalities who themselves are possessed by the Spirit. For example, who would dare to attempt a psychological analysis of the mystery of the personality of St. Francis? Our inability to provide a psychology of Jesus that would not sound a jarring note arises not so much from the type of sources at our disposal, as from the nature of his personality.

Even if objective documentation is plentiful, the most genuine sources concerning a charismatic personality are his utterances and the accounts of the faithful — read critically, of course. Together with these, the testimony of outsiders serves as a control. Let us take two modern examples. All that is significant about Joseph Smith (1805-1844), founder of the Mormons, can be learned mostly from his words and from Mormon documents.[1] There is also the case of the African, Simon Kimbangu, who performed miracles of healing in the Belgian Congo from March 18 to September 14, 1921. He died in exile in 1950. Following the Christian model, his followers believed him to be the Son of God, but the documents do not make it clear what he thought of himself. Because of the brevity of his public activity, no unequivocal answer can be given to the question of his own self-assessment.[2] The testimony of the Belgian authorities in the Congo is as helpful in his case as are the archives of the governor Pilate or the records in the chancellery of the high priest in the case of Jesus.

The early Christian accounts about Jesus are not as untrustworthy as scholars today often think. The first three Gospels not only present a reasonably faithful picture of Jesus as a Jew of his own time, but they even consistently retain his way of speaking about the Savior in the third person. An impartial reading of the Synoptic Gospels results in a picture not so much of a redeemer of mankind, but of a Jewish miracle-worker and preacher. There can be little doubt that this picture does not do full justice to the historical Jesus. Obviously such a picture did not require the Resurrection experience of the post-Easter church before it could be portrayed. A series of miracle-legends and sermons certainly cannot be interpreted to constitute a "kerygmatic" preaching of faith in the risen and glorified Lord, as most present-day scholars and theologians suggest. The only Gospel that teaches a post-Easter Christology is the Gospel according to St. John, and it is of less historical value than the three Synoptic Gospels. The

---

1. Fawn M. Brodie, *No Man Knows My History* (New York: Knopf, 1979).

2. See now W. Ustorf, *Afrikanische Initiative: Das aktive Leiden des Propheten Simon Kimbangu* (Bern: Herbert Lang, 1975). Nevertheless, the mystery of his self-awareness has not been resolved.

Jesus portrayed in the Synoptic Gospels is, therefore, the historical Jesus, not the "kerygmatic Christ."

For Jewish Christianity — even in later centuries when in general the church regarded Jewish Christianity's view as heretical — Jesus' role as miracle-worker, teacher, prophet, and Messiah was more important than the risen Lord of the kerygma. At an early date, the emphasis began to change among the Hellenistic Christian congregations founded by Greek Jews and composed predominantly of non-Jews. In these congregations, redemption through the crucified and risen Christ became the heart of preaching. It is no accident that the writings originating in these communities — for example, the letters of St. Paul — scarcely mention the life and preaching of Jesus.[3] It is perhaps a stroke of luck, as far as our knowledge of Jesus is concerned, that the Synoptic Gospels were written fairly late — apparently around A.D. 70 — when the dynamic creativity within the Pauline congregations had diminished. For the most part, this later stratum of the synoptic tradition found its first expression in the redaction of the separate Evangelists and was styled in Greek. If we examine this material with an unprejudiced mind, we learn from its content and its manner of expression that it is concerned not with kerygmatic statements, but with Christian platitudes.

Is it indeed credible to suggest that when the Synoptic Gospels are studied scientifically they present a reliable portrayal of the historical Jesus, in spite of the kerygmatic preaching of faith by the church? My research has led me to the conclusion that the Synoptic Gospels are based upon one or more non-extant early documents composed by Jesus' disciples and the early church in Jerusalem. These texts were originally written in Hebrew. Subsequently they were translated into Greek and passed through various stages of redaction. It is the Greek translation of these early Hebrew sources that were employed by our three Evangelists. Thus, when studied in the light of their Jewish background, the Synoptic Gospels do preserve a picture of Jesus that is more reliable than is generally acknowledged.

The question of the literary interdependence of the Synoptic Gospels is called the "Synoptic Problem." The scope of this book does not allow sufficient space to address this crucial issue thoroughly. My approach,

---

3. See the list in D. Flusser, *Judaism and the Origins of Christianity* [hereafter: *JOC*] (Jerusalem: Magnes Press, 1988), 621-625.

however, chiefly based on the research of the late R. L. Lindsey,[4] is that Luke preserves, in comparison with Mark (and Matthew when depending on Mark), the more primitive tradition. A critical reevaluation of the literary evidence thus indicates that Luke wrote before Mark. Mark then reworked the Gospel material and unfavorably influenced Matthew who followed Mark's version closely. Finally, it is important to add that Matthew, when independent of Mark, frequently preserves the earlier sources of the life of Jesus that lie behind Luke's Gospel.[5] Hence, Luke and Matthew together provide the most authentic portrayal of Jesus' life and teachings.

The present biography intends to apply the methods of literary criticism and Lindsey's solution to unlock these ancient sources. In order to understand the historical Jesus, it is not sufficient to follow the literary development of the Gospel material. We also need to possess intimate familiarity with Judaism in the time of Jesus. The Jewish material is important not just because it allows us to place Jesus in his own time, but because it also permits a correct interpretation of his original Hebrew sayings. Thus, whenever we can be sure that there is a Hebrew phrase behind the Greek text of the Gospels, we translate that, and not the literal Greek.

This book does not set out to build a bridge between the Jesus of history and the Christian faith. With no ax to grind, but at the same time not pretending to submerge my personality and milieu — for how can one do

4. R. L. Lindsey, *A Hebrew Translation of the Gospel of Mark* (Jerusalem: Dugith Publishers, 1973), 9-84; idem, *A Comparative Greek Concordance of the Synoptic Gospels* (Jerusalem, 1985), iii-xiv. See now the preface by R. S. Notley, *Jesus' Last Week: Jerusalem Studies in the Synoptic Gospels, Volume One* (Leiden: Brill, 2006), 1-16. The Gospel of Mark is not only rewritten according to the popular taste, even in a more vulgar Greek, but its author also betrays a gift of stylization of the content and of a successful dramatization. In this literary activity Mark is led by his own concept of the personality of Jesus; he describes Jesus as a supernatural, lonely, holy man and wonder-worker, different from all other contemporaries. They are not able to understand him, not even his inner circle. This tendency of Mark reaches a climax at the end of his Gospel, in his description of Jesus' crucifixion and death. Here not only do the Jewish people abandon Jesus, but it appears that the Crucified One deemed that his heavenly Father had forsaken him. Thus, I believe that the famous quotation of Ps. 22:1 [HMT 22:2] in Mark 15:34 (and Matt. 27:46) is a creative invention. By the way, in this point, and indeed in the whole chapter about Jesus' crucifixion, Matthew followed Mark.

5. See D. Flusser, "Die synoptische Frage und die Gleichnisse Jesu," in *Die rabbinischen Gleichnisse und der Gleichniserzähler Jesus* (Bern: Frankfurt am Main, 1981), 193-233; idem, *Jewish Sources in Early Christianity* (Tel Aviv: Sifriyat Po'alim, 1979), 28-49 [Hebrew]. I have discussed this also in my article, "The Last Supper and the Essenes," *JOC*, 204.

that when writing a biography? — this work seeks merely to present Jesus directly to the reader. The present age seems especially well disposed to understand him and his interests. A new sensitivity has been awakened in us by profound fear of the future and the present. Today we are receptive to Jesus' reappraisal of all our usual values. Many of us have become aware of his questioning of the moral norm, which was his starting point. Like Jesus, we feel drawn to the social pariahs, to the sinners. If he says that one should not oppose the wicked forces, he evidently means that by struggling against them one really only benefits the basically indifferent play of forces within society and the world at large (see, e.g., Matt. 5:25-26). This, I believe, is the feeling of many today. If we free ourselves from the chains of dead prejudices, we are able to appreciate Jesus' demand for an all-embracing love, not as philanthropic weakness, but as a realistic approach to our world.

The enormity of Jesus' life also speaks to us today: the call at his baptism, the severing of ties with his estranged family and his discovery of a new, sublime sonship, the pandemonium of the sick and possessed, and his death on the cross. Therefore, the words that Matthew (28:20) places on the lips of the risen Lord take on for us a new, non-ecclesiastical meaning, "Lo, I am with you always, to the close of the age."

CHAPTER 2

Ancestry

Jesus is the common Greek form of the name Joshua. In Jesus' day the name was pronounced "Yeshua." We find him named in ancient Jewish literature where he is sometimes called "Yeshu"[1] that, almost certainly, was the Galilean pronunciation. After the arrest of Jesus, Peter betrayed himself by his peculiarly Galilean pronunciation.[2] In those days, "Jesus" was one of the most common of Jewish names. For example, the ancient Jewish historian, Josephus Flavius, mentions twenty men with this name. The first is Joshua of the Bible, Moses' successor who conquered the Holy Land. Out of religious awe the ancient Jews avoided certain important biblical names such as David, Solomon, Moses, and Aaron, and it may be that the name Yeshua — Jesus — in those days had gained popularity as a kind of substitute for Moses.

Jesus' father and his brothers also bore very popular names. His brothers[3] were called James,[4] Joses, Judah, and Simon (Mark 6:3) — the names of the biblical patriarch Jacob and three of his sons. The names were as common in those days as Jack and Bill are today. Joses is short for Joseph — the name of Jesus' father.[5] Today it would be almost impossible

---

1. See the discussion by R. Travers Herford, *Christianity in Talmud and Midrash* (New York: Ktav Publishing, 1975), 35-96.

2. See Matt. 26:73; Mark 14:70; Luke 22:59.

3. On the view that Jesus' brothers and sisters were, in fact, his cousins, or children of Joseph by a previous marriage, see the excellent book by the Catholic scholar J. Blinzler, *Die Brüder und Schwestern Jesu* (Stuttgart: Verlag Katholisches Bibelwerk, 1967).

4. "James" is the anglicized form of the Hebrew and Greek name "Jacob." He seemingly was named for his grandfather, Jacob, the father of Joseph (cf. Matt. 1:15).

5. See e.g., Luke 1:59.

for a Jewish child to be named after his father, if the latter were still living. In ancient times, however, this was a fairly widespread custom. Jesus' mother was called Mary, which corresponds to the Hebrew, Miriam, another common name in those days. Although we know few women's names from ancient times — none of the names of Jesus' sisters have come down to us — Josephus mentions eight women called Miriam. The first is the sister of Moses, and the others are all named after her.

The miraculous account of Jesus' birth is to be found in the two independent literary versions of Matthew and Luke. It is not mentioned in Mark and John and is not presupposed in any other part of the New Testament. Apart from the New Testament writers, the first to mention the virgin birth is Ignatius of Antioch (d. A.D. 107).[6]

As is well known, Jesus Christ means "Jesus the Messiah." According to ancient Jewish belief, the Messiah was to be a descendant of David — the Son of David. Both Matthew (1:2-16) and Luke (3:23-38) provide a genealogical tree for Jesus leading back to David. In both of these genealogies, it is Joseph, not Mary, who is descended from King David. The most remarkable thing, moreover, is that Joseph's genealogies are to be found in those same Gospels — Matthew and Luke — that tell the story of the virgin birth. It would seem that neither of these Evangelists sensed any tension between the descent of Jesus from David through Joseph and the conception of Jesus without the agency of a human father. We should keep in mind that the two genealogies agree only from Abraham down to David.[7] The internal problems of both lists and their considerable differences leave us with the impression that both genealogies were constructed *ad hoc*, so to speak, in order to prove descent from David.[8]

It would have been quite natural that any expected Messiah be retrospectively legitimized by his followers as the Son of David. On the other hand, it has become clear that in Jesus' time there were indeed many real

6. Ign. *Smyrn.* 1:1.

7. See W. Bauer, *Das Leben Jesu im Zeitalter der neutestamentlichen Apokryphen* (Darmstadt: Wissenschaftliche Buchgesellschaft, 1967), 21-29. On the sonship of David, see A. Suhl, *Die Funktion der alttestamentlichen Zitate und Anspielungen im Markusevangelium* (Gütersloh: Gütersloher Verlagshaus G. Mohn, 1965), 89-94; F. Hahn, *Christologische Hoheitstitel; ihre Geschichte im frühen Christentum* (Göttingen: Vandenhoeck & Ruprecht, 1964), 242-279.

8. But see J. Jeremias, *Jerusalem in the Time of Jesus* (Philadelphia: Fortress Press, 1975), 276-277, 287, 291-297; J. T. Milik, ed., *The Books of Enoch* (Oxford: Clarendon Press, 1976), 257.

1. Bethlehem viewed from the south. The Church of the Nativity
is in the center of the photo.

descendants from the family of the famous King David[9] (as there are today many descendants of Charlemagne). In recent years there has even been found an ossuary designated for the bones of one from the "House of David."[10] So, knowledge that one was from the family of David would not necessarily legitimize a person for messianic claims. It is important to reiterate, moreover, that even though there were those in the first century who could trace their lineage to David, we cannot be certain that Jesus himself belonged to David's line.

Since Matthew and Luke provide the Davidic genealogy of Jesus, it is no surprise that it is they who set the place of his birth in Bethlehem, the city of David's birth. Nevertheless, here the two accounts display important differences. According to Luke 2:4, Jesus' family traveled to Bethlehem only because of the census. Before the birth of Jesus, they lived in Nazareth to

9. Jeremias, ibid. Davidic lineage was also attributed to Hillel the Elder (*y. Kil.* 9:3; *y. Ta'an.* 4:2; *b. Ketub.* 62:2).

10. Flusser, "'The House of David' on an Ossuary," *Israel Museum Journal* 5 (1986), 37-40.

which they returned. According to Matthew 2:23, however, the family resided in Bethlehem in Judea before the birth of Jesus and settled in Nazareth only after their return from Egypt.[11] It would seem, then, that both the
tradition that Jesus was born in Bethlehem, and the proof of his Davidic an-
cestry, arose because many believed that the Messiah would be of David's
line and would, like David, be born in Bethlehem. This follows plainly from
John 7:41-42. The passage tells of some who denied that Jesus was the Messiah, saying, "Is the Christ to come from Galilee? Has not the scripture said
that the Christ is descended from David, and comes from Bethlehem, the
village where David was?" John, therefore, knew neither that Jesus had been
born in Bethlehem, nor that he was descended from David. At the same
time, this incident shows how people demanded the fulfillment of these two
conditions as legitimization of the messianic claim.

Historically, Jesus was a Galilean Jew who was probably born in Nazareth. Certainly that was where he lived for about thirty years until the time
of his baptism by John (Luke 3:23). He was baptized in either A.D. 27/28 or
A.D. 28/29.[12] It is more difficult to determine the duration of his public
ministry, namely, the period between his baptism and crucifixion. On the
evidence of the first three Gospels, it appears that this period extended not
more than one year. Following John, on the other hand, we would have to
assume that it covered two, or even three years. It has become fairly clear
today that John, the theologian, had little intention of being a historian,
and thus it would be unwise to accept his chronology or his geographical
framework without careful examination.[13]

At the same time, we have to ask whether even the first three Gospels intended to provide a historical and geographical scheme, or to
what extent such a scheme was conditioned by the theological presuppositions of the individual Evangelists.[14] There is material evidence to

11. See Bauer, op. cit., 59.

12. On the chronology of Jesus, see M. Dibelius, *From Tradition to Gospel* (New York:
Scribner, 1965); K. L. Schmidt, *Der Rahmen der Geschichte Jesu: literarkritische Untersuchungen zur ältesten Jesus-überlieferung* (Darmstadt: Wissenschaftliche Buchgesellschaft,
1964), 1-17; Bauer, op. cit., 279-310.

13. On the historical value of St. John's Gospel, see C. H. Dodd, *Historical Tradition in
the Fourth Gospel* (New York: Cambridge University Press, 1963).

14. On Mark, see W. Marxsen, *Der Evangelist Markus* (Göttingen: Vandenhoeck &
Ruprecht, 1959). On Luke, see H. Conzelmann, *The Theology of St. Luke* (New York: Harper,
1961).

2. Nazareth today.

suggest that on these chronological and geographical points the Synoptists are to be trusted. Jesus may have ministered in Judea and in Jerusalem before his final journey to death, but his real sphere of operation was in Galilee on the northwest shore of Lake Gennesaret. It will also become evident that the events of Jesus' life are best understood on the presumption that the baptism and the crucifixion were separated by only a short space of time. There are scholars who suggest that Jesus died at Easter in the year 30 or 33. Most likely, Jesus was baptized in A.D. 28/29 and died in A.D. 30.

As we have mentioned, Jesus had four brothers and several sisters. The family at Nazareth, therefore, included at least seven children. If one accepts the virgin birth as historical and also concedes that the brethren of Jesus were his true brothers and sisters, one must conclude that Jesus was Mary's first-born child. Even those who regard the birth narratives of Matthew and Luke as unhistorical must admit that Jesus may well have been the eldest of the family. Luke (2:22-24) reports that the parents of Jesus took him to Jerusalem shortly after his birth to present him to the Lord, as the law prescribed, "Every male that opens the womb shall be called holy to the Lord." It is true that one could redeem one's first-born through an offering to a priest anywhere,[15] but there were devout people who took this opportunity to make a pilgrimage with their son to the Temple in Jerusalem. Did Luke or his source invent this story to proclaim the virgin birth, or was Jesus, in fact, Mary's eldest child?

It is almost certain that Jesus' father died before Jesus was baptized. He may have died when Jesus was still a child. When Jesus' public ministry begins, we meet his mother and his brethren, but there is no mention of his father. According to Luke (2:41-51), Joseph was still alive when Jesus was twelve years old.

> Now his parents went to Jerusalem every year at the feast of the Passover. And when he was twelve years old, they went up according to the custom; and when the feast was ended, as they were returning, the boy Jesus stayed behind in Jerusalem. His parents did not know it, but supposing him to be in the company they went a day's journey, and they sought him among their kinsfolk and acquaintances; and when they did not find him, they returned to Jerusalem, seeking him. After three days they found him in the temple, sitting among the teachers, listening to them and asking them questions; and all who heard him were amazed at his understanding and his answers.

This anecdote from the childhood of Jesus has special significance. It is a story of a precocious scholar, one might almost say of a young talmudist. Today a Jewish boy is regarded as an adult when he turns thirteen, but in those days a boy of twelve could be regarded as grown up. Luke's story may well be true. I myself have heard the widow of a great rabbinic scholar, A. Aptowitzer, tell how her husband was lost when his parents were visiting an annual fair. In the early hours of the morning, they found him in a synagogue keenly disputing scholarly problems with the rabbis. This woman had certainly never read St. Luke. If I am not mistaken, the Indian philosopher Gupta tells a similar story in his autobiography.[16]

---

15. Num. 18:15.

16. The Jewish historian Josephus Flavius provides a similar anecdote about himself: "While still a mere boy, about fourteen years old, I won universal applause for my love of letters; insomuch that the chief priests and the leading men of the city used constantly to come to me for precise information about some particular in our ordinances" (*Life* 9). Compare also the legends by Josephus and Philo about the precocity of young Moses (*Ant.* 2:230-237; *Mos.* 1:5).

The account Luke tells of the boy does not contradict the rest of what we know about Jesus' Jewish education. It may be suggested with some justification that Jesus' disciples were "uneducated, common men" (Acts 4:13). This led to the assertion — made, indeed, by the historically less reliable John (7:15) — that Jesus himself was uneducated, that he had "never studied." When Jesus' sayings are examined against the background of contemporaneous Jewish learning, however, it is easy to observe that Jesus was far from uneducated. He was perfectly at home both in holy scripture and in oral tradition, and he knew how to apply this scholarly heritage. Moreover, Jesus' Jewish education was incomparably superior to that of St. Paul.

Can we say that Jesus was one of the Jewish Sages of his days? This at least is the conclusion of Josephus Flavius some decades after the Cross. Although it is generally recognized that the passage concerning Jesus in the extant Greek manuscripts of his *Jewish Antiquities* (18:63-64) was distorted by later Christian hands, "the most probable view seems to be that our text represents substantially what Josephus wrote, but that some alterations have been made by a Christian interpolator."[17] As we will see below, the original wording is not completely lost. One can already detect the method of the Christian revisor in the beginning of the passage. "About this time there lived Jesus, a wise man — *if indeed one ought to call him a man.*" It is precisely this unhappy interpolation that guarantees the authenticity of Josephus' statement that Jesus was "a wise man."[18]

Evidently by these words Josephus identifies Jesus with the Jewish Sages. The Greek word for "wise" has a common root with the Greek term "sophist," a term that did not then possess the negative connotation it has today.[19] Elsewhere[20] Josephus refers to two outstanding Jewish Sages as

17. See L. H. Feldman's commentary, *Josephus, Jewish Antiquities Books XVIII-XIX,* The Loeb Classical Library (Cambridge, Mass.: Harvard University Press, 1998), 49 n. b.

18. Josephus' definition of Jesus as a "wise man" is confirmed by the Arabic translation of the supposed original wording of the passage. S. Pinés, "Arabic Version of the *Testmonium Flavianum*," in *The Collected Works of Shlomo Pinés: Studies in the History of Religion* (ed. G. G. Stroumsa; Jerusalem: Magnes Press, 1996), 48.

19. The Greek word "sophist" also appears in rabbinic texts as a designation for a Jewish Sage. See M. Jastrow, *A Dictionary of the Targumim, the Talmud Babli and Yerushalmi, and the Midrashic Literature* (New York: Pardes, 1950), 968; M. Sokoloff, *A Dictionary of Jewish Palestinian Aramaic* (Ramat Gan: Bar Ilan University Press, 1990), 371-372.

20. *Ant.* 17:152; *J.W.* 1:648, 650.

sophists, and he regularly used this title to designate prominent Jewish Sages.[21] The Greek author Lucian from Samosata (born ca. 120 and died after A.D. 180)[22] similarly refers to Jesus as "the crucified sophist." I am not sure that Jesus himself would have liked being seen as a Jewish rabbinic scholar, but this is not very important for our question. What is important is that Josephus' reference to Jesus as "a wise man" challenges the recent tendency to view Jesus as merely a simple peasant.[23]

External corroboration of Jesus' Jewish scholarship is provided by the fact that, although he was not an approved scribe,[24] some were accustomed to address him as "Rabbi," "my teacher/master."[25] Nevertheless, it should be noted that according to the oldest sources, as reflected by Luke, only outsiders addressed Jesus as "Rabbi." Those numbered among the inner circle of his followers and those who came to him in need addressed him as "lord" (*ha'adon*). Apparently this is the title that he preferred. This we know, again thanks to the report of Luke: "How can one say that the Messiah is the Son of David? For David himself says in the Book of Psalms (110:1), 'The Lord (God) said to my lord' (לַאדוֹנִי), 'Sit on My right hand until I make your enemies your footstool.' David calls him lord (i.e., אדון). How then can he be David's son?" (Luke 20:41-44 and par.). The title should not be confused as a sign of his deity (i.e., *Adonai*), but an indication of his high self-awareness.

The epithet "Rabbi" was in common use in those days and was especially popular for describing scholars and teachers of the Torah. It had not yet become restricted to expert and ordained teachers.[26] The generation following Jesus was the first to employ the title as an academic degree. Jesus did not approve of the pleasure so many Pharisees took in being addressed as rabbi. "Do not call yourselves master (רבי), for you have but one master (רבכם, i.e., God); call no man on the earth father (or: Abba), for there is but one who is

---

21. See the note in *Flavius Josephus, De bello judaico. Der Jüdische Krieg. Zweisprachige Ausgabe der sieben Bücher. Bd. I*, ed. M. Otto and O. Bauernfeind (Darmstadt: Wissenschaftliche Buchgesellschaft, 1959), 425.

22. Lucian, *The Passing of Peregrinus*, chapter 13. See above, n. 19.

23. See J. D. Crossan, *The Historical Jesus: The Life of a Mediterranean Jewish Peasant* (San Francisco: Harper, 1991).

24. Matt. 21:23-27; Luke 20:1-8. See D. Daube, *The New Testament and Rabbinic Judaism* (London: University of London Anthlone Press, 1956).

25. Hahn, op. cit., 74-81.

26. Hahn, op. cit., 75-76.

your father in heaven, and you are brothers" (Matt. 23:6-12). In those days "Abba" was another common form of address. Even the famous Bar Kokhba was addressed in a newly published letter as חביבי אבא (Dear Father).[27] In the generation before Jesus, a scribe had said much the same thing, "Love manual work and hate mastery."[28] Many others shared this view.

Arrogance may have been prevalent among the scribes, but they were not effete academicians. They demanded that everyone teach his son a trade, and many of them were themselves artisans. Carpenters were regarded as particularly learned. If a difficult problem was under discussion, they would ask, "Is there a carpenter among us, or the son of a carpenter, who can solve the problem for us?"[29] Jesus was a carpenter and/or the son of a carpenter.[30] This in itself is no proof that either he or his father was learned, but it counts against the common, sweetly idyllic notion of Jesus as a naïve and amiable, simple, manual workman.

Nietzsche was right when he wrote, "The attempts I know of to construct the history of a 'soul' from the Gospels seem to me to imply a deplorable psychological frivolity."[31] There is, however, a psychological element in the life of Jesus that we may not ignore: the tension between Jesus' familial ties and his understanding of his divinely appointed task. This element is to be found even in the historically less reliable John. At the marriage feast in Cana, Jesus' mother asked him to produce wine, and he replied, "O woman, what have you to do with me?" (John 2:4).[32] In a recently discovered apocryphal narrative, this theme of tension between Jesus and his family is heightened almost intolerably. The source[33] reports that, as Je-

---

27. See A. Yardeni, *Nahal Se'elim Documents* (Jerusalem: ha-Hevrah la-hakirat Erets-Yisra'el ve-'atikotehah, 1995), 91-92.

28. *M. Abot* 1:10.

29. J. Levy, *Wörterbuch über die Talmudim und Midraschim* (4 vols.; Berlin: B. Harz, 1924), 3:338.

30. Matthew 13:55 and Mark 6:3 present different information concerning who is "the carpenter." Furthermore, it should be noted that Luke omits any mention of the profession of carpentry in connection with either Joseph or Jesus (cf. Luke 4:22).

31. F. W. Nietzsche, *Antichrist. Complete Works* (18 vols.; New York: Russell & Russell, 1964), 164.

32. The expression, which appears frequently in the Gospels, comes from 1 Kings 17:18. See also R. E. Brown, *The Gospel according to John I-XII* (AB 29; Garden City, N.Y.: Doubleday, 1966), 99.

33. Pinés, "The Jewish Christians of the Early Centuries of Christianity according to a New Source," op. cit., 271.

sus was being crucified, his mother Mary and her sons James, Simon, and Judah, came and stood before him. Hanging upon the cross, he said to her, "Take your sons and go away!"

The heightening of this familial tension is also present in the Synoptic Gospels. According to Luke 8:21, Jesus recognized the religious piety of his family: "My mother and my brothers are those who hear the word of God and do it."[34] Yet, he elevated the importance of those who believe. On another occasion we hear that "a woman in the crowd raised her voice and said to him, 'Blessed is the womb that bore you, and the breasts that you sucked.' But he said, 'Blessed rather are those who hear the word of God and keep it!'" (Luke 11:27-28).[35] Even so, Mark's version of Luke 8:21 exaggerates Jesus' own familial tension and reads as a rejection by Jesus of his family: "'Who are my mother and my brothers?' And looking around at those who sat about him, he said, 'Here are my mother and my brothers! *Whoever* does the will of God is my brother, and sister, and mother'" (Mark 3:34-35; cf. Matt. 12:46-50).[36]

Notwithstanding the evidence of the Evangelists' editorial creativity, Jesus clearly understood that uncompromising religious commitment sometimes results in breaking family ties. "Truly, I say to you, there is no man who has left house or wife or brothers or parents or children, for the sake of the kingdom of God, who will not receive manifold more in this time, and in the age to come eternal life" (Luke 18:28-30). To another he said, "Follow me." But he said, "Lord, let me first go and bury my father." But he said to him, "Leave the dead to bury their own dead. . . ." Another said, "I will follow you, Lord; but first let me say farewell to those at my home." Jesus said to him, "No one who puts his hand to the plow and looks back is fit for the kingdom of God" (Luke 9:59-62). There is one more pertinent saying that does not sound so inhuman in Hebrew as in translation. "If any one comes to me and does not hate his own father and mother and wife and children and brothers and sisters . . . he cannot be my disciple" (Luke 14:26).[37]

---

34. See J. A. Fitzmyer, *The Gospel According to Luke I-IX* (AB 28; Garden City, N.Y.: Doubleday, 1981), 722-725.

35. B. H. Young, "Messianic Blessings in Jewish and Christian Texts," *JOC*, 280-300.

36. Mark's version of this saying seems to be influenced by his unique and unreliable report a few verses earlier that Jesus' family had come to seize him, because "people were saying 'He is beside himself'" (Mark 3:21). V. Taylor, *The Gospel according to St. Mark* (New York: St. Martin's Press, 1966), 235-236; see also Schmidt, op. cit., 122-123.

37. In Hebrew the verbs "hate and love" can be juxtaposed to suggest preference (e.g.,

An emotion-laden tension seems to have arisen between Jesus and his family in Nazareth, and it would appear to have been this psychological fact — the background to which we do not know — that contributed powerfully to his personal decision that was so decisive for mankind. The impetus for his departure from Nazareth probably lies in the fact that his family regarded the mission that led Jesus to his death as a dangerous illusion (John 7:5). Jesus correctly suspected that his own kith and kin would not favor his mission, and for this reason he did not return home after his baptism, but went to Capernaum. Later, when he returned to visit his native town, he proved that *no one is a prophet in his own country* (Matt. 13:57; Mark 6:4; Luke 4:24; John 4:44).

What happened to Jesus' family after his death? An interesting report (Acts 1:14)[38] tells us that Mary, the mother of Jesus, and his brethren joined the apostles in Jerusalem. The Lord's brother, James, came to believe as a result of a resurrection appearance.[39] In A.D. 62 a Sadducean high priest murdered James for his faith in his brother.[40] The other brothers were later converted to faith, and with their wives they accepted the hospitality of the congregations (1 Cor. 9:5). Having recognized their deceased brother as the Messiah, the brothers of the Lord then realized that they, too, were of David's line. An old account[41] tells us that the Emperor Domitian regarded the grandsons of the Lord's brother, Judah, with suspicion because they belonged to the Jewish royal house. The emperor is supposed to have interrogated them in Rome, but then set them free when he discovered that they were only poor peasants. They were leaders of Christian churches, apparently in Galilee, and they lived until the reign of Trajan.

James, the brother of the Lord, was succeeded as head of the Church in Jerusalem by Simeon, a cousin of Jesus. After Jesus' death, his family, therefore, overcame their disbelief, and assumed an honorable place in the

---

Gen. 29:31). The apostle Paul was also familiar with this idiomatic usage, "As it is written, 'Jacob I loved, but Esau I hated'" (Rom. 9:13).

38. See E. Haenchen, *Die Apostelgeschichte* (Göttingen: Vandenhoeck & Ruprecht, 1959); E. Meyer, *Ursprung und Anfänge des Christentums* (Stuttgart-Berlin: J. G. Cotta, 1921-23), 44-45.

39. 1 Cor. 15:7; Gal. 2:9. On the history of Jesus' family, see E. Hennecke and W. Schneemelcher, *New Testament Apocrypha*, vol. I, *Gospels and Related Writings* (Louisville: Westminster/John Knox Press, 1991), 470-488.

40. *Ant.* 20:200-201.

41. Eusebius, *Hist. eccl.*, III, 11, 19-20, 32.

young Jewish-Christian community. We can understand their action. It might be dangerous, indeed, to live as the Redeemer's relatives within an ordered society, but if they lived within a messianic community they would find it more compatible. Despite her inability to understand fully her son, this was also the case with the mother of Jesus. From her point of view, Mary's worries were justified. The dreaded catastrophe came and her own heart was pierced by a sword.[42] Did she find complete consolation later through faith in her risen son, and in the hope that she would see him again?

42. Luke 2:35. But on the original sense of this verse, see my comments in "The Magnificat and the Benedictus," *JOC*, 128 n. 10.

CHAPTER 3

Baptism

In those days, John the Baptist[1] went out into the wilderness preaching a baptism of repentance for forgiveness of sins. The prophecy of Isaiah (40:3) was being fulfilled, "The voice of one cries: In the wilderness prepare the way of the Lord" (cf. Mark 1:2-4). For the Essenes, whose writings were discovered near the Dead Sea, this prophecy was also a call "to depart from the habitations of men of sin, to go into the wilderness to prepare the way of the Lord."[2] John's words were so close to that of the Essenes that it is possible that at one time he may have belonged to one of their communities. He left later because he disapproved of the sectarian separatism of the Essenes and wanted to offer the opportunity of repentance and forgiveness of sins to the whole of Israel. Crowds streamed from far and wide to this grim, austere prophet of the wilderness. They listened to his threatening penitential sermons, confessed their sins, and were baptized by him in the river Jordan.

John's powerful influence over the people led to his execution by Herod Antipas, son of King Herod the Great. Josephus reports,

1. For bibliography, see J. Steinmann, *Johannes der Täufer* (Hamburg: Rowohlt, 1960). On John the Baptist and the Dead Sea Scrolls, see W. Brownlee, "John the Baptist in the Light of Ancient Scrolls," in *The Scrolls and the New Testament* (ed. K. Stendahl; New York: Harper, 1957), 33-53; see also Flusser, "The Baptism of John and the Dead Sea Sect," in *Essays on the Dead Sea Scrolls in Memory of E. L. Sukenik* (ed. Y. Yadin and C. Rabin; Jerusalem: H. Ha-Sefer, 1961), 209-239 [Hebrew]; idem, "Baptism," *JOC*, 50-54.

2. 1QS 8:13-16; 9:19-20. The syntactical division that we have given in our translation best reflects the sense of the verse in the Hebrew Old Testament, the Greek translation of the Septuagint, the Dead Sea Scrolls, and even in the New Testament! In other words, it is not "A voice crying in the wilderness: Prepare . . ." but "A voice crying: In the wilderness prepare."

When others too joined the crowds about him, because they were aroused to the highest degree by his sermons, Herod became alarmed. Eloquence that had so great an effect on mankind might lead to some form of sedition, for it looked as if they would be guided by John in everything that they did. Herod decided, therefore, that it would be much better to strike first and be rid of him before his work led to an uprising, than to wait for an upheaval, get involved in a difficult situation and see his mistake.[3]

We can learn more about the death of John from the Gospels.[4]

The thing that most attracted men to John was the baptism he conferred. Many hoped that the immersion would expiate their sins, and thus they would escape the coming wrath of God's judgment. John, however, first demanded true repentance. According to Josephus, John was a holy man who

> had exhorted the Jews to lead righteous lives, to practice justice towards their fellows and piety towards God, and so doing to join in baptism. In his view this was a necessary preliminary if baptism was to be acceptable to God. They must not employ it to gain pardon for whatever sins they committed, but as a purification of the body implying that the soul was already thoroughly cleansed by right behavior.[5]

This understanding of baptism is exactly in line with the Essene view.

Traditional Jewish baptismal baths merely washed ritual uncleanness from the body. In the Essene view, however, a sin committed brings ritual uncleanness, and so, "no one may enter the water . . . unless he has repented of his evil, because uncleanness clings to all transgressors of His word."[6] Only he "who bows his soul to the law of God, has his flesh purified by the sprinkling of the purifying waters, and is sanctified in the water of purity."[7] Or again — almost in the very words that express the view of John the Baptist — water can cleanse the body only if the soul has first been purified through righteousness. But what is it in repentance that pu-

---

3. *Ant.* 18:118-119.
4. Matt. 14:3-12; Mark 6:17-29; see Luke 3:19-20.
5. *Ant.* 18:117.
6. 1QS 5:13-14.
7. 1QS 3:8-9.

3. Earliest known depiction of Jesus' baptism. This fresco was found in the late second-century crypt of Lucina in the Roman catacombs.

4. Large mikveh (Jewish ritual immersion bath) from Qumran. Photo by J. H. Charlesworth.

rifies the soul? "By the spirit of holiness . . . a man is cleansed from all sins."[8] In this way, Essene baptism linked repentance with the forgiveness of sins, and the latter with the Holy Spirit. Just as John's notion of baptism coincided with that of the Essenes, he also reflects their understanding of the Holy Spirit at work in baptism.[9]

We can well imagine the holy excitement of that crowd who had listened to the words of the Baptist. Having confessed their sins and awaiting the gift of the Holy Spirit to cleanse their souls from all the filth of sin, they plunged their defiled bodies into the cleansing water of the river. Can it be that none of them would have had a special pneumatic-ecstatic experience in that hour when the Spirit of God touched them? "Now when all the people were baptized, and when Jesus also had been baptized and was praying, the heaven was opened, and the Holy Spirit descended upon him in bodily form, as a dove, and a voice came[10] from heaven, 'Thou art my beloved Son;[11] with thee I am well pleased.'" Thus spoke the heavenly voice according to Matthew (3:17) and Mark (1:11). Yet many scholars[12] are right in thinking that in the original account, the heavenly voice announced to Jesus, "Behold My servant, whom I uphold, My chosen, in whom My soul delights; I have put My Spirit upon him, he will bring forth justice to the nations" (Isa. 42:1). This form is probably the original, for the reason that the prophetic word fits the situation.

The gift of the Holy Spirit assumed significance for Jesus that was different than for others who were baptized by John. Heavenly voices were not an uncommon phenomenon among the Jews of those days, and frequently these voices were heard to utter verses from scripture. Endowment with the Holy Spirit, accompanied by an ecstatic experience, was apparently something that happened to others who were baptized in John's pres-

8. 1QS 3:7-8.

9. Another opinion, dictated by apologetics, is to be found in Acts 19:1-7.

10. Luke 3:21-22.

11. The Greek word translates the Hebrew "the only one." See C. H. Turner, "Ho Hyios mou ho agapetos," *JTS* 27 (1926), 113-129; see also M. D. Hooker, *Jesus and the Servant: The Influence of the Servant Concept of Deutero-Isaiah in the New Testament* (London: S.P.C.K., 1959), 71, 183.

12. Jeremias, "παῖς θεοῦ?" in *TDNT* (ed. G. Friedrich; Grand Rapids: Eerdmans, 1967), 5:700-704; K. Stendahl, *The School of St. Matthew* (Uppsala: C. W. K. Gleerup, Lund, 1954), 110, 144; Flusser, "Blessed Are the Poor in Spirit," *JOC*, 110-111 and note 25; Hahn, op. cit., 340-346; Pinés, op. cit., 273. These scholars have seen that the end of Luke 3:21 and Matthew 3:17, "with thee I am well pleased," alludes to Isaiah 42:1, "with whom my soul delights."

ence in the Jordan. If Jesus really did hear these words from Isaiah, the phrase "I have put my Spirit upon him" was a wonderful confirmation of the gift of the Holy Spirit. There was something else, however, that possesses unique significance.

If we accept the traditional form of the heavenly message, Jesus is described as "My Son." If, however, the heavenly voice intoned the words of Isaiah, Jesus must have understood that he was being set apart as the Servant of God, the Chosen One. For him the gift of the Holy Spirit, which was part of John's baptism, held another special significance that was to become decisive for his future. None of the designations Son, Servant, or Chosen One were exclusively messianic titles — the last two could also denote the special status of the prophetic office. By these titles, Jesus learned that he was now chosen, called, set apart. Nothing that we have learned casts any doubt upon the historicity of Jesus' experience at his baptism in the Jordan.

According to Mark (1:9) and Matthew (3:13), Jesus came to John from his home in Nazareth. If we are to believe the words of the archangel reported by Luke (1:36), Mary was related to John's mother. We cannot learn any more than this about the psychological background to Jesus' decision to join the crowd and be baptized by John. On the other hand, if we use the documents properly, we can form a fairly clear idea of what happened to Jesus after his baptism and call. The only serious problem seems to be that we have no reliable report of the place of the Baptist's activities.[13] Moreover, this prophet of the wilderness did not remain in the same place. Perhaps John baptized John not far from the point where the Jordan enters the Lake of Gennesaret in the north. In the area is Bethsaida, the home of the brothers Andrew and Peter, whom according to John (1:40-44), Jesus met at his baptism.

The first disciples — Peter, his brother Andrew, and the brothers James and John the sons of Zebedee — were all fishermen on the Lake of Gennesaret. Peter was married to a woman from nearby Capernaum, where they lived in the home of his mother-in-law.[14] The disciple's

13. C. H. Kraeling, *John the Baptist* (New York: Scribner, 1951), 9-16; E. Lohmeyer, *Das Urchristentum. Johannes der Täufer* (Göttingen: Vandenhoeck, 1932), 26. See now A. F. Rainey and R. S. Notley, *The Sacred Bridge: Carta's Atlas of the Biblical World* (Jerusalem: Carta Jerusalem, 2006), 350-351.

14. Matt. 8:14; Luke 4:38. Mark (1:29) includes the doubtful addition that Andrew, James, and John also resided in the house. Matthew (8:14) and Luke (4:38) are in agreement in omitting Mark's expansion of "Peter's household."

mother-in-law became a believer after Jesus cured her of a fever. Her house became almost a second home for Jesus. Later, after the unsuccessful visit to his native Nazareth, Jesus returned to the district around Capernaum.

The geographical setting for Jesus' public ministry may result from the vicinity of his baptism and from his acquaintance with Peter. This is not a theological, but a strictly factual background. It is confirmed by Jesus' own words.

> Then he began to upbraid the cities where most of his mighty works had been done, because they did not repent. "Woe to you, Chorazin! woe to you, Bethsaida! for if the mighty works done in you had been done in Tyre and Sidon, they would have repented long ago in sack cloth and ashes. But I tell you, it shall be more tolerable on the day of judgment for Tyre and Sidon than for you. And you, Capernaum, will you be exalted to heaven? You shall be brought down to Hades. For if the mighty works done in you had been done in Sodom, it would have remained to this day. But I tell you that it shall be more tolerable on the day of judgment for the land of Sodom than for you. (Matt. 11:20-24; Luke 10:12-15)

The northwest corner of the Sea of Galilee was densely populated and well cultivated. Nearby Chorazin — whose wheat was famous — is not mentioned anywhere else in the New Testament. The wretched Mary Magdalene "from whom seven demons had gone out" (Luke 8:2) came from the neighboring Magdala. Many fishermen lived there and sailed routinely across to the east bank where fish were plentiful. Contrary to popular notions today, the inhabitants of this district were not rude backwoodsmen.

More important than establishing the geographical setting of Jesus' public ministry is defining the relationship between John the Baptist and Jesus after the baptism. Only after correcting some common misconceptions can we portray Jesus in his true significance. The root of the distortion lies in the chronology of salvation history[15] found in Mark. Because, in the Christian view, John the Baptist was justifiably regarded as the forerunner of Jesus, and because Jesus' entry on the scene did follow that of John, Mark makes John the precursor of Jesus in the literal sense. Thus, according to Mark, Jesus could appear publicly only after John had been ar-

---

15. J. Weiss in Schmidt, op. cit., 34. The psychological premise for the incorrect chronology in Mark is attested in Acts 13:25 (for the expression, see Acts 20:24).

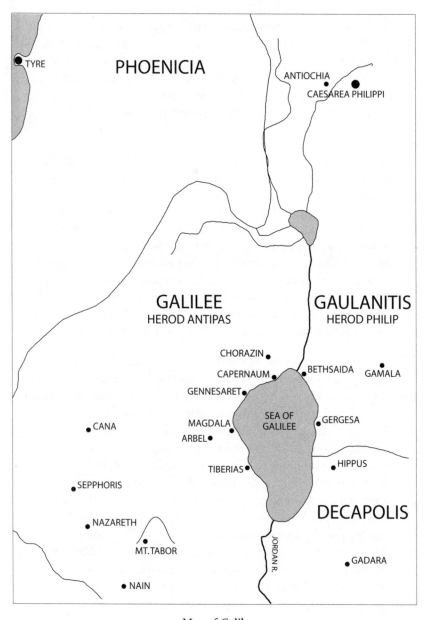

5. Map of Galilee.

rested. "Now after John was arrested, Jesus came into Galilee, preaching the gospel of God" (Mark 1:14).

Matthew goes a step further. He followed Mark's chronological framework (see Matt. 4:12-13) that assumed that John had been seized before the first appearance of Jesus. Accordingly, only after John had been imprisoned was Matthew able to portray John sending messengers to Jesus to ask him if he was the "one who was to come." Matthew's version "corrected" the original chronology under the influence of Mark. Thus, Luke 4:1 is right while Matthew 11:2 is wrong. Moreover, Matthew displays a tendency to conflate John's words with elements of Jesus' speech (and vice versa).[16] He thus puts Jesus' preaching, word for word, in the Baptist's mouth (Matt. 3:2; cf. 4:17). The change in the original chronology by Mark and Matthew and the new distorted order of events have given birth to unnecessary reconstructions of Jesus' beginnings.

Mark's mistaken chronology is usually taken to prove that Jesus' prime purpose in stepping into public life was to fill the gap left in Israel by the arrest of the Baptist. This impression seems to find confirmation in Matthew. At first, according to that Gospel, Jesus merely continued to preach John's message. If this were indeed so, it would have been the height of human tragedy that, shortly before his death, John, who had spent his whole life waiting for the Messiah, received news of Jesus' emergence, and sent messengers to him. No wonder that Flaubert described this moving scene in his story, *Herodias!*

Again, the original historical picture is altered first by Mark and Matthew for theological reasons, then through the psychological reinterpretation of many scholars. Yet, even the less reliable Gospel of John knows that "John had not yet been put in prison" (3:24). Luke and his sources, too, never report that Jesus appeared only after John had disappeared. Having now removed the secondary distortions, we can proceed to tell the story of the beginning of Jesus' public ministry.

John the Baptist certainly had a circle of disciples, but obviously most of the men whom he baptized in the Jordan left him after their baptism and went home. John did not want to found a sect; he thought it better to send each man back to his own trade (Luke 3:10-14). On the other hand, Jesus did not return to his former lifestyle after the voice at baptism announced his election. "From that time Jesus began to preach, saying, 'Re-

---

16. C. H. Dodd, *The Parables of the Kingdom* (London: Fontana Books, 1961), 39 n. 20.

pent, for the kingdom of God is at hand'" (Matt. 4:17). He called his disciples, taught in the synagogues, "and they brought him all the sick . . . and he healed them" (Matt. 4:17-25).[17]

It is possible that John the Baptist believed himself to be the prophet who was to come at the end of time. The people saw him as the biblical prophet Elijah who was to precede the Messiah. He himself preached that one would soon come who was stronger than he, and who would inaugurate God's judgment. When John heard of the excitement over Jesus in the villages around the Sea of Galilee — so the sources tell us[18] — he sent two of his disciples to inquire of Jesus. In those days, it was a Jewish custom to send not one but two men on a commission. Jesus, too, sent his disciples out in pairs (Mark 6:7; Luke 10:1), and Christians continued this custom on their early missionary journeys.[19]

John the Baptist asked Jesus through his two disciples, "Are you the coming one or shall we look for another?" The meaning of these words becomes clear when we read them in connection with the well-known verse from Daniel 7:13, "I saw one like a son of man *coming* with the clouds of heaven." Later on, in a separate chapter, we will treat the apocalyptic figure of the Son of Man. We will see that his main task in the eschatological future will be to separate the righteous from the sinners, to save the former and to cast the others into the fires of hell (see, e.g., Matt. 25:31-46).

This is precisely what John preached about the one mightier than he who *is coming* and "whose winnowing fork is in his hand, to clear his threshing floor, and so gather the wheat into his granary, but the chaff he will burn with unquenchable fire" (Luke 3:16-17; Matt. 3:11-12). The Son of Man is a figure that appears exclusively in Jewish apocalyptic writings, mostly in those that are close to the Essene movement. As we will see, Jesus himself also accepted this belief. Unlike the Baptist, however, he did not see the coming of the Son of Man and the last judgment as imminent.[20] His different perspective is expressed in the parable of the tares (Matt. 13:24-30; see also the parable of the dragnet in Matt. 13:47-50).

17. I have discussed the temptation of Jesus by Satan in "Die Versuchung Jesu und ihr jüdischer Hintergrund," *Jud* 45 (1989), 110-128.

18. Matt. 11:2-6; Luke 7:18-23.

19. A. von Harnack, *Die Mission und Ausbreitung des Christentums in den ersten drei Jahrhunderten* (2 vols.; Leipzig: Hinrichs'sche Buchhandlung, 1924), 1:344.

20. See Flusser, "Die jüdische Messiaserwartung Jesu," in the collected papers, *Das Christentum — eine jüdische Religion* (Munich: Kösel-Verlag, 1990), 37-52.

6. First-century fishing boat being excavated from the mud
near the western shore of the Sea of Galilee.
Courtesy of the Israel Government Press Office.

These parables stand in marked contrast to the acute eschatology of
the Baptist, heard in the above-mentioned metaphor in Luke 3:16-17 and
Matthew 3:11-12. Jesus' parable of the tares may have been meant as an indirect reaction to the words of the Baptist. According to John, the saving of
the righteous and the destruction of the sinners will take place in the im-

mediate future. Jesus, on the other hand, rightly saw that even in the period of the kingdom of heaven, which had begun to be realized, the good and the wicked coexist.

The idea of the Son of Man belongs to an apocalyptic system of thinking in which there is no place for the concept of the present kingdom of heaven. As we will see, the idea of the kingdom of heaven is particularly rabbinic, and it is well known that this idea is pivotal for Jesus. It is precisely here that we see the clear difference between the prophet of doom[21] and Jesus.

Jesus sent his reply to the Baptist: "Go and tell John what you hear and see. The blind receive their sight and the lame walk, lepers are cleansed and the deaf hear, and the dead are raised up, and the poor have good news preached to them. And blessed is he who is not wrong about me" (Matt. 11:2-6; Luke 7:18-23).[22] Jesus' doubts about the Baptist were justified. John never accepted Jesus' claim.

What is important is that Jesus affirmed in principle the Baptist's question about the eschatological meaning of his activities, without explicitly declaring that he was the coming Messiah. He established his claim to the eschatological office by pointing to his preaching of salvation and to his supernatural works of healing. Jesus saw these things as an unmistakable sign that the era of salvation had already dawned. "But if it is by the finger of God that I cast out demons, then the kingdom of God has come upon you" (Luke 11:20). Disease is of the devil, and the kingdom of God comes when Satan is conquered and rendered powerless.

According to Luke (10:18), Jesus once said, "I saw Satan fall like lightning from heaven." According to a book[23] that was written when Jesus was a child, "Then will his kingdom over all creation appear, Satan will be destroyed and grief will depart with him." The coming of the kingdom is thus bound up with the overthrow of Satan and his spirits. When Jesus heals the sick and casts out unclean spirits, he is the victorious conqueror who

---

21. Only in Matt. 3:2 does John the Baptist speak about the kingdom of heaven. "But Matthew cannot be trusted to distinguish between the words of John and the words of Jesus," Dodd, op. cit., 39.

22. See Isa. 26:19; 29:18; 35:5; 61:1 and the relevant parallel in 4Q521, fragments 2ii and 4, lines 6-13, especially line 12. See E. Puech, "Une apocalypse messianique (4Q521)," *RevQ* 60 (Oct. 1992), 475-522. Only the cleansing of lepers is lacking in the parallels. As to the last sentence of the passage, compare the end of Hosea.

23. *As. Mos.* 10:1.

makes real the kingdom of God.[24] "When a strong man, fully armed, guards his own palace, his goods are in peace; but when one stronger than he assaults him and overcomes him, he takes away his armor in which he trusted, and divides his spoil. He who is not with me is against me, and he who does not gather with me scatters" (Luke 11:21-23).

In addition to the miracles of healing, Jesus gives the Baptist a second proof of his claim. The poor have salvation preached to them. This is an allusion to words of the prophet Isaiah (61:1-2), which were especially important to Jesus. "The Spirit of the Lord God is upon me, because the Lord has anointed me to bring good tidings to the afflicted; he has sent me to bind up the brokenhearted, to proclaim liberty to the captives, and the opening of the prison to those who are bound; to proclaim the year of the Lord's favor, and the day of vengeance of our God; to comfort all who mourn." These were the words that — according to Luke 4:17-18 — Jesus read in the synagogue at the start of his ministry. Then he rolled up the scroll, handed it back to the attendant, sat down, and said, "Today this scripture has been fulfilled in your hearing" (Luke 4:18-21).

The words of the prophet ring out, too, in Jesus' beatitudes. He opens the kingdom of heaven to the poor in spirit and the meek, and gives comfort to them that mourn. It was to them that the good news of Jesus was sent. The word used in Greek was *euangelion,* derived from the verb used in the verse from Isaiah to denote the preaching of salvation (see Isa. 61:1; cf. 40:9; 52:7). For Jesus, this passage from scripture was the bridge between his calling — announced when John baptized him in the Jordan — and his present vocation. He knew that the Spirit of the Lord had come upon him, because the Lord had anointed him to proclaim salvation to the meek and the poor.

As John's messengers were departing to report Jesus' answer,

Jesus began to speak to the crowds concerning John, "What did you go out into the wilderness to behold? A reed swayed by the wind? Why then did you go out? To see a man clothed in soft raiment? Behold, those who wear soft raiment are in kings' houses. Why then did you go out? To see a prophet? Yes, I tell you, and more than a prophet. This is he of whom it is written,[25] 'Behold, I send my mes-

24. See Jeremias, *The Parables of Jesus* (New York: C. Scribner's Sons, 1963), 122-123.
25. Mal. 3:1.

senger before thy face, who shall prepare thy way before thee.' Truly I say to you, among those born of women there has risen no one greater than John the Baptist; yet he who is least in the kingdom of heaven is greater than he. From the days of John the Baptist until now the kingdom of heaven is breaking through, and those who break through, take it in possession. For all the prophets and the law prophesied until John; and if you are willing to accept it, he is Elijah who is to come. He who has ears to hear, let him hear." (Matt. 11:7-15)

Buber once said, in a conversation, that if a man has the gift of listening, he can hear the voice of Jesus himself speaking in the later accounts of the Gospels. This authentic note can, I believe, be detected in Jesus' comments regarding the Baptist. These are at once simple and profound, naive and full of paradox, tempestuous and yet calm. Can anyone plumb their ultimate depths? Jesus was addressing those who had made their pilgrimage out into the wilderness to see the new prophet. That was no place to find finely clothed courtiers, who live in palaces, and bend like a reed in the wind to every change of opinion. We observe that the imagery is taken from a well-known fable of Aesop,[26] with which the rabbis, too, were familiar.[27]

The reed outlives the storm because it bends to the wind, whereas a stronger tree, that refuses to bend, is often uprooted by the storm. Now we know who was the target of Jesus' scorn: Herod Antipas and his fawning courtiers, against whom the unbending, fearless desert prophet, dressed in a garment of camel hair, hurled his preaching of doom. It can surely be no accident that Jesus recast a fable of Aesop. Clearly he regarded the tetrarch and his court as a kind of "animal farm." Later, in Aesop's style, he was to describe Herod as "that fox" (Luke 13:32).[28]

26. See *Fabulae aesopicae collectae* (ed. K. Halm; Leipzig: B. G. Teubneri, 1875), nos. 179a,b,c.

27. H. L. Strack and P. Billerbeck, *Kommentar zum Neuen Testament aus Talmud und Midrasch. Das Evangelium nach Matthäus* (5 vols.; Munich: C. H. Beck'sche Verlagsbuchhandlung, 1961), 1:596-597.

28. Nevertheless, in Palestinian Hebrew and Aramaic the term "fox" was sometimes used to designate someone of insignificance. Thus, Jesus' nickname for Antipas should be read as a not-so-subtle insult directed at the Galilean tetrarch. See Jastrow, op. cit., 1538; Sokoloff, op. cit., 587; R. Buth, "That Small-fry Herod Antipas, or When a Fox Is Not a Fox," *Jerusalem Perspective* 40 (Sept./Oct. 1993), 7-9, 14.

In Jesus' view, John was a prophet, if you like, the one who was preparing the way of God at the end of time, the Elijah who was to return. With John, the end-time begins — the decisive eruption into the history of the world. All the prophets have prophesied until the time of John the Baptist; but from now on, "the kingdom of heaven is breaking through, and those who break through, take it in possession." These enigmatic words are connected with the saying of the prophet Micah (2:13). "He who opens the breach will go up before them; they will break through and pass the gate, going out by it. Their king will pass on before them, the Lord at their head."

A medieval commentator, David Kimchi, offered the following interpretation for this verse:[29] "The 'one who opens up the breach' is Elijah and 'their king' is the scion of David." According to this interpretation, an earlier form of which Jesus seems to have known, Elijah was to come first to open the breach, and he would be followed by those who broke through with their king, the Messiah. According to Jesus, Elijah-John has already come, and those men who have the courage of decision are now taking possession of the kingdom.

With John's coming, the kingdom of heaven broke through. Yet, although John was the greatest among "those born among women," the least in the kingdom of heaven would be greater than he. John the Baptist made the breach through which the kingdom of God could break, but he himself was never a member of that kingdom. We may state it another way. At his baptism Jesus was illuminated by the heavenly voice concerning the beginning of the messianic kingdom. John was the precursor, "the breaker," for the advent of that kingdom, but he himself did not belong to the kingdom. He was, so to speak, a member of the previous generation. This paradoxical insight on the part of Jesus highlights both the distinction between John and the messianic kingdom, as well as the historic link between Jesus and the Baptist. Nevertheless, Jesus' experience at his baptism invested him

29. B. H. Young (*Jesus the Jewish Theologian* [Peabody, Mass.: Hendrickson, 1995], 65-66, 73-76) remarks that Edward Pococke, *A Commentary on the Prophecy of Micah* (Oxford: Printed at the Theatre, 1677), 22-25, had already seen the connection between Matt. 11:12 and Mic. 2:13. Pococke's explanation is also based upon the commentary of David Kimchi to Mic. 2:13. See Flusser, *Gleichnisse*, 272-273; R. S. Notley, "The Kingdom of Heaven Forcefully Advances," in *The Interpretation of Scripture in Early Judaism and Christianity: Studies in Language and Tradition*, JSPSS 33 (ed. C. A. Evans; Sheffield: Sheffield Academic Press, 2000), 279-311.

with a new and separate function. Jesus could not become a disciple of John. He would have to move on to the villages around the Sea of Galilee and proclaim the kingdom of heaven.

Now we understand why Jesus' reply to the Baptist's inquiry ended with a warning, "Blessed is he who is not wrong about me." The Hebrew verb that in those days was expanded to mean, "to be led into sin, to go astray from the right understanding of the will of God," was rendered in the Greek of the Gospel literally "to stumble." Following a later document (1 Pet. 2:7-8), Jesus is, as it were, the touchstone, a cornerstone for believers, a rock of offense, and a stone of stumbling (Luke 20:18; cf. 2:34) for unbelievers. When the Baptist sent his inquiry to Jesus, Jesus rightly guessed that he could not go along with him, because John, the greatest member of the former generation, did not belong to the kingdom of God. It may even be that Jesus had concrete indications of John's hesitation. We are not told what the Baptist's reaction was to Jesus' message. Nevertheless, the movement he started carried on an independent life parallel to that of emergent Christianity (cf. Acts 19:1-7).

As we have seen, many thought that John was Elijah come again. The Old Testament itself tells us that Elijah never died, but was transported up to heaven. How, then, could this immortal one, having returned at the end of time as John, be irrevocably killed by Herod? There were indeed men who thought that John the Baptist had risen from the dead (Luke 9:1) and had reappeared in Jesus. It is obvious that many of John's disciples shared this belief in their master's resurrection. Nevertheless, John's own preaching rules out the possibility that he regarded himself as the Messiah. He looked for another to come who was greater than himself (Luke 3:16). Yet, there were those among his disciples who, even during his life, toyed with the idea that he was the greater. In any event, after his death there is evidence of belief in the Baptist as the Messiah. Clearly, however, because he belonged to a priestly line, he was regarded as the priestly, not the Davidic, Messiah.

The logic of the accounts requires that Herod must have been quick to see the danger that the Baptist represented. He did not leave him free for long. Jesus' activity, too, after John's arrest, was obviously restricted to a short space of time. Herod, the fox, had not been asleep. After he had executed John, "Herod, the tetrarch, heard about the fame of Jesus; and he said to his servants, 'This is John the Baptist, he has been raised from the dead'" (Matt. 14:1). Later, some of the Pharisees warned Jesus that Herod was seeking his life. Thereupon, Jesus sent word to Herod that he would spend two or three days more in the district, and then move on to Jerusalem, "for it cannot be that a prophet should perish away from Jerusalem" (Luke 13:31). As we shall see, Herod had his share in the blame for the crucifixion.

After John's execution, Jesus pointed out to his disciples the tragic connection between that execution and the end that threatened himself. "And the disciples asked him, 'Then, why do the scribes say that first Elijah must come?' He replied, 'Elijah does come, and he is to restore all things;[30] but I tell you that Elijah has already come, and they did not know him, but did to him whatever they pleased. So also the Son of man will suffer at their hands.' Then the disciples understood that he was speaking to them of John the Baptist" (Matt. 17:10-13).

Earlier than this, at the beginning of his ministry, when John the Baptist was still preaching in the wilderness, Jesus had compared himself with John the Baptist. "But to what shall I compare this generation? It is like children sitting in the market places calling to their playmates, 'We piped to you, and you did not dance; we wailed, and you did not mourn.' For John came neither eating nor drinking, and they say, 'He has a demon'; the Son of man came eating and drinking, and they say, 'Behold, a glutton and a drunkard, a friend of tax collectors and sinners!' Yet wisdom is justified by her deeds" (Matt. 11:16-19).[31] It was impossible to please anybody. They said that the ascetic desert preacher, John, was mad — as they said later that Jesus was using an evil spirit — and they found fault with Jesus, too, on account of his openness to the world. From this saying of Jesus we learn indirectly that the content of each man's preaching was closely linked with his character. The good news of love was related to Jesus' Socratic nature; penitential preaching was related to John's somber inclination toward asceticism.

---

30. Jesus alludes here to the tradition of the "scribes," reflected in *m. 'Eduyyot* 8:7.
31. Jesus evidently depends here on the fable of Aesop. See *Fabulae aesopicae*, nos. 27a,b.

CHAPTER 4

Law

Paul and his entourage "went through the region of Phrygia and Galatia, having been forbidden by the Holy Spirit to speak the word in Asia . . .; so, passing by Mysia, they went down to Troas. And a vision appeared to Paul in the night; a man of Macedonia was standing beseeching him and saying, 'Come over to Macedonia and help us'" (Acts 16:6-10).

This episode in Paul's mission to the heathen in the West was of enormous importance. It was the will of God for Christianity to spread westward into Europe. Christianity, thus, penetrated into the Graeco-Roman world and from there later became a European religion. In contrast to the cultural setting of Judaism and the religions of eastern Asia beginning with Persia, Western culture contributed to Christianity's de-emphasis on ritual or ceremonial prescriptions concerning "food and drink and various ablutions" (Heb. 9:10). In the European view one may eat whatever is sold in the meat market without raising any question on the grounds of conscience. For, "the earth is the Lord's, and everything in it" (1 Cor. 10:25-26).

One of the tasks taken up by Paulinism and other movements in early Christianity was the creation of an ideological framework based upon this concept of freedom from the law. In the course of Christianity's history, the superstructure has changed. On the whole, however, it has had to remain because this "liberalism" is an intrinsic characteristic of European civilization. Had Christianity spread first to the eastern Asiatic regions, it would have developed specific ritual and ceremonial practices based on the Jewish law in order to become a genuine religion in that part of the world.

It would be a mistake, therefore, not to recognize the unease experienced by many Christian thinkers and scholars. They have felt obliged to deal with the fact that the founder of their religion was a Jew, faithful to the law, who never had to face the necessity of adapting his Judaism to the European way of life. For Jesus there was, of course, the peculiar problem of his relationship to the law and its precepts, but this arises for every believing Jew who takes his Judaism seriously.

In the Gospels, we see how Jesus' attitude to the law has sometimes become unrecognizable as the result of "clarification" by the Evangelists and touching up by later revisers. Nevertheless, the Synoptic Gospels, if read through the eyes of their own time, still portray a picture of Jesus as a faithful, law-observant Jew. Few people seem to realize that in the Synoptic Gospels, Jesus is never shown in conflict with current practice of the law — with the single exception of the plucking of heads of grains on the Sabbath. In this incident, Luke (6:1-5) is the closest to the original account. "On a Sabbath, while he was going through the grain fields, his disciples plucked and ate some heads of grain, rubbing them in their hands. But some of the Pharisees said, 'Why are you (pl.)[1] doing what is not lawful to do on the Sabbath?'"

The general opinion was that on the Sabbath it was permissible to pick up fallen heads of grain and rub them between the fingers. According to Rabbi Yehuda, also a Galilean, it was even permissible to rub them in one's hand.[2] Some of the Pharisees found fault with Jesus' disciples for behaving in accordance with their Galilean tradition. The Greek translator of the original evidently was unacquainted with the customs of the people. To make the scene more vivid, he added the statement about plucking the wheat and thus introduced the one and only act of transgression of the law recorded in the Synoptic tradition.[3]

In the case of washing hands before a meal, the Synoptic tradition is not to blame for the misunderstanding. The precept about washing hands

---

1. Or "your disciples" (Matt. 12:2); "they" (Mark 2:24).

2. See *b. Shabb.* 128a; Pinés, op. cit., 273. The plucking is lacking not only in the text mentioned by Pinés, but also in the *Diatessaron* of Tatian. See *Diatessaron de Tatien: texte arabe établi, traduit en français, collationné avec les anciennes versions syriaques, suivi d'un évangéliaire diatessarique syriaque et accompagné de quatre planches hors texte* (ed. A. S. Marmardji; Beirut: Imprimerie Catholique, 1935), 66; and in Ephraem's commentary on the *Diatessaron, Commentaire de l'Évangile concordant texte syriaque* (*Manuscrit Chester Beatty* 709) (ed. L. Leloir; Dublin: Hodges Figgis, 1963), 104. See now also Pinés, op. cit., 452-453.

3. See M. Kister, "Plucking on the Sabbath and Christian-Jewish Polemic," *Imm* 24-25 (1990), 35-51.

7. A "seat" of Moses carved from basalt found in the ruins of the
synagogue at Chorazin, third-fourth century A.D.
Courtesy of the Israel Museum, Jerusalem.

was part of neither written nor oral teaching. In Jesus' time the precept
ran, "Washing hands before a meal is advisable, ablution after a meal is
obligatory."[4] This custom concerned rabbinic regulations that are first
found, perhaps, in the generation before Jesus. Even the most bigoted, village Pharisee of those days would have shaken his head uncompre-
hendingly had anyone asserted that Jesus had broken the Law of Moses,
because his disciples did not always wash their hands before eating. "It is
reasonable to suppose that till the time of the Destruction of the Temple,
and possibly even later, washing of the hands for ordinary food was not accepted by *all the Sages* nor practiced by *all Israel*."[5]

4. *T. Ber.* 5:13; Billerbeck, op. cit., 1:696-698. The phrase "advisable" may be understood
to be "a matter of a (formal) prescript of the authority." Other examples of this meaning are
found in G. Alon, *Studies in Jewish History in the Times of the Second Temple, the Mishna, and
the Talmud* (Tel Aviv: ha-Kibuts ha-Me'uhad, 1958), 111-119 [Hebrew]. This interpretation fits
better the debate in the Gospels.

5. G. Alon, *Jews, Judaism and the Classical World* (Jerusalem: Magnes Press, 1977), 221
[the italics are Alon's].

Viewed from the standpoint of the gradation of Jewish precepts, the scribes in conversation with Jesus described the washing of hands as no more than "a tradition of the fathers" (Mark 7:5). Jesus, too, was using the concepts of his own time when he described the rabbinical prescription of washing hands — not wholly obligatory in those days — as "a tradition of men" (Mark 7:8) in contrast to the commandments of written and oral teaching. The prescription of washing hands before a meal was not generally binding in those days for the simple reason that it was one of those rules of purification that did not affect all Jews. It was only incumbent upon those particular groups of Jews who had accepted them as an obligation for life.

The degree and extent of this obligation varied. The Pharisees were a society whose rules of ritual purity were still much looser than those of the Essene community. It would have been natural, therefore, that in the debate on washing of hands, Jesus enlarged the scope of our whole problem of ritual purity by saying, "not what goes into the mouth defiles a man, but what comes out of the mouth, this defiles a man" (Matt. 15:11). By the way, this dictum is completely compatible with the Jewish legal position. A person's body does not become ritually impure even when one has eaten animals forbidden by the Law of Moses!

What Jesus said, thus, has nothing to do with a supposed abrogation of Judaic law, but is part of a criticism directed at the Pharisees. The general truth that strict observation of ritual purity can encourage moral laxity was applicable even in Jesus' day. A Jewish writer[6] of those days certainly had the Pharisees in mind when he spoke of "pestilential and impious men . . . Hypocritical. . . . And although their hands and minds are occupied with things unclean, they will make a fine show in words, even saying, Do not touch me, lest you pollute me. . . ." Here, as with Jesus, the contrast between morally unclean thought and speech, and the craving for ritual purity is stressed.

Jesus spoke on this topic on another occasion, "Woe to you, scribes and Pharisees, hypocrites! For you clean the outside of the cup and plate, but inside they are full of extortion and rapacity. You blind Pharisees! First clean the inside of the cup and plate, so that the outside also may become clean" (Matt. 23:25-26). He also called them "blind guides, straining at a

---

6. *As. Mos.* 7:3-9; *The Apocryphal Old Testament* (ed. H. F. D. Sparks; Oxford: Oxford University Press, 1984), 611.

gnat and swallowing a camel!" (Matt. 23:24). This last saying sounds like a proverb. Perhaps Jesus' terminology about internal and external purity was not invented by him either.

If we are right in thinking that this saying is an important one, we ought to inquire into the precise meaning it had for Jesus himself. Following the custom, Jesus used to pronounce a blessing over wine and bread. Could he, at the same time, believe that material things are in themselves religiously neutral? A few decades later Rabban Yohanan ben Zakkai said to his pupils, "In life it is not the dead who make you unclean, nor is it water, but it is an ordinance of the King of kings. God has said, 'I have established My statute. I have settled My ordinance. No man has the right to transgress My ordinance.' For it is written,[7] 'This is the statute of the law which the Lord has commanded.'"[8]

Jesus would not have spoken thus — for one thing, it is too rationalistic. We may say — provisionally — that for Jesus, moral values far overshadowed all ritual values, but that is far from the whole truth. Would Jesus, in any case, think in such sharply defined theoretical categories? On the matter of washing hands[9] and plucking heads of grain, it was the disciples, not the master, who were less strict in their observance of the law.[10] Even this is not usually noticed. When his disciples' negligence was pointed out to the master, he not only came to their defense, but replied with far more force than it would seem the case merits.

Jesus seized the opportunity to elucidate an important point. His replies here and elsewhere were not so revolutionary as the uninitiated might imagine. His saying about purity and impurity is almost a piece of popular moral wisdom, and the kernel of Jesus' words in the debate about

---

7. Num. 19:2.

8. Billerbeck, op. cit., 1:719. It is important to note that Rabbi Yohanan ben Zakkai was speaking about a biblical commandment, whereas the washing of hands was merely a late precept, and the purification precepts of the Pharisees were voluntary.

9. See also the important extra-canonical history of the clash between Jesus and the Pharisaic high priest in the forecourt of the Temple in Jerusalem, Jeremias, *Unknown Sayings of Jesus* (London: S.P.C.K., 1957), 37-49.

10. Joseph Frankovic brought to my attention a similar situation that is described about Rabban Gamaliel, the grandson of Paul's teacher, who instructed his disciples in a more lenient understanding of a matter of law, while he himself maintained a more strict practice for himself. When the disciples challenged him to set aside his more strict understanding of the precept for his wedding night, he responded, "I will not heed you to cancel for myself the kingdom of heaven even for one hour" (*m. Ber.* 2:5).

grain on the Sabbath is completely in harmony with the views of the moderate scribes. On that occasion, Jesus said, among other things, "The Sabbath was made for man, not man for the Sabbath. So, man[11] is lord even of the Sabbath" (Mark 2:27-28). The scribes, too, said, "The Sabbath has been handed over to you, not you to the Sabbath."[12]

Jesus knew how to capitalize on a suitable occasion for a pedagogic offensive against the bigots.[13] He did this, for example, when he performed a miracle of healing on the Sabbath. To understand the situation properly, we must keep in mind that if there was even a slight suspicion of danger to life, any form of healing was permitted. Moreover, even when the illness was not dangerous, while mechanical means were not allowed, healing by word was always permitted on the Sabbath. According to the Synoptic Gospels, Jesus adhered to these restrictions in all of his healings.[14] Not so with John, who was less interested in history. He reports the healing of the blind man, a story that is reminiscent of Mark 8:22-26. According to John 9:6, Jesus healed the man by placing mud made from earth and spittle on the blind man's eyes. In contrast to Mark, John adds, "Now it was a Sabbath day when Jesus made clay and opened his eyes. . . . Some of the Pharisees said, 'This man is not from God, for he does not keep the Sabbath'" (John 9:14-16). If Jesus had acted thus, the objection of the Pharisees would have been legitimate. We have noted, however, that Jesus had no desire to oppose the Law of Moses. He only wanted to expose the rigidity of the bigots, using this case as an example.

Not only did Jesus use the criticism of his opponents for teaching purposes, he actually knew how to create situations that would highlight aspects of his teaching. "On another Sabbath, when he entered the synagogue and taught, a man was there whose right hand was withered. And

11. Literally, "the son of man." Here it means simply "man." This was already recognized in the seventeenth century by the famous Dutch scholar Hugo Grotius in his commentary on Matt. 12:8, *Annotationes in Novum Testamentum denuo emendatius editae* (9 vols.; Groningen: W. Zuidema, 1826-1834) 1: 358. See also chapter nine in the present book.

12. *Mek. Rab. Ishmael* on Exod. 31:14 (103b); S. Horovitz and I. A. Rabin, *Mechilta d'Rabbi Ismael* (Jerusalem: Bamberger & Wahrmann, 1960), 341; see W. Bacher, *Die Agada der Tannaiten* (2 vols.; Strassburg: K. J. Trübner, 1890-1903), 2:493 n. 2. See also V. Taylor, op. cit., 218-220.

13. Flusser, "It Is Not a Serpent That Kills," *JOC*, 550.

14. See J. N. Epstein, *Introduction to Tannaitic Literature; Mishna, Tosephta and Halakhic Midrashim* (Tel Aviv: Devir, 1957), 280-281 [Hebrew].

they watched him, to see whether he would heal on the Sabbath. But he said to them, 'Which is lawful on the Sabbath: to do good or to do evil, *to save a soul* or to destroy it?' And he said to the man, 'Stretch out your hand.' He did so, and his hand was restored like the other. But they were at a loss and asked one another, 'What are we to do with Jesus?'" (Luke 6:6-11).

Since the mention of the Pharisees is inconsistent in all three of the Synoptic traditions, it is probable that those who stood by watching were not in fact Pharisees. Their description as such is the product of the hand of a later redactor. Moreover, the statement regarding their motivation, "they were looking for a reason to accuse Jesus," is also secondary. Jesus' assertion that it is lawful to save a person and not to let him perish was surely not foreign to many of his hearers. Jesus alluded to a well-known classical expression of the Jewish humane approach to the other, as it is contained in the important rabbinical saying:[15]

> Therefore only a single man was created in the world, to teach that if any man has caused a single soul to perish Scripture imputes it to him as though he had caused a whole world to perish; and if any man *saves alive a single soul* Scripture imputes it to him as though he had saved alive a whole world.

Jesus' creative innovation was that he applied this common Jewish principle to the attitude toward the Sabbath and healing on it. But for some of his hearers the allusion to the well-known sentence only strengthened their perplexity.

Jesus, already known to be a healer, meets a man with a withered hand in the synagogue on the Sabbath. The man is chronically, not dangerously, ill. Is Jesus going to heal this man? Yes! But in a manner consistent with Sabbath observance. By this deed, and by what he said, he showed the true meaning of the Sabbath. Naturally, he roused the sanctimonious people who had been unable to catch him breaking the law. Furthermore, in the original account, which lies behind much of Matthew's narrative (Matt. 12:9-14), the Pharisees were not explicitly mentioned.[16] The reference to

---

15. *M. Sanh.* 4:5. The sentence was certainly known to the Alexandrian Jewish philosopher Philo (20 B.C.–A.D. 40), *On the Decalogue* 37, *Philo VII*, LCL (trans. F. H. Colson; Cambridge, Mass.: Harvard University Press, 1958), 25.

16. See also R. Bultmann, *History of the Synoptic Tradition* (New York: Harper & Row, 1963), 52ff.

the Pharisees in Matthew's conclusion (Matt. 12:14) is not drawn from the original account but a dependency at this point on Mark's Gospel. In Mark, the story ends not with the impotent confusion of the bigots, but in this way: "The Pharisees went out, and immediately held counsel with the Herodians against him, how to destroy him." This is a plain reference to the coming crucifixion (cf. Mark 15:1). It is most unlikely that the Pharisees would have acted in that way. The wickedest among them would never have resolved to kill Jesus because he had performed a work of healing on the Sabbath — a permissible deed anyway. For this reason Luke's conclusion (Luke 6:11) is preferable here.[17]

If Jesus, then, emphasized the moral side of life in preference to the purely formal side of legal observance, we can give a little more depth to this provisional affirmation by leaving the question of the law and addressing two of his other controversial conversations. The first has the same polemical overtone as the saying on the occasion of the healing of the man's withered hand. "And behold, they brought to him a paralytic, lying on his bed; and when Jesus saw their faith he said, 'My son, your sins are forgiven.' And behold, some of the scribes said to themselves, 'This man is blaspheming. Who can forgive sins but God?' But Jesus, knowing their thoughts said, 'What are you thinking in your hearts? For which is easier, to say, "Your sins are forgiven," or to say, "Rise and walk"? But that you may know that man[18] has authority on earth to forgive sins' — he then said to the paralytic, 'Rise, take up your bed and go home.' And he rose and went home. And all were afraid, and they glorified God, who had given such authority to men" (cf. Matt. 9:1-8).

As in the episode of the healing of the withered hand, Jesus again links word with deed. The healing was not intended as an end in itself but as a striking proof of his message. Because people believed that illnesses were a consequence of sins committed, forgiveness of sins could even imply heal-

17. Few scholars have noted the distinctively different ending to Luke's account or the tendentious English translation of ἄνοια, "But they were filled with *fury*." The English translators have rendered Luke's Greek word in light of Mark's ending (cp. Mark 3:6; Matt. 12:14). The Greek term, however, is never elsewhere translated "anger, fury, wrath." See H. G. Liddell and R. Scott, *A Greek-English Lexicon* (Oxford: Clarendon Press, 1996), 145. Instead, those watching were filled with "frustration, bafflement." See my discussion in the introduction to *JOC*, xxv n. 35, or my foreword to Lindsey, op. cit., 5. See below, chapter 8 n. 10.

18. Literally, "the son of man"; Taylor, op. cit., 197.

ing.[19] By healing the paralytic, Jesus proved that God had given authority to men to pronounce forgiveness of sins even when those sins had not been committed against them. It is also important that Jesus forgave the sick man his sins after having perceived the faith of those present, and also, apparently, the faith of the sick man. The original account makes no mention of belief in Jesus himself — only later did it become an integral part of the Christian faith (e.g., in John's Gospel) — but the power of faith itself was already recognized by Jesus. "If you had faith as a grain of mustard seed, you could say to this mulberry tree, 'Be rooted up, and be planted in the sea' and it would obey you" (Luke 17:6).

There is another controversy regarding the forgiveness of sins. It was alleged that Jesus' healing power came from Beelzebub, the prince of spirits, by whose power Jesus drove out the spirits. One of his replies to this calumny is reported in Matthew 12:32, "And whoever says a word against the son of man (i.e., a man) will be forgiven; but whoever speaks against the Holy Spirit will not be forgiven, either in this age or the age to come." The special significance of this saying, which has parallels in Jewish writings,[20] lies in the fact that, since his baptism, Jesus knew he possessed the Holy Spirit.

The saying is important, also, because it shows us the substance to which Jesus is pointing in his controversies, even in those concerned with the observance of the law; namely, with human sin and human dignity. In the course of subsequent stages of revision, the protagonists in Jesus' controversial dialogues become more sharply delineated — and increasingly distorted. In the original accounts Jesus' opponents are often anonymous, self-appointed spokesmen of local bigotry. Later they are described unhesitatingly as scribes and Pharisees.[21] It is worthwhile to follow the progressive development of the text in order to see how Jesus' opponents increasingly become his enemies, inspired by boundless wickedness, having as their ultimate goal his demise and destruction.

There is some justification, however, in describing Jesus' opponents-in-argument as Pharisees. In the narrower sense, the Pharisees were a soci-

---

19. Flusser, "A Lost Jewish Benediction in Matthew 9:8," *JOC*, 535-542.

20. See P. Volz, *Der Geist Gottes und die verwandten Erscheinungen im Alten Testament und im anschliessenden Judentum* (Tübingen: J. C. B. Mohr, 1910), 164; Flusser, "Die Sünde gegen den heiligen Geist," in *Wie gut Sind deine Zeite, Jaakow . . .": Festschrift zum 60. Geburtstag von Reinhold Mayer* (ed. E. L. Ehrlich, B. Klappert, and U. Ast; Gerlingen: Bleicher, 1986), 139-147.

21. See n. 16.

ety whose members — as we have said — had voluntarily accepted certain prescriptions of purity, and other obligations. In Jesus' time, this society numbered about six thousand members in Jerusalem. They were founded in the turbulent period of the second century B.C. They had been the opponents of the Maccabean ruling dynasty, that had made an alliance with the politico-religious movement of the Sadducees.

Early Sadducean ideology is reflected by drawings found in Jerusalem in a tomb of a certain Jason. This Jason bears a Greek name, and a Greek inscription in his tomb invites living men to enjoy their life. The man was evidently a Sadducee who did not believe in an afterlife.[22] In the tomb is also a drawing of three ships.[23] The middle ship is a merchant (or fishing) vessel. The warship on the right is pursuing the two other ships. Apparently, the scene portrays a sea battle between the pursuing ship and the merchant vessel before it.

> There is little doubt that the picture of naval action was meant to refer to the occupation of one important member of the family buried here. . . . In the present instance, there is reason to assume that the scene is one in which the deceased took a leading part, and that it is he who is clearly shown on the forecastle of his ship.[24]

Thus, the man who is chasing the merchant or fishing vessel and another warship is Jason himself. Apparently Jason was a Sadducean buccaneer in the time of Alexander Jannaeus (103-76 B.C.). We know of such activities, that are depicted in the inscription through Pompey's expressed concern for Arab and Jewish attacks (i.e., by sea) on Syria. He finally disallowed the throne to the last Seleucid, saying "that he would not know how to defend, lest he should again expose Syria to the depredations *(latrocinia)* of the Jews and Arabs."[25]

The Pharisaic movement became involved in the civil war of the late Maccabean period, and by Jesus' time they had become recognized as the

---

22. L. Y. Rahmani, "Jason's Tomb," *IEJ* 17/2 (1967), 95.

23. Rahmani, ibid., 69-73.

24. Rahmani, ibid., 96-97.

25. *Justinus, Epitoma historiarum Philippicarum Pompei Trogi* (ed. O. Seel; Stuttgart: B. G. Teubner, 1972), 276; M. Stern, *Greek and Latin Authors on Jews and Judaism. Edited with Introductions, Translations and Commentary* (3 vols.; Jerusalem: Israel Academy of Sciences and Humanities), 1:343.

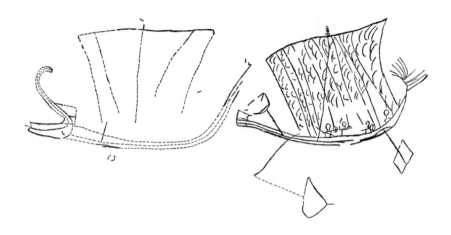

8. Drawing of two ships pursued by warship

teachers of the masses, consciously identifying themselves with popular faith. The Sadducees, on the other hand, formed a small but powerful group among the priestly aristocracy of the temple in Jerusalem. Fundamentally, the Pharisaic philosophy of life was in line with non-sectarian universal Judaism, while the Sadducees turned into a counter-revolutionary group that denied the validity of the oral tradition and saw belief in a future life as an old wives' tale.

The Pharisees were not identical with the later rabbis, but the two groups may, in practice, be regarded as forming a unity. In the rabbinic literature the sages are never designated as Pharisees. We do, however, know two men who called themselves Pharisees: the historian Josephus Flavius[26] and St. Paul.[27] While Paul's teacher, Rabban Gamaliel, in the rabbinic sources is never called a Pharisee, in Acts 5:34 Luke speaks about "a Pharisee named Gamaliel, a teacher of the law, who was honored by all the people." Gamaliel's son, Simon, is described as a Pharisee only in

26. *Life* 12. About the name "Pharisee" and its various meanings, see now Flusser, "Ein Sendschreiben aus Qumran (4QMMT) und der Ketzersegen," *Bulletin der Schweizerischen Gesellschaft für judaistische Forschung* 4 (Basel, 1995), 27-31.

27. Phil. 3:5; Acts 23:6; 26:5.

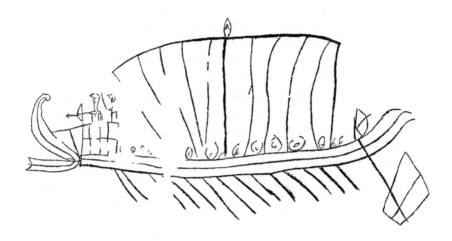

Josephus.[28] These exceptions to the rule are because they wrote in Greek. The term "Pharisee" in Hebrew usually bore a negative connotation. In those days, if one said, "Pharisee," one immediately thought of a religious hypocrite. On his deathbed, the Sadducean King Alexander Jannaeus warned his wife not against the true Pharisees, but against the "painted ones, whose deeds are the deeds of Zimri, but who expect to receive the reward of Phinehas."[29]

The Sadducean king spoke of "the painted ones." The Essenes called the Pharisees "the whitewashed,"[30] and Jesus said, "Woe to you, scribes and Pharisees, hypocrites! For you are like whitewashed tombs, which outwardly appear beautiful, but within they are full of dead men's bones and all uncleanness. So you also outwardly appear righteous to men, but within you are full of hypocrisy and iniquity" (Matt. 23:27-28). The Sadducean king distinguished between the wicked deeds of the "whitewashed" and their claim to be honored as righteous. The Essenes, too, condemned the deeds of the Pharisees: "And they lead thy people astray, for they utter

28. *Life* 191.
29. *B. Soṭah* 22b. This is an allusion to the story told in Num. 25:6-15.
30. CD 8:12; 19:25 (according to Ezek. 13:10).

smooth speeches to them. False teachers, they lead astray, and blindly they are heading for a fall, for their works are done in deceit."[31]

Jesus identified the hypocrisy of the Pharisees in the discrepancy between their doctrine and their deeds, "for they preach, but do not practice" (Matt. 23:3). It is worth noting that this same anti-Pharisaic polemic also occurs in rabbinic literature, which is an expression of true Pharisaism. The talmudic list of the *seven* kinds of Pharisee[32] is a fivefold variation on the theme of hypocrisy — the last two kinds of hypocrisy are replaced by two positive kinds of Pharisee. It is thus no accident that in the Pharisee discourse of Matthew 23:1-36, Jesus addresses *seven* "Woes" to the Pharisees. The first type in the talmudic list is the "shoulder-Pharisee who lays commandments upon men's shoulders."[33] Jesus likewise said that the Pharisees "bind heavy burdens, hard to bear, and lay them on men's shoulders; but they themselves will not move them with their finger" (Matt. 23:4).

The Essene writings are full of the bitterest attacks upon the party of the Pharisees — although the name is not directly mentioned. The Pharisees were described as "slippery exegetes," their actions were hypocrisy, and by means of "their deceitful doctrine, lying tongues and false lips" they were able to lead almost the whole people astray.[34] In all this, "they closed up the fountain of knowledge to the thirsty and gave them vinegar with which to quench their thirst."[35] This reminds us of Jesus' words. "Woe to you lawyers! For you have taken away the key of knowledge; you did not enter yourselves, and you hindered those who were entering" (Luke 11:52; cf. Matt. 23:13).

Nevertheless, the gap between the Essene attack upon the Pharisees and Jesus' criticism of them is great. The Essenes sharply rejected the doctrine of the Pharisees,[36] whereas Jesus said, "The scribes and Pharisees sit

---

31. 1QH^a 4:6-8.

32. *B. Soṭah* 22b; *j. Ber.* 14b.

33. So it is, according to *j. Ber.* 14b.

34. 4Q169 2:7-10.

35. 1QH^a 4:11.

36. Flusser, "Pharisäer, Sadduzäer und Essener in Pescher Nahum," in *Qumran* (Darmstadt, 1981), 121-166; idem, "Miqsat Maaseh ha-Torah u-Birkat ha-Minim," in *Judaism of the Second Temple Period, Qumran and Apocalypticism* (ed. Serge Ruzer; Jerusalem: Izhak Ben-Zvi Press and Magnes Press, 2002), 58-100 [Hebrew], and the German translation of this study, above n. 26.

on Moses' seat; so practice and observe whatever they tell you, but not what they do; for they preach, but do not practice" (Matt. 23:2-3). In the Pharisees, Jesus saw the contemporary heirs of Moses, and said that men should model their lives upon their teaching. This makes sense, for although Jesus was apparently indirectly influenced by Essenism, he was basically rooted in universal non-sectarian Judaism. The philosophy and practice of this Judaism was that of the Pharisees.

It would not be wrong to describe Jesus as a Pharisee in the *broad* sense. However, even if his criticism of the Pharisees was not as hostile as that of the Essenes, nor as contradictory as that of the contemporaneous writing we have cited (i.e., *As. Mos.*, chap. 7), he did view the Pharisees as an outsider, and did not identify himself with them. We have still to discuss the inevitable tension between the charismatic Jesus and institutional Judaism. Neither dare we forget that the revolutionary element in his preaching of the kingdom heightened this tension. It will become evident also that the authentic teaching of Jesus questioned the very foundations of the social structure. Nonetheless, we should bear in mind that this tension never implied negation, nor were the views of Jesus and the Pharisees contrary or ever degenerated into enmity.

Even if it were not possible to detect by philological method the heightening of tensions by the Evangelists, it would be difficult to understand the existence of a genuine hostility toward Jesus from the "scribes and Pharisees" — allegedly a contributory cause of his death. Obviously, there were some petty minds among the Pharisees — such people are found in all societies — who were suspicious of this wonder-worker. These would gladly have caught him in some forbidden action so that they could drag him before the rabbinic court. Yet, Jesus always succeeded in stating his opinion without giving them the slightest excuse for prosecuting him.

Those who have studied the scribes of those days are well aware that their leaders were not without faults. At the same time, they know also that they were far from being petty-minded. If Jesus had lived in the stormy days of the last Maccabean kings, it would certainly have been possible for him to have been persecuted by the Pharisees, because he was the leader of a messianic movement. When the Pharisees came to power under Queen Salome Alexandra, by no means did they spare their Saducean opponents.[37] The Dead Sea Scrolls tell us that they also unleashed systematic

---

37. *Ant.* 13:409-411; *J.W.* 1:110-114.

persecution against the Essenes. But all that belonged to a past of which the Pharisees were ashamed. Jesus has something fine to say on this topic. "Woe to you, scribes and Pharisees, hypocrites! for you build the tombs of the prophets and adorn the monuments of the righteous, saying, 'If we had lived in the days of our fathers, we would not have taken part with them in shedding the blood of prophets.' Thus you witness against yourselves, that you are the sons of those who murdered the prophets" (Matt. 23:29-31).[38]

The testimonial that Jesus has involuntarily given the Pharisees of his time is confirmed by the report of his trial. It is hardly ever pointed out that the Pharisees, so often mentioned in the Gospels as Jesus' opponents, do not appear in any of the Synoptic accounts of the trial. The fact that it would have been easy to smuggle the word "Pharisees" into these relatively late accounts is proved by the less historical John, who had no qualms mentioning them in Jesus' arrest. "So Judas, procuring a band of soldiers and some officers from the chief priests and the Pharisees, went there with lanterns and torches and weapons" (John 18:3). The reason that not only the original accounts, but the first three Gospels as well, avoid mentioning the Pharisees in the story of the trial of Jesus, becomes clearer if we recall the role of the Pharisees in the first decades of the Christian church.

When the Saducean high priest persecuted the apostles, Rabban Gamaliel took their side and saved them (Acts 5:17-42). When Paul was taken before the high council in Jerusalem, he found sympathy among his hearers by appealing to the Pharisees (Acts 22:30–23:10). When in A.D. 62, the Lord's brother James, and apparently other Christians, were illegally put to death by the Saducean high priest, the Pharisees appealed to the king, and the high priest was deposed.[39] Taking the last case along with the two earlier ones, we can hardly avoid the impression that the Pharisees regarded the Saducean hierocracy's persecution of the early Christians as further proof of the manifestly unjust cruelty of this group. Out of it they forged a moral-political weapon against the Saducean priesthood — politics is not always an evil business. This explains the Pharisees' apparently consistent opposition to the persecutions of the Christians by the Saducean high priests, one of whom lost his office as a result of this opposition.

---

38. Even if in the parallel in Luke 11:47-48 it is not sure that these words were addressed directly against the Pharisees, I believe that they were included in Jesus' criticism. This was also Matthew's opinion.

39. *Ant.* 20:200-201.

The reason that the early Christians became a bone of contention between the two Jewish parties is that the Pharisees regarded the handing over of Jesus to the Romans as a repulsive act of sacerdotal despotism. Moreover, the handing over of a Jew to the foreign power was generally considered a crime.[40] We can assume also that the Pharisees do not figure as accusers of Jesus at his trial in the first three Gospel accounts, because at that time people knew that the Pharisees had not agreed to hand Jesus over to the Romans. The Synoptists could not name the Pharisees as present at the trial without risking credibility. On the other hand, the Synoptists could not mention the protest of the Pharisees, because they had already portrayed Jesus as an anti-Pharisee in the earlier part of their narratives.

How curious the changes a movement can undergo in the course of its history! As early as the second century, Christians of Jewish origin, who continued to follow the Law of Moses, were being marginalized.[41] Later, all Christians were forbidden to keep the precepts of the old covenant, even though Jesus had said, "For truly, I say to you, till heaven and earth pass away, not an iota, not a dot, will pass from the law.[42] Whoever then relaxes one of the least of these commandments and teaches men so, shall be called least in the kingdom of heaven; but he who does them and teaches them shall be called great in the kingdom of heaven" (Matt. 5:18-20).[43]

40. See the brief discussion by J. Klatzkin, "Informers," in *EncJud* (16 vols.; Jerusalem: Keter Publishing, 1972), 8:1364, and my study mentioned above in n. 36, 13-15. In the second-century midrash, *Seder Olam,* chapter 3 (see C. J. Milikowsky, *Seder Olam: A Rabbinic Chronography, A Dissertation Presented to the Faculty of the Graduate Schools of Yale University,* May 1981, 458) the "informers, betrayers" (מוסרים) are listed among those whose sins are "unforgivable" and who are punished forever. A study of the Greek linguistic equivalent (παραδίδωμι) in the Gospels indicates a similar pejorative notion (see W. Bauer, *A Greek-English Lexicon of the New Testament* [Chicago, 1957], 619-620). The illegality of the action probably rests behind Caiaphas' attempt to justify handing Jesus over to the Romans in John 11:49-50. It might also explain the concern by the high priest that what had happened clandestinely would become public knowledge (Acts 5:28). See the critique of Bauer in W. Klassen, *Judas: Betrayer or Friend of Jesus?* (Minneapolis: Fortress Press, 1996), 48, 50-51, 59-60.

41. Justin Martyr, *Dialogue with Trypho,* chapter 47.

42. The words, "till all shall have come to pass," do not seem to be spoken by Jesus. On the meaning of these words, see Billerbeck, op. cit., 1:143-144. I personally am sure that the natural place for these words is in Matthew 24:34b (and par.). Matthew also cited them in 5:18 because of the *external* verbal similarity between that verse and 24:34-35.

43. It would be absurd to believe that after such statements Jesus intended to say there was a contrast between his teaching and the Mosaic Law. I know that "everything is permis-

The abrogation of the Jewish laws within the early centuries of the church is connected with the fact that already at an early stage Christianity was turning into a religion of non-Jews. It was possible for this to happen because, in the ancient world, many people, "God-fearers," regarded the God of the Jews as the one true God. While some in those days took the final step, and became fully converted to Judaism, others remained on the periphery. The expansion of Christianity into the Gentile world first reached these who already were sympathetic to aspects of ancient Judaism but not yet converted.[44]

The liberal school of Hillel was not distressed to see Gentiles becoming Jews. By contrast, the school of Shammai made conversion as difficult as possible. The following sayings show that Jesus shared the strict standpoint of Shammai. "Woe to you, scribes and Pharisees, hypocrites! for you traverse sea and land to make a single proselyte, and when he becomes a proselyte, you make him twice as much a child of hell as yourselves" (Matt. 23:15). A non-Jew who lives according to certain fundamental moral laws, without following the whole Mosaic law, is blessed. The proselyte, the Gentile who has converted to Judaism, however, is bound by the whole law.[45] If a proselyte fails to fulfill the whole law, which formerly did not obligate him, his conversion to Judaism is itself the cause of his becoming a child of hell. Quite needlessly he has thrown away his blessedness.

As far as the sources allow us to judge, Jesus had a poor opinion of

---

sible — but not everything is beneficial" (1 Cor. 6:12). It has already been seen that the famous "but I tell you" is not an expression of Jesus' opposition to Moses. In reality Jesus' personal opinion, which follows after this phrase, is mostly attested also in the other Jewish sources. He has chosen one of two contrasting Jewish opinions, which better fits his ethics. Even Matt. 5:44, "love your enemies," is within the framework of Judaism (see below, 57-61 and 71-73). Nothing of what Jesus says in the Sermon particularly conflicts with the content of the Mosaic legislation. See also Flusser, "Die Tora in der Bergpredigt," *Entdeckungen*, 1:21-31; idem, "'Den Alten ist gesagt' — Interpretation der sogenannten Antithesen der Bergpredigt," *Jud* 48 (Basel, 1992) 35-39; S. Ruzer, "The Technique of Composite Citations in the Sermon on the Mount (Matt 5:21-22, 33-37)," *RB* 103 (1996), 65-75.

44. See Acts 10, particularly the description of Cornelius in verse 2. Flusser, "Paul's Jewish-Christian Opponents in the Didache," in *Gilgul: Essays on Transformation, Revolution, and Permanence in the History of Religions, Dedicated to R. J. Zwi Werblowsky* (ed. S. Shaked, D. Shulman, and G. G. Stroumsa; Leiden: Brill, 1987), 71-90; D. Flusser and Sh. Safrai, "Das Aposteldekret und die Noachitischen Gebote," in *Wer Tora vermehrt, mehrt Leben: Festgabe für Heinz Kremers* (Neukirchen-Vluyn: Neukirchener Verlag, 1986), 173-192.

45. Gal. 5:3; Jas. 2:10.

the non-Jews, the Gentiles. They are anxious about their material future and do not know that "tomorrow will be anxious for itself" (Matt. 6:32-34). They "heap up empty phrases" in prayer, thinking "that they will be heard for their many words" (Matt. 6:7). They know nothing of the Jews' command to love one's neighbor and mix only with their friends (Matt. 5:47). The first and the third sayings give us the feeling that Jesus is speaking about vices that still afflict European and Western society to some extent.

Another profound saying seems directed chiefly against the Romans. According to Luke's wording (22:24-27), during the Last Supper Jesus indicated that he would be handed over. His apostles began discussing among themselves who would be Jesus' successor, or, in Luke's words, "Then arose a dispute among them, which of them was to be regarded as the greatest. And he said to them, 'The kings of the Gentiles exercise lordship over them. But not so with you! Rather let the greatest among you become as the youngest, and the leader as one who serves. For which is the greater, one who sits at the table, or one who serves? Is it not the one who sits at the table?[46] But I am among you as one who serves.'"[47]

For a full understanding of these words of Jesus, some knowledge of Hebrew is necessary. The apostles were arguing over who would be their future leader (Hebrew: *Rav*, great one). Jesus opposed any kind of lordship over men, as was the custom of Gentile kings: "But not so with you!" In order to express his opposition to any kind of nationalistic imperialism, Jesus alluded to Genesis 25:23: "The great one (*Rav*, here in the meaning of 'the elder') shall serve the younger." This was said in connection with Esau ("the elder") who would serve Jacob ("the younger"), and was seen as a prophecy of the waning power of the elder Esau under the ascendancy of the younger Jacob.

In Jesus' time Esau was taken as symbolizing Rome. Jesus, in an anti-imperialistic mood, purposely de-politicized the contemporary understanding of the biblical verse. He wanted to say, thereby, that the Roman rulers of the nations have power in their hands; but for us the biblical words mean that the greater, the leader, shall serve the lesser. It is self-evident that those who are sitting at the table are more important than the waiter. Nevertheless, Jesus, the master, now performs on the eve of the

46. Billerbeck, op. cit., 2:257.
47. Billerbeck, op. cit., 2:257-258.

Passover the task of a waiter and serves the apostles at the table.[48] Jesus' acted with uncommon humility, even if a similar act is reported about the grandson of the Gamaliel mentioned in Acts.[49]

In any event, Jesus as a rule did not heal non-Jews. On one occasion a Syro-Phoenician woman entreated him to heal her daughter, and he reiterated what he had said to his disciples, [50] "I was sent only to the lost sheep of the house of Israel." But she came and knelt before him, saying, "Lord, help me." And he answered, "It is not fair to take the children's bread and throw it to the dogs." She said, "Yes, Lord, even the dogs eat the crumbs that fall from their master's table." Jesus was moved by what the woman said and her daughter was healed from that hour (Matt. 15:21-28).

There is only one more report of Jesus healing a non-Jew, the servant of the Roman centurion at Capernaum (Matt. 8:5-13; Luke 7:1-10). Luke tells us that the centurion was no heathen, but a man who feared God. He said to Jesus, "Lord . . . I am not worthy to have you come under my roof; . . . but say the word, and let my servant be healed." This devout Roman wanted to avoid the possibility of Jesus contracting impurity through contact with a non-Jew — the dwelling places of Gentiles were considered impure — so he asked Jesus to heal his servant from a distance.[51] He based his belief in the power of this wonder-working teacher to heal in this way, upon a comparison with his own office. "'For I am a man set under authority, with soldiers under me; and I say to one, "Go," and he goes; and to another, "Come," and he comes; and to my slave, "Do this," and he does it.' When Jesus heard this he marveled at him, and turned and said to the multitude that followed him, 'I tell you, not even in Israel have I found such faith.'"[52]

---

48. Mark (10:41-45; so also Matt. 20:24-28) has placed the scene in an earlier connection and replaced the end of the story (Luke 18:27) by another, christological conclusion (Mark 10:45; Matt. 20:28).

49. See *b. Qidd.* 32b in Billerbeck, op. cit., 1:830. However, this story is *not* connected with the Passover.

50. See Matt. 10:6.

51. See *t. Ahilut* 18:11 (cf. John 18:28; Acts 10:28). G. Alon, "The Levitical Uncleanness of Gentiles," in *Jews, Judaism and the Classical World: Studies in Jewish History in the Times of the Second Temple and Talmud* (Jerusalem: Magnes Press, 1977), 154 n. 12, 186 n. 75. In connection with the God-fearing centurion, see *Tractate Gerim* 3:2.

52. I venture that here "faith" means the same attitude in Judaism as in Christianity; namely, a special attitude to God. I have opposed the common opinion about the difference between faith in Judaism and Christianity in my concluding remarks to Buber's *Zwei Glaubensweisen* (Gerlingen: Lambert Schneider, 1994), 185-247.

9. Synagogue at Capernaum.

These are the only two stories in which Jesus healed non-Jews. In both, the decisive words are spoken not by Jesus, but by the Gentile, and these words make a deep impression on Jesus. We ought to note as well that none of the rabbinical documents say that one should not or may not heal a non-Jew. The picture preserved for us by the first three Gospels is clear. Jesus, the Jew, worked among Jews, and he wanted to work only among them (cf. Matt. 10:5-7). Even Paul, apostle to the Gentiles, confirms this fact. Jesus was "born under the law" (Gal. 4:4). He was "a servant to the circumcised to show God's truthfulness, in order to confirm the promises given to the patriarchs" (Rom. 15:8).

That Jesus worked only among the children of Israel was surely not a sign of his nationalistic narrow-mindedness. He acted so because this restriction was, as he believed, the will of the heavenly Father. He said it explicitly to the Syro-Phoenician woman, "I was sent only to the lost sheep of the house of Israel" (Matt. 15:24; see also Matt. 10:6). Jesus accepted this restriction, although he knew, as other Jews did,[53] that Gentiles are more

---

53. See the pertinent passage about the prophet Jonah in the *Mek. Rab. Ishmael* on Exod. 12:1 (Horowitz and Rabin, eds.), 3-4.

prone to repent than many of the children of Israel. In this spirit Jesus said about the cities of Galilee and their Jewish inhabitants, "Woe to you, Chorazin, woe to you, Bethsaida! for if the mighty works done in you had been done in Tyre and Sidon, they would have repented long ago in sackcloth and ashes . . ." (Matt. 11:20-24; Luke 10:13-15). The same attitude is expressed in Jesus' critique of his generation (Matt. 12:38-42; Luke 11:29-32).[54] Perhaps it was intended as divine providence that at the beginning the message was restricted to the children of Israel — and Jesus accepted this restriction.[55]

Were the various Jewish-Christian sects right then in thinking that by living as Jews they were following the will of Jesus? Expelled from the synagogues as heretics, stigmatized by the Gentile church as unorthodox, these Jews lived by the firm conviction that they alone cherished the true heritage of their master. They were also confident that they were the only ones who grasped the true meaning of Judaism. History passed them by. They became embittered and so, among them, the preaching of Jesus gradually turned into a rigid, apologetic caricature. As late as the tenth century they were to be found somewhere in Mossul, utterly lonely in their superhuman loyalty.[56]

54. These words of Jesus mention the prophet Jonah in the same way that the rabbinic passage cited in the previous note does.

55. Later on, Paul (Rom. 1:16b) speaks about "the power of God for the salvation of everybody who believes: first for the Jew, then for the Gentile" (see also Rom. 2:9-10).

56. See Pinés, op. cit., 255-257.

CHAPTER 5

Love

The germ of revolution in Jesus' preaching does not emerge from his criticism of Jewish law, but from other premises altogether. These premises did not originate with Jesus. On the contrary, his critical assault stemmed from attitudes already established before his time. Revolution broke through at three points: the radical interpretation of the commandment of mutual love, the call for a new morality, and the idea of the kingdom of heaven.

In about 175 B.C. a Jewish scribe bearing the Greek name Antigonos of Socho said, "Be not like slaves who serve their master for the sake of reward, but like slaves who serve their master with no eye on any reward; and may the fear of heaven be among you."[1] This saying is characteristic of the change in the intellectual and moral atmosphere that had taken place in Judaism since the time of the Old Testament.[2] At the same time, it exemplifies the expression of a new and deeper sensitivity within Judaism, which was an important precondition for the preaching of Jesus.

The religion of Israel preaches the one righteous God. His iconoclastic exclusiveness is linked with his inflexible moral will. The righteousness of the Old Testament sought concrete expression in a new and just social order. God's righteousness is also his compassion. He espouses especially the cause of the poor and oppressed, for he does not desire men's physical

---

1. M. 'Abot 1:3; K. Schlesinger, *Die Gesetzeslehrer; von Schimon dem Wahrhaftigen bis zum Auftreten Hillels* (Berlin: Schocken Verlag, 1936), 25. On what follows, see Flusser, "A New Sensitivity in Judaism and the Christian Message," *JOC,* 469-489.

2. See also the legends in *'Abot R. Nat.* 5:1 in Schlesinger, ibid.

power and strength, but rather their fear of him. Judaism is an ethical religion in which the principle of justice is indispensable; that is why the division of mankind into the righteous and the sinners is so important. For the Jew, the concept that God rewards the just and punishes the wicked is confirmation of God's steadfast truth. How, otherwise, could the righteousness of God rule in the world?

Man's destiny in this world, however, seldom corresponds to his moral endeavor. Often guilt goes conspicuously unpunished and virtue unrewarded. It is thus easy for us to conclude that something is amiss. No ethics and no religion has yet succeeded in solving the problem of evil. In the Old Testament, the book of Job is devoted to the topic of the bitter lot of the righteous. Eastern pagan wisdom literature, too, knows the cry: "They walk on a lucky path, those who do not seek a god. Those who devoutly pray to a goddess become poor and weak."[3]

It was not this problem that caused the revolution that sparked the moral imperative of Jesus. As we have noted, the moral religious maxim, according to which the righteous flourish and the evil come to a bad end, is constantly refuted by life itself. For the Jew of ancient times, the statement was also doubtful from another point of view. Even if the maxim had been confirmed by experience, the question would still have to be asked: Is the simple division of men into righteous and sinners itself appropriate? We know that no one is perfectly just or utterly evil, for good and evil struggle within the heart of every person. The question also arises whether there are any limits to the mercy of God and his love for people. Even if there were no problems regarding the reward of the just and the punishment of the sinner, would one be performing a truly moral act if he or she were motivated to act because of a reward? As we have said, already Antigonos of Socho rejected such a shallow, slavish attitude as basically vulgar. One ought to act morally, and at the same time give no thought to the reward that will surely come.

The rigid morality of the old covenant was clearly inadequate for the new sensitivity of the Jews in the Greek and Roman period. Having recognized that people are not sharply divided into the categories of the righteous and sinners, one is compelled to admit the impossibility of loving those who are good and hating the wicked. Because of the difficulty of

---

3. *Ancient Near Eastern Texts Relating to the Old Testament* (ed. J. B. Pritchard; Princeton: Princeton University Press, 1955), 439.

knowing how far God's love and mercy extended, many concluded that one ought to show love and mercy toward all, both righteous and wicked. In this they would be imitating God himself. Luke puts this saying into the mouth of Jesus: "Be merciful, even as your Father is merciful" (Luke 6:36). This is also an old rabbinical saying.[4]

Luke 6:36 is a parallel to Matthew 5:48: "You must be perfect, as your heavenly Father is perfect." The best way of translating this saying is, "There must be no limit to your goodness, as your heavenly Father's goodness knows no bounds."[5] Matthew 5:48 is merely the conclusion to a short homily where Jesus teaches that God reaches out in love to *all* people, regardless of their attitude and behavior toward him, "for he makes his sun rise on the evil and on the good, and sends rain on the just and on the unjust." In this Jesus is not far from the humane attitude of other Jews. Rabbi Abbahu said, "Greater is the day of rainfall than the day of resurrection. For the latter benefits only the pious, whereas the former benefits pious and sinners alike."[6] Rabbi Abbahu lived about A.D. 300, but there is a similar saying dating from Jesus' time.[7] Thus, it is no wonder that in such a spiritual atmosphere Jesus drew his daring conclusion: "Love your enemies!" (Matt. 5:44).[8] In other words, "Return love to those who hate you" or: "Do good to those who hate you" (Luke 6:27).

In those circles where the new Jewish sensitivity was then especially well developed, love of one's neighbor was regarded as a precondition to reconciliation with God. One rabbi said shortly after Jesus,[9] "Transgressions between a man and his neighbor are not expiated by the Day of Atonement unless the man first makes peace with his neighbor." Similarly, we hear Jesus say, "For if you forgive men their trespasses, your heavenly Father also will forgive you; but if you do not forgive men their trespasses, neither will your Father forgive your trespasses" (Matt. 6:14-15).

The best summary of the new Jewish ethics is found in its oldest manifesto, *Ecclesiasticus*, or the *Wisdom of Jesus the Son of Sirach* (27:30-28:7).[10]

---

4. *Mek. Rab. Ishmael* on Exod. 15:2.

5. This is the translation of Matt. 5:48 in the New English Bible.

6. *B. Ta'anit* 7a; Flusser, op. cit., 482.

7. *Deut. Rab.* on Deut. 7:7; Flusser, "Johanan ben Zakkai and Matthew," op. cit., 490-493.

8. Flusser, *Entdeckungen*, 1:22-23.

9. *M. Yoma* 8:9; H. D. Danby, *The Mishnah* (New York: Oxford University Press, 1985), 172.

10. This was written about the year 185 B.C.

Wrath and anger are loathsome things
   which the sinful person has for his own.
The vengeful will suffer the Lord's vengeance,
   for he remembers their sins in detail.
Forgive your neighbor's injustice;
   then, when you pray, your own sins will be forgiven.
Should a person nourish anger against another,
   and expect healing from the Lord?
Should a person refuse mercy to another,
   yet seek pardon for his own sins?
If one who is but flesh cherishes wrath,
   who will forgive his sins?
Remember your last day, set enmity aside;
   remember death and decay, and cease from sin!
Think of the commandments, hate not your neighbor;
   of the Most High's covenant, and overlook faults.

The notion that a man must be reconciled with his brother before praying for himself is linked in Sirach with a modification of the old idea of reward that is typical of the period. The old compensatory justice whereby the righteous man was rewarded according to the measure of his righteousness, and the sinner punished according to the measure of his sins, discomfitted many in those days. So, they began to think, if you love your neighbor, God will reward you with good; if you hate your neighbor, God will visit you with evil. Jesus too said something like this: "Judge not, and you will not be judged; condemn not and you will not be condemned; forgive, and you will be forgiven; give, and it will be given to you; good measure, pressed down, shaken together, running over, will be put into your lap. For the measure you give will be the measure you get back" (Luke 6:37-38).

The beginning of this saying reminds us of something the celebrated Hillel had already said: "Judge not your neighbor lest you find yourself in his place!"[11] The saying, "The measure you give will be the measure you get back,"[12] was a Jewish proverb in those days. The saying of Jesus reported by Luke finds an important parallel in the Lord's words as reproduced by Clement of Rome about A.D. 96: "Be merciful, and you will find

11. M. 'Abot 2:3; Danby, op. cit., 448.
12. Billerbeck, op. cit., 1:444-446.

mercy; forgive, and you will be forgiven; as you do, so it will be done to you; as you give, so it will be given to you; as you judge, so you will be judged; as you do good, so will good be done to you; with the same measure in which you give, it will be given to you" (1 Clem. 13:2). This saying came from the Mother Church, or perhaps from Jesus himself.[13]

The themes in which the new sensitivity in Judaism expressed itself in those days were interwoven. This dynamic method of thematic interplay is recognizable within Jesus' own didactic style. By his manner of teaching, he was able to interlace his sayings as well as link them with the broader web of Jewish motifs. Clement of Rome reports the Lord to say, "As you do, so it will be done to you." That is to say, as you treat your neighbor, so God will treat you. This is a fascinating variation on the so-called Golden Rule, accepted as a moral imperative by many nations. Jesus quoted this maxim when he said, "Whatever you wish that men should do to you, do so to them, for this is the law and the prophets" (Matt. 7:12). Among the Jews,[14] even before the time of Jesus, it was regarded as the summation of the entire law. Hillel had said, "What is distasteful to yourself, do not do to your neighbor; that is the whole law, the rest is but deduction." The Jews of that time probably interpreted the precept as follows: God metes out to you in the same measure in which you mete out to your neighbor. The consequence is, "As a person makes request from the Lord for his own soul, in the same manner let him behave toward every living soul."[15]

Both Jesus and Hillel before him saw the Golden Rule as a summary of the Law of Moses. This becomes intelligible when we consider that the biblical saying, "You shall love your neighbor as yourself" (Lev. 19:18), was esteemed by Jesus and by the Jews in general as a chief commandment of the law.[16] An old Aramaic translation of this biblical precept runs like this,

13. It certainly was not first compiled from the Greek Synoptic Gospels. Its Semitisms, among other things, prove this. *Mart. Pol.* 2:3 is dependent upon Clement, as the introduction to the Lord's saying shows (*1 Clem.* 13:1b). See A. Jaubert, *Épître aux Corinthiens, Sources chrétiennes* No. 167 (Paris: Éditions du Cerf, 1971), 52.

14. Billerbeck, op. cit., 1:459-460. On Hillel's dictum in *b. Shabbat* 31a, see Bacher, op. cit., 1:4. On the Golden Rule, see especially A. Dihle, *Die goldene Regel: eine Einführung in die Geschichte der antiken und frühchristlichen Vulgärethik* (Göttingen: Vandenhoeck & Ruprecht, 1962); P. S. Alexander, "Jesus and the Golden Rule," in *Jesus and Hillel* (ed. J. H. Charlesworth and L. L. Johns; Minneapolis: Fortress Press, 1997), 363-388.

15. *2 En.* 61:2; *The Old Testament Pseudepigrapha* (ed. J. H. Charlesworth; 2 vols.; Garden City, N.Y.: Doubleday, 1983-1985), 1:187; Billerbeck, op. cit., 1:460.

16. Billerbeck, op. cit., 1:358. Earlier, on page 354 he argues against the assertion of mod-

"Love your neighbor, for whatever displeases you, do not to him!"[17] This periphrastic translation turns the phrase "as yourself" into the negative form of the Golden Rule. The saying, "Love your neighbor," was understood as a positive commandment, and the words "as yourself" as the negative commandment included in it. You are not to treat your neighbor with hatred, because you would not like him to treat you in that way. Therefore, by means of Jewish parallels we are able to see how the Golden Rule (Matt. 7:12) and the commandment to love our neighbor (Matt. 22:39) are related within Jesus' teaching.

There was yet another explanation of the phrase "as yourself" in the biblical commandment to love one's neighbor, so important in those days. In Hebrew the phrase can also mean, "as though he were yourself." The commandment then reads, "Love your neighbor for he is like yourself." Sirach knew of this interpretation when he demanded that one forgive one's neighbor his trespasses, for it is a sin to withhold mercy from "a man like himself" (Sir. 28:3-5). Rabbi Hanina, who lived approximately one generation after Jesus, explicitly taught that this commandment to love one's neighbor is "a saying upon which the whole world hangs, a mighty oath from Mount Sinai. If you hate your neighbor whose deeds are wicked like your own, I, the Lord, will punish you as your judge; and if you love your neighbor whose deeds are good like your own, I, the Lord, will be faithful to you and have mercy on you."[18]

A man's relationship to his neighbor ought, therefore, to be determined by the fact that he is one with him both in his good and in his evil characteristics. This is not far from Jesus' commandment to love, but Jesus went further and broke the last fetters still restricting the ancient Jewish commandment to love one's neighbor. We have already seen that Rabbi Hanina believed that one ought to love the righteous and not hate the sinner. Jesus said, "I say to you, Love your enemies and pray for those who persecute you" (Matt. 5:44). It is true that in those days semi-Essene circles had reached similar conclusions from different presuppositions, and Jesus' moral teaching was influenced by these circles. Yet, influences do not explain everything.

---

ern Jewish scholars, "that the old synagogue, even in New Testament times, had understood the command to love one's neighbor to be contained in the universal obligation to love others." Let us assume that he is right. With what certainty, however, can we conclude that Jesus specifically extended the command to love one's neighbor to embrace Gentiles?

17. *Tg. Ps.-J.* on Lev. 19:18.

18. *'Abot R. Nat.* Ver. B (Schechter ed.), 53.

He who avoided his parental home in Nazareth and became the "friend of publicans and sinners" felt himself sent to "the lost sheep of the house of Israel." It was not simply his total way of life that urged Jesus to express loving devotion to sinners; this inclination was deeply linked with the purpose of his message. From the beginning until his death on the cross, the preaching of Jesus was, in turn, linked with his own way of life. The commandment to love one's enemies is so much his definitive characteristic that his are the only lips from which we hear the commandment in the whole of the New Testament. Elsewhere we hear only of mutual love, and blessing one's persecutors. In those days it was obviously very difficult for people to rise up to the heights of Jesus' commandment.[19]

Jesus mentioned the biblical commandment when he was explaining the sum and substance of the Law of Moses. "You shall love the Lord your God with all your heart, and with all your soul, and with all your mind (Deut. 6:5). This is the great rule in the law. And the second is similar to it, You shall love your neighbor as yourself (Lev. 19:18). On these two commandments depends all the law" (Matt. 22:35-40).[20]

It is almost certain that here Jesus was teaching an older tradition, because he saw it as important for his own message. This happened on other occasions, too. He simply borrowed a saying of a scribe. "And he said to them, 'Therefore every scribe[21] . . . is like a householder who brings out of his storeroom what is new and what is old'" (Matt. 13:52). Jesus' saying about the double commandment of love clearly was coined before his time. We have already seen that the biblical saying about love of one's neighbor was also described elsewhere as "the great commandment in the law."[22] This commandment is truly like the other — the commandment to love God — for both verses from the Bible (Deut. 6:5 and Lev. 19:18) begin with the same word. It was typical of rabbinical scholarship to see similarly phrased passages from the Bible as connected in content also. The first great commandment of Jesus — love of God — was thus in harmony with

---

19. H. W. Kuhn, "Das Liebesgebot Jesu," in *Vom Urchristentum zu Jesus, für Joachim Gnilka* (ed. H. Frankemölle and K. Kertelge; Freiburg: Herder, 1989), 194-230.

20. The phrase "and the prophets" was added later. We have tried to reconstruct the beginning of the Lord's saying according to the manner of speech of that time. The saying could be possible in its present form only if the inquirer had wanted to discover whether Jesus knew the answer. Luke (10:25-28) spotted this difficulty and wanted to overcome it.

21. The saying does not come from Jesus. It has undergone Christian elaboration.

22. See n. 14.

the spirit of contemporary Pharisaism.[23] In the list of the seven kinds of Pharisees that we have already mentioned,[24] two positive types are named: the Pharisee of fear, like Job, and the Pharisee of love, like Abraham. The many rabbinical passages that compare fear of God and love of God elevate love much higher than fear, for it was in harmony with the new Jewish sensitivity to serve God out of unconditional love rather than from fear of punishment.[25]

All that has been said explains how the double commandment of love existed in ancient Judaism before, and alongside, Jesus.[26] The fact that it does not appear in the rabbinical documents that have come down to us is probably accidental.[27] Mark (12:28-34) and Luke (10:25-28) show that on the question of "the great commandment" Jesus and the scribes were in agreement.

Jesus' saying in Matthew 22:35-40 is but one example where the uninitiated reader mistakenly thinks he has found a uniquely characteristic teaching of Jesus. In fact, however, he has failed to recognize the sayings that are truly revolutionary. All the same, such sayings as "the great commandment" fulfill a significant function within the total preaching of Jesus. From ancient Jewish writings we could easily construct a whole gospel without using a single word that originated with Jesus. This could only be done, however, because we do in fact possess the Gospels.

The same is true with the Sermon on the Mount in which Jesus presumably defines his own personal attitude toward the Law of Moses (Matt. 5:17-48). In the sermon, Jesus in a certain sense brings things old and new out of his storeroom. The sensitivity within ancient Judaism evolved a whole dialectic of sin, in contrast to the simple view of the Old Testament. When man ceases to be regarded as an unproblematic being,

---

23. *M. 'Abot* 1:3.

24. See chapter four, n. 32.

25. *Sipre* on Deut. 6:5. The correct text reads according to *Midr. Tannaim* on this passage.

26. *Jub.* 36:1-24; *Did.* 1:2; *T. Dan* 5:3; *T. Iss.* 5:2; 7:6; *T. Zeb.* 5:1; F. M. Braun, "Les Testaments des XII Patriarches," *RB* 67 (1960), 531-532.

27. The double precept of love does indeed appear in a medieval rabbinic compilation, but one cannot be sure whether the passage was somehow influenced by the Gospels. See Flusser, "The Ten Commandments and the New Testament," in *The Ten Commandments in History and Tradition* (ed. B. T. Segal and G. Levi; Jerusalem: Magnes Press, 1990), 241-243; idem, op. cit., 86-87.

10. Synagogue at Chorazin, a town upon which Jesus pronounced woe.

sins themselves become a problem. If a person is not careful, one sin can lead to another. Even an action that does not appear sinful can cause him to become entangled in a real sin. There was a saying, "Flee from what is evil and from what resembles evil."[28] If we apply this concept to the commandments, we discover that the lesser commandments are as serious as the greater.

Jesus' exegesis in Matthew 5:17-48 should be understood in this sense. The exegesis proper is preceded by a preamble (5:17-20) where Jesus justifies his method. It would seem that exaggerated importance has been attached to the first sentence (5:17) of this introduction. Jesus simply intended to say, "Think not that I come to cancel the law;[29] I do not come to cancel, but to uphold it." Thus, following the customary language[30] of his

28. About this saying, see Flusser, "Which Is the Right Way That a Man Should Choose for Himself?" *Tarbiz* 60 (1991), 172-173 [Hebrew]; idem, *Das essenische Abenteuer*, 88-91; M. van Loopik, *The Ways of the Sages and the Way of the World* (Tübingen: J. C. B. Mohr, 1991), 194-197.

29. The phrase "or the prophets" does not seem to be original.

30. For a parallel to Jesus' use of the idiom "to fulfill," see Rom. 3:31.

time, he avoided the accusation that the exegesis of the law that followed abrogated the original meaning of the words of the Bible. He could not have wanted to do this because the law, as written, is mysteriously bound up with the existence of this world. Even the minor commandments are to be obeyed. This implies a tightening up of the law, not regarding ritual, but in respect to the relationships between people. This attitude was also present in Judaism at that time, as the following saying exemplifies: "Everyone who publicly shames his neighbor sheds his blood."[31]

The first two biblical expositions of Jesus in the Sermon on the Mount are constructed on this conceptual and formal scheme. It is not just the murderer, but he who is angry with his brother, who is condemned (Matt. 5:21-22), and "every one who looks at a woman lustfully has already committed adultery with her in his heart" (5:28). According to a later traditional Jewish saying, three classes of sinners are consigned to hell for all eternity: the adulterer, he who publicly puts his neighbor to shame, and he who insults his neighbor.[32] Jesus, too, had something to say regarding this last type: "Whoever insults his brother shall be liable to the council, and whoever says, 'You fool!' shall be liable to hell" (5:22).

The continuation (Matt. 5:29-30) has an interesting parallel in rabbinical literature. Jesus said, "If your eye causes you to sin, pluck it out, for it is better to lose it than for your whole body to go into hell."[33] The same is said about the hand and the foot. Earlier (5:28), Jesus said that every one who looked at a woman lustfully had already committed adultery with her in his heart. There was a Jewish opinion[34] that the word "to commit adultery" in Hebrew had four letters in order to warn us that adultery could be committed by hand, foot, eye, and heart. Jesus began his exegesis of the scriptures by stressing the importance of the lesser commandments. In this spirit he was then able to equate anger with murder and lust with adultery.

In the Jewish "Two Ways" which is preserved in the early Christian document,[35] the *Didache*, we read, "My child, flee all evil, and from all that is like unto it. Be not prone to anger, for anger leadeth to murder.... My

---

31. *B. B. Mesi'a* 58b.
32. Ibid.
33. Matthew abridges the saying, and Mark 9:43-48 elaborates it.
34. *Midr. Hagadol* on Exod. 20:14.
35. J. P. Audet, "Affinités litteraires et doctrinales du Manuel de Discipline," *RB* (1952), 219-238; Flusser, "Die Zwölfapostellehre und Jesu," op. cit., 79-96.

child, be not lustful, for lust leadeth to fornication . . . for from all these are generated adulteries."[36] We have already met the first statement as a Jewish moral rule, and the two applications of the rule correspond to the sixth and the seventh of the Ten Commandments that Jesus expounds in exactly the same way in the Sermon on the Mount.

The second half of the Decalogue can be seen as the background to Jesus' scriptural exegesis, as it is also seen in the "Two Ways." These biblical commandments speak of our relation to our neighbor, and so the real conclusion of Jesus' exegesis is his commentary (Matt. 5:43-48) on the great commandment, "Love your neighbor as yourself." Those who listened to Jesus' preaching of love might well have been moved by it. Many in those days thought in a similar way. Nonetheless, in the clear purity of his love they must have detected something very special. Jesus did not accept all that was thought and taught in the Judaism of his time. Although not really a Pharisee himself, he was closest to the Pharisees of the school of Hillel who preached love, and he led the way further to unconditional love — even of one's enemies and of sinners. As we shall see, this was no mere sentimental teaching.

---

36. *Did.* 3:1-3; Flusser, *JOC*, 508.

CHAPTER 6

Ethics

One day someone said to Jesus, "I will follow you wherever you go." To this he replied, "Foxes have holes, and birds have nests; but man[1] has nowhere to lay his head" (Matt. 8:19-20). This answer is in reality a social protest. The African-American social outcasts knew well what Jesus meant, when they sang,

> De foxes have holes in de groun',
> An de birds have nests in de air,
> An ev'ryting have a hiding place,
> But we poor sinners have none.[2]

With Jesus the social overtone is louder than with the rabbis. It forms the core of his authentic message. He, however, was no social revolutionary in the usual sense of the word. The Essenes were of a different stamp. Originally they were an apocalyptic revolutionary movement that developed an ideological amalgamation of poverty and double predestination. They were the true sons of light who were the divinely chosen poor. At the imminent end of time, by the power of arms and the assistance of the heavenly hosts, they would inherit the land and conquer the whole world. The sons of darkness — including the rest of Israel, the Gentiles, and the demonic powers who rule the world — would then be annihilated. Even if, by Jesus' time, the Essenes had mollified their activist ideology and become

---

1. Literally, "the son of man."
2. *Negro Spirituals* (ed. J. Jahn and A. M. Dauer; Frankfurt am Main: Fischer Bücherei, 1962), 48.

11. Caves 4B, 4A, and 5 at Qumran. Writings of the Essenes were discovered in these and other caves near the Dead Sea. Photo by J. H. Charlesworth.

12. Room at Qumran. Photo by J. H. Charlesworth.

a more contemplative mystic sect, they still lived in communities with common ownership, prized poverty highly, and kept themselves strictly apart from the rest of Jewish society.

The Essene sons of light restricted their economic ties with the surrounding world as much as possible. "None of them will eat of their food or drink of their drink or take anything from their hands, unless it has been bought from them . . . for, all who despise His word He will destroy out of the world, all their deeds are as filth before Him, and all their possessions are stained with uncleanness."[3] The Essenes, then, were obliged "to separate themselves from the sons of destruction and keep free from the possession of wickedness."[4]

Obviously, Jesus was unwilling to assent to their ideological and economic separation. "The sons of this world are wiser in dealing with their own generation than the sons of light. And I tell you, make friends for yourself from the wealth of [the men of] unrighteousness.[5] . . . If then you have not been faithful with the unrighteous mammon, who will entrust to you true riches? And if you have not been faithful in that which is another's, who will give you that which is your own?" (Luke 16:8-12). Using their own self-description — sons of light — Jesus made an ironic allusion to the Essenes.

Like the Essenes of his own time, Jesus too regarded all possessions as a threat to true piety. "No one can serve two masters; for either he will hate the one and love the other, or he will be devoted to the one and despise the other. You cannot serve God and mammon" (Matt. 6:24).[6] The dualism of this saying is Essene in outlook. The Essenes endeavored "to love everything that he has chosen, to hate everything that he has repudiated, to keep far from evil, and cleave to all good works."[7] Between good and evil there is eternal enmity, and so also between the sons of light and the sons of darkness, between God and Belial, the devil. Jesus could not

---

3. 1QS 5:14-20.

4. CD 6:14-15.

5. Prior to the discovery of the Dead Sea Scrolls, the preposition ἐκ was usually translated in our verse as "through," because the context was not understood. Linguistically this is impossible. In the original, moreover, the Aramaic *mammona* (Hebrew, *mammon*) means "possession." For the translation and whole concept, see "Jesus' Opinion about the Essenes," *JOC*, 150-168.

6. Flusser and Safrai, "The Slave of Two Masters," *JOC*, 169-172.

7. 1QS 1:4-5.

accept this attitude. He did not embrace Essene theology, but only certain social aspects of their philosophy of life. Therefore, the two masters who figure in his saying are not God and the devil, Belial, but God and mammon.

According to Jesus, possessions are an obstacle to virtue. "Children, how hard it is for those who trust in riches to enter the kingdom of God! It is easier for a camel to go through the eye of a needle than for a rich man to enter the kingdom of God" (Mark 10:24-25). For both the Essenes and Jesus, poverty, humility, purity, and unsophisticated simplicity of heart were the essential religious virtues. Jesus and the Essenes thought that in the very near divine future, the social outcasts and oppressed would become the preferred, "for theirs is the kingdom of heaven," and "those who mourn will be comforted." Jesus certainly did not mean for us to give a sentimental slant to these sayings, as the immediately following "woes," addressed to the "rich," the "satiated," and "those who laugh" prove (Luke 6:24-26). These people will have sorrow and weep when the end comes. Now for the first time, because of the Dead Sea Scrolls, we can understand the phrase "the poor in spirit." It was a title of honor among the Essenes.[8] These are the poor to whom the Holy Spirit is given. In one passage from the Essene hymnbook (1QH[a] 18:14-15) the author thanks God for having appointed him preacher of his grace. He is destined "to proclaim to the *meek* the multitude of Thine mercies and to let them that *are of contrite spirit* hear salvation from his everlasting source, and to them *that mourn* everlasting joy." These correspond to "the meek," "the poor in spirit," and "those who mourn" of the first three beatitudes of Jesus.

An even more significant parallel to Jesus' "beatitudes" and "woes" occurs in Jewish writings that are not Essene, but belong to the fringe of the Essene movement.[9] These are the so-called *Testaments of the Twelve Patriarchs* that we possess in a Christian recension. It is easy, however, to detect the Jewish provenance of these writings. The work is presented in the form of the valedictory speeches of the twelve sons of Jacob. Judah speaks about salvation at the end of time:[10]

---

8. Flusser, "Blessed Are the Poor in Spirit," *JOC*, 102-114. Over them God's Spirit is hovering. See 4Q 521, frag. 2ii + 4, line 6; E. Puech, "Une apocalypse messianique (4Q521)," *RevQ* 15 (1992), 485-486.

9. See Flusser, "Some Notes to the Beatitudes," *JOC*, 117.

10. *T. Jud.* 25:3-5; Sparks, op. cit., 550-551.

And there will be one people of the Lord and one language;
And there will be no spirit of error of Beliar anymore,
For he will be thrown into the fire forever.
And those who have died in grief will rise again in joy,
And those who are in penury[11] will be made rich,
And those who are in want will eat their fill,
And those who are weak will receive their strength,
And those who have been put to death for the Lord's sake
    will awake to life.
And the harts of Jacob will run with gladness,
And the eagles of Israel will fly with joy
(But the ungodly will mourn and sinners weep),
And all the peoples will glorify the Lord forever.

The similarity between the beatitudes and woes of Jesus and the *Testament of Judah* is obvious. The Jewish author has poetically expanded the common tradition and especially elaborated on the resurrection of the dead. He says that those who have died for the Lord's sake will awaken to life, whereas Jesus promises that the persecuted will inherit the kingdom of heaven. This suggests that the *Testaments of the Twelve Patriarchs* are a semi-Essene work. It is true that genuine Essenes believed in paradise, and hell, and in eternal life; but they did not believe, as did the Pharisees and, later, the Christians, in the resurrection of the dead. It is remarkable that in the first three Gospels, Jesus too speaks about eternal life, but never explicitly of the resurrection of the dead — with the exception of his conversation with the Sadducees "who say there is no resurrection" (Luke 20:27-39 and par.), and when, in apparently secondary passages, he is speaking about his own resurrection. Is this coincidental?

Having said this about the Essenes, we need to explain how it is that the profoundly human beatitudes of Jesus breathe the spirit of the Essenes who, although less hostile in his times, still had not discarded their misanthropic theological impulse. It should be noted in this connection that radical sects can often be quite amiable. The Essene writings are distinguished by their fervent piety. Both the Jewish classical historian Josephus and the philosopher Philo of Alexandria are not far afield when they depict the Essenes as Tolstoy-like men. In the course of time, an inhuman

---

11. The following, "for the Lord's sake," is evidently an interpolation.

ideology can produce almost human consequences. This happened with the Essenes. Humanization was fully realized in Jewish circles that existed on the fringes of Essenism and were simultaneously influenced by the sensitivity of rabbinic Judaism. Jesus was familiar with the ideas current in these circles, and incorporated them into his transvaluation of all values.

The Essenes believed that God had predestined their final victory and the annihilation of evil. If the end has not yet come, one is still subject to the evil powers of this world. Hence the way one lives in these times is regulated as follows: "Show eternal, secret hatred to the men of destruction, leaving them property and the produce of labor, as a slave shows humility to him who rules over him. But at the same time let everyone be mindful of the predestined time — the day of vengeance."[12] This view gave rise to a kind of inhuman humanity, so that the Essenes could say of themselves, "I will repay no one with evil; I will visit men with good, for God judges all things that live and he will repay. . . . I will not give up the struggle with the men of destruction until the day of vengeance, and I will not turn away my anger from wicked men and will not rest until God appoints judgment."[13]

The Essene discovery that evil can be overcome with good has proved a mighty weapon in the history of the world. As we shall see, this idea was developed further by Jesus and adopted by Christianity — even independently of Jesus' doctrine of love.[14] The rule, "Do not resist one who is evil" (Matt. 5:39), has also penetrated into modern times. It reached Gandhi, who learned of it through Christianity and grafted it into ancient Indian ideas. This originally Essene idea thus helped to liberate India by passive resistance.

History has shown that an enemy can be overcome by goodness, even if one does not love him, and even if he becomes no better as a result of the good that is done to him. This was what the Essenes wanted; but it is hard to fulfill these two conditions. It is only human nature to begin to love the one for whom we are doing good. More important, when we genuinely do good for someone — even though we might only love them a little — as a rule, they become a better human being. Those groups which occupied the fringe of Essenism outgrew the Essene theology of hate, and eventually began to affirm these same consequences of doing good to one's enemy. In

12. 1QS 9:21-26.
13. 1QS 10:17-20.
14. See especially Rom. 12:9–13:7.

the *Testaments of the Twelve Patriarchs,* especially in the *Testament of Benjamin,* the loving conquest of the sinner becomes an important moral imperative.[15]

> The good man has not an eye that cannot see; for he shows mercy to all men, sinners though they may be, and though they may plot his ruin. This man, by doing good, overcomes evil, since he is protected by the good. . . . If, then, your minds are predisposed to what is good, children, wicked men will live at peace with you, the profligate will reverence you and turn towards the good, and the money-grubbers will not only turn their backs on the things they have been striving for, but even give what they have got by their money-grubbing to those who are in distress. . . . His good mind will not let him speak with two tongues, one of blessing and one of cursing, one of insult and one of compliment, one of sorrow and one of joy, one of quietness and one of tumult, one of hypocrisy and one of truth, one of poverty and one of wealth; but it has a single disposition only, simple and pure, that says the same thing to everyone. It has no double sight or hearing; for whenever such a man does, or says, or sees anything, he knows that the Lord is looking into his soul in judgment. And he purifies his mind so that he is not condemned by God and men. But everything that Beliar does is double and has nothing single about it at all.

The same spirit was expressed by Jesus, when he said,

> You have heard that it was said, "An eye for an eye and a tooth for a tooth . . . stripe for stripe" [Exod. 21:24-25].[16] But I say to you, Do not resist one who is evil. If any one strikes you on the right cheek, turn to him the other also; and if any one would sue you and take your coat, let him have your cloak as well; and if any one forces you to go one mile, go with him two miles. Give to him who begs from you, and do not refuse him who would borrow from you.[17] You

15. *T. Ben.* 4:2-3; 5:1; 6:5-7; Sparks, op. cit., 595-597.

16. The ending of the biblical saying is missing in Matthew, although it is precisely its closing words that Jesus explains.

17. So, according to Luke 6:30. See the correct comment by G. Strecker, *Der Weg der Gerechtigkeit; Untersuchung zur Theologie des Matthäus* (Göttingen: Vandenhoeck & Ruprecht, 1966), 134.

have heard that it was said, "You shall love your neighbor[18] [Lev. 19:18] and hate your enemy." But I say to you, Love your enemies[19] and pray for those who persecute you,[20] so that you may be sons of your Father who is in heaven; for He makes His sun rise on the evil and on the good, and sends rain on the just and on the unjust. . . . You, therefore, must be perfect, as your heavenly Father is perfect. (Matt. 5:38-48)

According to *The Testament of Benjamin,* one must not have "two tongues, one of blessing and one of cursing . . . but everything that Beliar does is double and has nothing simple about it at all." According to Jesus, in loving one's neighbor one must be undivided, as God is undivided. Even in the Old Testament the saying "an eye for an eye" (Exod. 21:24) was not taken literally. Jesus wanted to take the interpretation of this verse from Exodus further by explaining, "stripe for stripe" to mean turning the other cheek to receive yet another stroke. This, too, was in harmony with the pietistic spirit of the Essene fringe. According to *The Testaments of the Twelve Patriarchs,*[21] the leading patriarch, Zebulon, went so far as to take a garment surreptitiously to a poor man he saw shivering in the winter's cold. On one occasion, being able to find nothing to give to a poor man, he accompanied him seven stages of his journey, wailing all the time, for his heart went out in sympathy to the man.

It was from the Essene fringe, too, that Jesus took over both the idea that one ought not to resist one who is evil, and the concept of good news addressed particularly to the poor and the outcast. The doctrine of the Essene fringe about maintaining a consistent relationship with all men

---

18. Instead of "as yourself," Matthew has, "and hate your enemy." These words are a secondary explanation of the (lacking) "as yourselves." Those who did so (evidently Sadducees) explained these words: "Act with the neighbor as he treats you. If he is good to you, he is your friend and then be friendly to him, but if he wrongs you, hate him." This fits the ancient (pagan) vulgar ethics of retribution. About this kind of ethics, see Dihle, op. cit. The early Greek poet Archilochos (seventh century B.C.) boasts: "I know to love a man who loves (me) and to hate the enemy." See *Archilochos: griechisch und deutsch* (ed. M. Treu; Munich: Heimeran, 1959), 10.

19. The correct interpretation of this love of the enemy is given in Luke 6:27: "Love your enemies, do good to those who hate you."

20. See the interesting rabbinic parallel in *t. B. Qam.* 9:29-30 (ed. M. S. Zuckermandel; Jerusalem: Wahrmann Books, 1970), 365.

21. *T. Zeb.,* chap. 7.

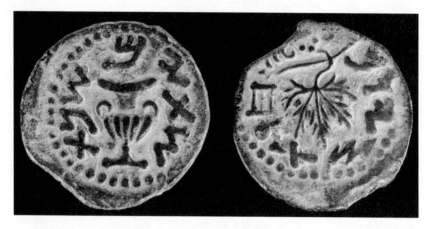

13. Bronze prutah of the Jewish war against Rome, struck in Jerusalem in A.D. 67, depicting amphora and vine leaf. Hebrew inscription around amphora: "Year 2"; around vine leaf: "Freedom of Zion."

without distinction was developed by Jesus to become the command to love one's enemies, and in particular to love sinners. When the Pharisees upbraided him for eating in the company of publicans (who are sinners),[22] he replied, "Those who are well have no need of a physician, only those who are sick." And to this he added, "I came not to call the righteous, but sinners" (Luke 5:30-32 and par.).

The paradox of Jesus' break with the customary old morality was marvelously expressed in the parable of the workers in the vineyard (Matt. 20:1-16). A proprietor went out to hire workers for his vineyard, and promised each one a daily wage of one denarius. In the evening he paid them all the same wage irrespective of the length of time they had worked. Those who had started work early began to complain, and so the proprietor said to one of them, "'Friend, I am doing you no wrong; did you not agree with me for a denarius? Take what belongs to you, and go; I choose to give to this last as I give to you. Am I not allowed to do what I choose with what belongs to me? Or do you begrudge my kindness?' So the last will be first, and the first last."

22. "And sinners" is rightly lacking in two important manuscripts of Luke 5:30, because eating "with sinners" is, according to classical Judaism, an overly abstract accusation. It crept into Luke 5:30 (and in the two Synoptic parallels) from Jesus' answer in Luke 5:32 (and par.).

Here as elsewhere, the principle of reward is accepted by Jesus, but all the norms of the usual concepts of God's righteousness are abrogated. One might think that this comes about because God, in his all-embracing love and mercy, makes no distinctions between men. With Jesus, however, the transvaluation of all values is not idyllic. Even misfortune does not distinguish between the sinner and the just man. On one occasion someone brought the news to Jesus about the Galileans whose blood Pilate mixed with their sacrifices. The bystanders obviously expected a political reply, but Jesus said, "Do you think that these Galileans were worse sinners than all other Galileans, because they suffered thus? I tell you, No! But unless you repent, you will all likewise perish. Or those eighteen upon whom the tower in Siloam fell and killed, do you think that they were worse offenders than all the others who dwelt in Jerusalem? I tell you, No! But unless you repent you will all likewise perish" (Luke 13:1-5).

It was then, more or less, a general opinion that calamity — and illness — was a punishment for sin. It could be argued, therefore, that these men were greater sinners than other Galileans. Jesus did not reject this general opinion, but at the same time he rejected the current application of this view as simplistic. Instead of the vulgar ethics, he called to Israel, "Repent or perish!" He illustrated his call for a national repentance by the following parable of the barren fig tree (Luke 13:6-9). Later on, being in Jerusalem he saw the imminent catastrophe as almost inevitable (Luke 19:40-44). The future destruction of Jerusalem could have been avoided, if it had chosen the way of peace and repentance.[23]

Jesus' concept of the righteousness of God, therefore, is incommensurable with reason. Man cannot measure it, but he can grasp it. It leads to the preaching of the kingdom in which the last will be first and the first last. It leads also from the Sermon on the Mount to Golgotha, where the just man dies a criminal's death. It is at once profoundly moral, and yet beyond good and evil. In this paradoxical scheme, all the "important," customary virtues, and the well-knit personality, worldly dignity, and the proud insistence upon the formal fulfillment of the law, are fragmentary and empty. Socrates questioned the intellectual side of man. Jesus questioned the moral. Both were executed. Can this be mere chance?

---

23. See I. H. Marshall, *The Gospel of Luke*, NIGTC (Exeter: Paternoster Press, 1978), 553, 717; Grotius, op. cit., 3:343-344.

CHAPTER 7

The Kingdom of Heaven

One day they sent spies to watch and to catch Jesus in what he said. "'Teacher,' they said to him, 'we know that you speak and teach rightly, and show no partiality. Is it lawful for us to give tribute to Caesar, or not?' But he perceived their craftiness, and said to them, 'Show me a coin. Whose likeness and inscription are on it?' They said, 'Caesar's.' He said to them, 'Then render to Caesar the things that are Caesar's, and to God the things that are God's'" (cf. Luke 20:20-26).

Once again Jesus had succeeded in evading capture, while at the same time making his meaning unmistakably clear. One cannot serve two masters, God and mammon. Money comes from Caesar, and so it must be handed over to him. Quite certainly the saying did not express friendship toward the Romans, but it also showed that Jesus was no supporter of revolt against them. His ethical teaching made that impossible. He was well aware of social reality, but that was not his most important concern. Once one has allowed oneself to enter the game, one must play according to the rules. "Settle matters quickly with your accuser while you are going with him to court, lest your accuser hand you over to the judge, and the judge to the guard, and you be put in prison; truly I say to you, you will never get out till you have paid the last penny" (Matt. 5:25-26).

It is hard to agree with those who maintain[1] that Pilate was right when he executed Jesus because he was a political agitator, or the leader of a gang

---

1. See especially the discussion by W. G. Kümmel, "Jesusforschung seit 1950," *TRu* 31 (1966), 312-313. The one saying of Jesus that can seriously be taken in an active sense is Luke 22:35-38, but see my comments in "Jesus' Opinion about the Essenes," *JOC*, 165 n. 40.

in the Jewish war of liberation against Rome. In addition to the trial of Jesus, the chief evidence cited in support of this view is that Jesus had preached the kingdom of heaven. "Heaven" is a circumlocution for "God" (cf. 1 Macc 4:5), and people in general believed that when the kingdom of God came, Israel would be freed from the yoke of Rome. At that time most Jews hated the occupying Roman power. The party known as the Zealots[2] believed that armed struggle against Rome was divinely ordained, and their terrorist activists made the country unsafe. One of the twelve apostles had been a Zealot at one time.[3]

The fundamental teaching of the Zealots was "the demand for the sole rule of God, which led to a radical breach with the Roman Caesar's claims to sovereignty; it was linked with the expectation that, through battle with the Roman oppressor, the eschatological liberation of Israel at the end of time would be ushered in."[4] Although it is possible that the Zealots, too, spoke about the kingdom of heaven, at that time the phrase had in fact become an anti-Zealot slogan. Because there are clear similarities between the rabbinic idea of the kingdom and that of Jesus, we may assume that Jesus embraced and developed their idea.[5]

Although Israel now languishes under a foreign yoke, at the end God alone will rule in Zion. The anti-Zealot parties, too, cherished this hope, and some of the disciples of Jesus thought likewise. According to Acts 1:6 they asked the risen Lord, "Lord, will you at this time restore the kingdom to Israel?" In the book of Revelation (chap. 18) we hear jubilation at the fall of Rome, but the "historical Jesus" of the Gospels is silent on this point. Could the friend of the poor and the persecuted be a friend to the Romans? It seems that Jesus indirectly hinted to the end of foreign occupation of his homeland (Luke 21:24, 28). Yet, even if Jesus did foresee the fall

---

2. See M. Hengel, *Die Zeloten: Untersuchungen zur jüdischen Freiheitsbewegung in der Zeit von Herodes I bis 70 n. Chr, Arbeiten zur Geschichte des Spätjudentums und Urchristentums* (2 vols.; Leiden: Brill, 1961).

3. Acts 1:13; Mark 3:18; Luke 6:15.

4. Hengel, op. cit., 1:384.

5. For the whole theme, see Flusser, "Die jüdische Messiaserwartung Jesu," *Das Christentum — eine jüdische Religion* (Munich: Kösel-Verlag, 1990), 37-62; idem, "The Dead of Masada in the Eyes of Their Contemporaries," in *Jews and Judaism in the Second Temple, Mishna and Talmud Period: Studies in Honor of Shmuel Safrai* (ed. I. Gafni, A. Oppenheimer, and M. Stern; Jerusalem: Yad Izhak Ben-Zvi, 1993), 116-146 [Hebrew]. B. H. Young, *Jesus and His Jewish Parables* (New York: Paulist Press, 1989), 189-235.

of Rome, the Evangelists might not have mentioned it, so as not to cast even more suspicion upon the founder of their religion.

The domination of Israel by a foreign power was seen as a punishment for her sins. "If the house of Israel transgresses the law, foreign nations will rule over her, and if they keep the law, mourning, tribulation, and lamentation will depart from her."[6] In other words, "If Israel kept the words of the law given to them, no people or kingdom would rule over them. And what does the law say? 'Take upon you the yoke of My kingdom and emulate one another in the fear of God and practice kindness to one another.'"[7] Thus, even at present, there may be individuals who are, so to speak, living in the kingdom of God. "Every one who takes upon himself the yoke of the law removes from his shoulders the yoke of government and daily sorrows. But whoever removes the yoke of the law will be burdened with the yoke of government and daily sorrows."[8]

When Israel wants to do only the will of God, the kingdom of heaven will be revealed to them. "If Israel at the Red Sea had said, 'He is king for all eternity,' no nation or language would have ruled over them; but they said (Ex. 15:18), 'the Lord will reign for ever and ever.'"[9] This saying was apparently not only directed against the futuristic hopes of the apocalyptists, but against the Zealots who wanted to take heaven by force. When the Zealots had forcibly assumed government and the rebellion had been bloodily suppressed by Rome, one of the scribes complained of "the rulers of the cities of Judah, who have put off the yoke of heaven and assumed the yoke of the government of flesh and blood."[10] This view was shared by Rabbi Yohanan ben Zakkai.[11] After the destruction of Jerusalem, when he saw the daughter of Nicodemus assuaging her hunger with grains of barley picked from the dung of an Arab horse, he wept and said, "As long as Israel is doing the will of God, no nation or kingdom shall rule over it. But if they are not doing the will of God, he will deliver them into the hand of the lowest nation and not only this, but under the legs of the beast of the lowest nation."[12]

6. *Tg. Ezek.* 2:10.

7. *Sipre* on Deut. 32:29.

8. *M. 'Abot* 3:6.

9. *Mek. Rab. Ishmael* (Horovitz and Rabin, ed.), 150-51.

10. *'Abot R. Nat.* (Schechter, ed.), 72.

11. *T. Sotah* 14:4.

12. *Sipre* on Deut piska 304 (Finkelstein, ed.), 325; *Mek. Rab. Ishmael* on Exod. 19:1 (Horovitz and Rabin, ed.), 203. See Bacher, op. cit., 1:42.

According to Jesus, the coming of God's rule, and hope in the eschatological savior were two distinctly different aspects of the expectation of the end. The idea of the kingdom of God and the Son of Man were never confused in his mind.[13] According to both Jesus and the rabbis, the kingdom of heaven emerges, indeed, out of God's might, but it is realized upon earth by men. Man, then, can and should work for the realization of the kingdom. "Repent, for the kingdom of heaven is at hand" (Matt. 4:17).

The first to suggest the eschatological orientation of the message of Jesus through his preaching of the kingdom of God was Hermann Samuel Reimarus (1694-1768). G. E. Lessing, as we know, subsequently published fragments of his writings. Starting from Lessing's text, Albert Schweitzer then elaborated his own "consistent eschatology": "To be worthy of consideration, Jesus' mode of thought must be either completely eschatological or completely non-eschatological."[14] Reimarus certainly would not have agreed with this. In the final version of his work, Reimarus distinguished between Jesus' non-eschatological moral preaching of repentance and "his main purpose, which was to establish the kingdom."[15] Modern portrayals of Jesus, however, often trace his eschatology along a different line. The warning of the great Christian and religious socialist Leonhard Ragaz was in vain.

> The notion is quite untenable, that Jesus built a kind of ethic and theology upon his expectation of the imminence of the kingdom of God. This sort of thing may well happen in the study of a theologian or a philosopher. . . . The relationship is quite the reverse from what the eschatological systematizers imagine. It is not the eschatological expectation which determines Jesus' understanding of God and of man . . . but, conversely, his understanding of God and of man which determines his eschatological expectation. . . . To fail to see this one must have already put on a professor's spectacles.[16]

13. See P. Vielhauer, *Aufsätze zum Neuen Testament* (2 vols.; Munich: Chr. Kaiser Verlag, 1965-1979), 1:vii.

14. A. Schweitzer, *In Quest of the Historical Jesus: A Critical Study of Its Progress from Reimarus to Wrede* (New York: Macmillan, 1968), viii.

15. H. S. Reimarus, *Apologie; oder, Schutzschrift für die vernünftigen Verehrer Gottes* (2 vols.; Frankfurt am Main: Insel Verlag, 1972), 2:147-148.

16. L. Ragaz, *Die Botschaft vom Reiche Gottes: Ein Katechismus für Erwachsene* (Bern: Herbert Lang, 1942), 280; idem, *Die Geschichte der Sache Christi: Ein Versuch* (Bern: Verlag Herbert Lang & Cie, 1945), 112-113.

Schweitzer was still concerned with the painful truth, but the later eschatologists fell into a non-committal admiration of an alleged pan-eschatologism of Jesus. If we understand every saying of Jesus in a purely eschatological sense, so that eschatology becomes unrealistic and purely existential, then we arrive at the conclusion that the demands of Jesus are not morally binding. One New Testament scholar has said that turning the other cheek is only allowed because it is a "messianic license" — otherwise, this sort of thing would be revolutionary. This is a correct assessment, for the preaching of Jesus is indeed revolutionary and subversive.

For Jesus and the rabbis, the kingdom of God is *both* present and future, but their perspectives are different. When Jesus was asked when the kingdom was to come, he said, "The kingdom of God is not coming with signs to be observed; nor will they say, 'Lo, here it is!' or 'There!' For behold, the kingdom of God is in the midst of you" (Luke 17:20-21). Elsewhere he said, "But if it is by the finger of God that I cast out demons, then the kingdom of God has come upon you" (Luke 11:20). According to Jesus, therefore, there are individuals who are already in the kingdom of heaven. This is not exactly the same sense in which the rabbis understood the kingdom. For them the kingdom had always been an unchanging reality, but for Jesus there was a specific point in time when the kingdom began to break out upon earth. "From the days of John the Baptist until now the kingdom of heaven is breaking through, and those who break through, seize it" (Matt. 11:12). According to Luke 16:16, "every one forces his way in." Both of these dominical sayings reflect an ancient Jewish homily on Micah 2:13.

This, then, is the "realized eschatology" of Jesus. He is the only Jew of ancient times known to us who preached not only that people were on the threshold of the end of time, but that the new age of salvation had already begun.[17] This new age had begun with John the Baptist who made the great break-through, but he himself was not a member of the kingdom. The eruption of the kingdom of God also meant its expansion among the people. "The kingdom of heaven is like leaven which a woman took and hid in three measures of meal, till all was leavened" (Matt. 13:33). On the growth of the kingdom of heaven Jesus also said, "It is like a grain of mustard seed which a man took and sowed in his garden; and it grew and became a tree, and the birds of the air made nests in its branches" (Luke 13:18-19).

17. Jeremias, *Parables*, 227.

A similar image is to be found in the Essene hymnbook.[18] The poet compares the congregation to a tree: "all the beasts of the forest fed on its leafy boughs . . . and its branches sheltered all the birds, but all the trees by the water rose above it." This is a symbol of the wicked world all around. The tree of life itself is concealed — "the seal of its mystery remains unobserved, unrecognized." God himself guards its secret; the outsider "sees but does not recognize, and thinks but does not believe in the source of life." This reminds us of the words of Jesus. "To you it has been given to know the secrets of God, but to them it has not been given" (cf. Matt. 13:11-15).[19] What is much more important is that the parable of the mustard seed resembles the Essene symbol for the community.

Thus, for Jesus, the kingdom of heaven is not only the eschatological rule of God that has dawned already, but a divinely willed movement that spreads among people throughout the earth. The kingdom of heaven is not simply a matter of God's kingship, but also the domain of his rule, an expanding realm embracing ever more and more people, a realm into which one may enter and find one's inheritance, a realm where there are both great and small. That is why Jesus called the twelve to be *fishers of men*[20] and to heal and preach everywhere. "The kingdom of heaven is at hand" (Matt. 10:5-16). For this reason he demanded of some that they should leave everything behind and follow him. We do not mean to assert that Jesus wanted to found a church or even a single community, but that he wanted to start a movement. Stated in exaggerated ecclesiological terms, we might say that the eruption of the kingdom of heaven is a process in which ultimately the invisible Church becomes identical with the visible.

That which Jesus recognized and desired is fulfilled in the message of the kingdom. There God's unconditional love for all becomes visible, and the barriers between sinners and righteous are shattered. Human dignity becomes null and void, the last become first and the first become last. The poor, the hungry, the meek, the mourners, and the persecuted inherit the kingdom of heaven. In Jesus' message of the kingdom, however, the strictly social factor does not seem to be the decisive thing. His revolution has to do chiefly with the transvaluation of all the usual moral values, and hence his promise is especially for sinners. "Truly, I say to you, the tax collectors

---

18. 1QH[a] 8:4-14; 6:15-16.
19. Flusser, *Gleichnisse*, 273-277.
20. Matt. 4:19.

and the harlots go into the kingdom of God before you" (Matt. 21:31-32). Jesus found resonance among the social outcasts and the despised, just as John the Baptist had done before him.

Even the non-eschatological ethical teaching of Jesus can presumably be oriented toward his message of the kingdom.[21] Since Satan and his powers will be overthrown and the present world-order shattered, it is to be regarded almost with indifference, and ought not to be strengthened by opposition. Therefore, one should not resist evildoers; one should love one's enemy and not provoke the Roman Empire to attack.[22] For when the kingdom of God appears, all this will vanish.

The rabbinical concept of the kingdom of heaven does not appear among the Essenes.[23] Yet, with the help of the writings of the Dead Sea Sect — the Essenes — and pertinent Jewish Apocalyptic literature, it has become clear that John the Baptist shared their fascinating spiritual world of thought. Jesus' ideas, on the other hand, were mainly shaped by Israel's Sages. In his redemptive timetable there was no room for his oft-assumed "acute eschatology." For him, the day of the Son of Man lay still in the future (Luke 17:22-24).

The ideological polarity between John and Jesus finally led to the separation of these two spiritual giants. When the Baptist heard about the activity of Jesus, he sent two of his disciples to ask: "Are you the one who has to come — or should we expect another?" (Matt. 11:2-4; Luke 7:18-21). John expected "the one who was to come." Previously, he had hinted with this term in his "messianic preaching" (Matt. 3:4-6; Mark 1:7; Luke 3:16) to Daniel 7:13, where it speaks about the "one like a son of man, *coming* with the clouds of heaven." Apparently, John the Baptist expected the coming of the well-known eschatological Son of Man.[24]

While the figure of the Son of Man is known from Daniel 7, it does not belong to rabbinical eschatology. On the other hand, the eschatological Son of Man is an important person in trends associated to Jewish Apocalyptic and Jesus. In fact, this notion for Jesus was central. Similar to the

21. See Ragaz n. 18.

22. *J.W.* 2:350-351.

23. Flusser, *Das Christentum*, 37-52; idem, *Jesus* (Reinbek bei Hamburg: Rowohlt Taschenbuch Verlag, 1999), 32-43 and 135 n. 43; Young, *Jesus the Jewish Theologian*, 49-74. See also Jeremias, *Die Verkündigung Jesu* (Gütersloh: Gütersloher Verlagshaus G. Mohn, 1971), 99-110.

24. See chapter nine.

apocalyptic writings, he describes the Son of Man as the almighty super-human judge of the Last Judgment.

> When the Son of Man comes in his glory, and all the angels with him, he will sit on the throne of his glory. All the nations will be gathered before him and he will separate men into two groups as a shepherd separates the sheep from the goats. He will put the sheep on his right and the goats on his left. Then the King will say to those on his right, "Come you who are blessed by my Father, take your inheritance, the kingdom prepared for you since the creation of the world." . . . Then he will also say to those on his left, "Depart from me, you who are cursed, into the eternal fire prepared for the devil and his angels." . . . There they will go away to eternal punishment, but the righteous to eternal life. (Matt. 25:31-46)

The designation, Son of Man (בן אדם or בר אנש), likewise does not appear in the writings of the Dead Sea Sect. In a fragment from Qumran,[25] however, the function of the judge of the Last Days is fulfilled by Melchizedek. During the Last Judgment he will separate the righteous from the wicked. He will not only pass judgment, but he will also execute it. According to the writings of the Essene Dead Sea Sect and related apocalyptic writings (as well as earlier biblical eschatology), the Last Judgment will close the current history of humanity. According to some writings, it will even mean an end to the existence of our earth. Wherever in apocalyptic texts the figure of the Son of Man appears, he is always the sublime judge of the Last Judgment. John the Baptist was sure that the Last Judgment was imminent (Matt. 3:10; Luke 3:9). In John's eschatology there is no place for any intermediary period between this wicked age and the end of this world — where the Son of Man shall be revealed. Consequently, within such an eschatological timetable, which is represented by the Dead Sea Sect, there is no place for the rabbinical concept of the kingdom of heaven.[26]

---

25. See "Melchizedek and the Son of Man," *JOC*, 186-191. See the commented edition of 11QMelch by Puech, "Notes sur le manuscrit de 11Q Melchisedeq," *RevQ* 48/12 (1987), 483-513.

26. Only in Matthew does John the Baptist speak about the kingdom of heaven. "But Matthew cannot be trusted to distinguish between the words of John and the words of Jesus." C. H. Dodd, *The Parables of the Kingdom* (London: Fontana Books, 1969), 39.

Jesus sent to the Baptist a partially affirmative answer. A new era had been opened by John. Jesus said to the Baptist's messengers, "Go and tell John what you hear and see. The blind receive their sight and the lame walk, lepers are cleansed and the deaf hear, and the dead are raised up, and the poor have good news preached to them. And blessed is he who is not wrong about me" (Matt. 11:2-6; Luke 7:18-23).

There is a very close parallel from Qumran that confirms the authenticity of Jesus' message to the Baptist.[27] In the fragment it is God himself who will perform all these marvelous deeds, as in the words of Jesus — he will revive the dead and bring good news to the poor. Jesus concluded his message to John with a warning, "Blessed is he who is not wrong about me." Jesus' doubts about the Baptist were justified. John never accepted Jesus' claim because of his different eschatological timetable.

What is important is that Jesus affirmed in principle the Baptist's question about the eschatological meaning of his activity without explicitly declaring that he was the Messiah. He established his claim to the eschatological office by pointing to his supernatural works of healing. Jesus saw this as an unmistakable sign that the new era had already begun. "But if it is by the finger of God that I cast out demons, then the kingdom of God has come upon you" (Luke 11:20). In the first redemption, one from the Egyptian yoke, the magicians recognized in the mighty works of Moses "the finger of God," God's direct redemption (Exod. 8:15[19]). According to Jesus, this was also the meaning of his healings.

In order to fully understand the contrast between the messianic view of John and the position of Jesus, one has to hear the second half of his esteem of the Baptist.

> Truly I say to you, among those born of women there has risen no one [like][28] John the Baptist, yet he who is least in the kingdom of

---

27. This text is 4Q521, fragments 2ii and 4, lines 6-13, especially line 12. See E. Puech, "Une apocalypse messianique" (4Q521), *RevQ* 60 (1992), 477-522. See also Isa. 26:19; 29:18; 35:5; 61:1. Only the cleansing of the lepers is lacking in the parallel.

28. The word "greater" in Matt. 11:11 seems to be an interpretative addition of the Evangelist caused by the second "greater" in the same verse. Jesus evidently has said that "among those born of women" there has not *risen* anyone like John the Baptist." Jesus hinted here to Moses, about whom is written in Deut. 34:10 that "no prophet *has risen* in Israel *like Moses*." Also the phrase "those born of women" was in Judaism connected with Moses. When Moses ascended to heaven in order to receive the Law from God, "as soon as the angels became

heaven is greater than he. From the days of John the Baptist until now the kingdom of heaven is breaking through, and those who break through, take it in possession. For all the prophets and the law prophesied until John; and if you are willing to accept it, he is Elijah to come. He who has ears, let him hear. (Matt. 11:11-15)

With John's coming, the kingdom of heaven broke forth. Yet, although John was the greatest among "those born among women" (cf. Deut. 34:10), the least in the kingdom of heaven would be greater than he. John the Baptist made the breach through which the kingdom of God could break, but he himself was never a member of that kingdom. He was, so to speak, a member of the previous generation. The prophets and the law prophesied until John — he marks the end of the "Old Testament" era.[29]

The root of the contrast between the "precursor," John, and Jesus was that although John was right that a new era was beginning, he believed that it would be the time of the Last Judgment and the end of human history. Jesus, however, was sure that through him the age of the kingdom of heaven was inaugurated before the end of days. One sees that in the eschatological system of the Baptist — and in the whole apocalyptic trend to which both John and the Dead Sea Sect belonged — an additional period *before* the judgment was unthinkable. Jesus, on the other hand, recognized a period *after* the kingdom of heaven — the unknown day of the coming of the Son of Man and the Last Judgment (see, e.g., Luke 17:22-24; Mark 13:22; Matt. 24:26). It is true that the bipartite division between this world and the eschatological world to come is older than the tripartite framework of Jesus. Nevertheless, among his contemporaries he was certainly not the only Jewish thinker who believed that subsequent to present history and before the purely eschatological age, there would be a type of transitional age. For the moment, however, we want to return to the differences between Jesus and the Baptist.

John believed that the Last Judgment was imminent; the ax is already at the root of the tree, and the Mighty One will come "and his winnowing

---

aware of Moses in heaven they said to God: 'Why is he who is born of women here?'" See L. Ginzberg, *The Legends of the Jews* (7 vols.; Philadelphia: Jewish Publication Society, 1947), 3:113. Apparently, Jesus considered John as a type of second Moses.

29. Flusser, *Gleichnisse*, 270-273 and 280-281. According to the rabbinical sources the messianic age was indeed revealed to the biblical prophets, while "the age to come" was hidden. This is the opinion of Rabbi Yohanan (*b. Sanh.* 98a).

fork is in his hand, and he will clear his threshing-floor, gathering his wheat into the barn and burning up the chaff with unquenchable fire" (Matt. 3:12; Luke 3:17). Jesus rejected such a perspective and expressed his view in the parable of the weeds (Matt. 13:24-30).[30] "While you are pulling up the weeds, you may root up the wheat with them. Let both grow together until the harvest" (Matt. 13:29). Judgment must wait until the harvest. "Then one shall collect the weeds and tie them in bundles to be burned and gather the wheat and bring it into the barn" (Matt. 13:30). It even seems that Jesus' parable was a fitting answer to John's harvest metaphor. Today, in the intermediary period, it is inevitable that the sinners live in same world with the righteous. Only at the end, in the Last Judgment, the Son of Man "will separate them into two groups, as a shepherd separates the sheep from the goats."[31] The sinners "will go away to eternal punishment, but the righteous to eternal life" (Matt. 25:31-46).

Jesus adopted the idea of the intermediary period between the historical past and the end of history. Yet, he is the only known thinker who drew from this scheme the logical conclusion that until the final destruction of the wicked, the righteous and the sinners would necessarily coexist. This insight was necessary for him, because he identified the intermediary period with the rabbinical concept of the kingdom of heaven — according to which the coexistence of the wicked and the righteous is indisputable.

Additionally, the only one who identified "the kingdom of heaven" with the second stage of a tripartite eschatology was Jesus. There were two primary causes for this. The first was that the foundations for Jesus' views and teaching were in rabbinical Judaism. Indeed, the concept that held central importance for Jesus was the kingdom of heaven, and it was exclusively rabbinical. The second reason for his identification of the intermediary stage as the kingdom of heaven was Jesus' belief that he was sent to lead a movement whose task was to announce that the kingdom of heaven was already at hand. I would even venture that the message of the kingdom of

---

30. See also the parable of the dragnet (Matt. 13:47-50) and the parable of the fig tree (Luke 13:6-9).

31. See Ezek. 37:16-17. There is an old Hebrew poem that the Jews pray in the Jewish New Year in which it is said: "Like a shepherd pasturing his flock, making sheep pass under his staff, so shall You cause to pass, count, calculate, and consider the soul of all the living; and You shall apportion the final needs of all Your creations and inscribe their verdict." *The Complete ArtScroll Machzor: Rosh Hashanah: A New Translation and Anthologized Commentary* (ed. N. Scherman and M. Zlotowitz; Brooklyn, N.Y.: Mesorah Publications, 1985), 483.

heaven and his role in it was for Jesus of such importance that any other components in his eschatological system were insignificant by comparison.

Not only was Jesus the only Jew who introduced the concept of the kingdom of heaven into the tripartite messianic scheme, he is also unique in his identification of the kingdom of heaven with the rabbinical "Days of the Messiah." It has already been recognized[32] that the coming of the Redeemer and the concept of the kingdom of heaven are two independent eschatological structures. The concept of the kingdom of heaven, both in rabbinical thought and in Jesus' view, is not purely futuristic. One scholar has called this notion "realized eschatology."[33]

The dangers inherent in a purely futuristic idea of God's kingship were understood by the Greek translators of the book of Exodus. The closing words of the Song of Moses (Exod. 15:18), "The Lord *will reign* forever and ever," are translated into Greek, "the Lord *is reigning* for ever and ever."[34] Later on, Rabbi Yose from Galilee (beginning of the second century A.D.) recognized the same dangers,[35] "If Israel at the Red Sea had said, 'He *is king* for all eternity,' no nation or language would have ruled over them, but they said (Exod. 15:18), 'the Lord *will reign* forever and ever.'"

According to rabbinical Judaism the kingdom of heaven means that the one and only God presently rules *de jure*, but in the eschatological future "the kingdom of God [will] be revealed to all the inhabitants of the world"[36] *de facto*. There should be no doubt that both for rabbinical Judaism and for Jesus the kingdom of heaven is a present reality: "The kingdom of heaven is in your midst" (Luke 11:20-21; cf. Exod. 25:8 and see the Aramaic Targumim there). The sages taught that there may even be individuals who are already living, so to speak, in the kingdom of heaven, if they take upon themselves "the yoke of the kingdom of heaven."[37] So also, we have heard that Jesus believed there were already men who had taken the kingdom of heaven into possession (Matt. 11:12). He evidently saw in them pioneers of the expansion of the kingdom of God among men. To this point, Jesus accords with the Sages in his view of the kingdom of heaven.

32. See Vielhauer, op. cit., 80-94; Young, op. cit., 51-83.
33. See Dodd, op. cit., 8.
34. Similar translations are preserved in the Aramaic Targums.
35. Horovitz and Rabin, op. cit., 150-151.
36. *Tg. Zech.* 14:9.
37. See, e.g., *m. 'Abot* 3:6.

In the pre-Christian Assumption of Moses (10:1) one reads about the Last Days. "And then shall his (God's) kingdom appear throughout all His creation; and then shall the Devil meet his end, and sorrow shall depart with him." In this apocalyptic writing, the kingdom of heaven is purely eschatological and not, as in the rabbinism, both future and present. Even so, there is one point of contact between the apocalyptic view and Jesus' idea of the kingdom of heaven, which does not appear in rabbinism; namely, Jesus' concept of the victory over Satan. When Jesus' envoys returned and announced to him, "Lord, even the demons submit to us in your name," he replied, "I saw Satan fall like lightning from heaven" (Luke 10:17-20). We have seen in Jesus' answer to the Baptist (Matt. 11:4-6; Luke 7:22-23) that he understood his healings to be proof that a new era had already begun.

As we have seen (Luke 11:20-22; Matt. 12:28-30), Jesus expressed his opinion about the nature of the kingdom of heaven and his task in advancing it. "If I drive out demons by the finger of God, then the kingdom of God has come to you" (Luke 11:20). At present the devil is not completely defeated, as we read in the Assumption of Moses. Instead, he is weakened. Jesus has overpowered him and has taken the armor in which Satan trusted and divided up his spoils (Luke 11:21-22). Jesus explained in the parable of the tares (Matt. 13:26-30; cf. the parable of the dragnet, Matt. 13:47-50) that in the period of the kingdom of heaven the righteous and the wicked will coexist until the coming of the Son of Man. Although the Jewish sages did not say explicitly that presently persons who take upon themselves the yoke of the kingdom of heaven live among sinners, they would certainly not have opposed the content of Jesus' parables on the theme.

At the end of the parable Jesus adds: "He who is not with me is against me, and he who does not gather with me scatters" (Matt. 12:30; Luke 11:23).[38] A movement had begun in Israel. This revival was the realization of the kingdom of heaven on earth (Matt. 6:10). The movement necessarily centered around the person of Jesus; separate initiatives, independent of Jesus, would not gather but scatter. One can recognize again how important for Jesus was the concept of the kingdom of heaven. His main task was to be the center of the movement which realized the kingdom of God among mankind — with the aid of co-laborers. "From the days of John the

---

38. About this saying, see also Flusser, "Hillel's Self-Awareness and Jesus," *JOC*, 510-511.

Baptist until now the kingdom of heaven is breaking through and *those who break through, take it in possession*" (Matt. 11:12). He urged his disciples, "The harvest is plentiful, but the laborers are few; pray therefore the owner of the harvest to send out laborers into his harvest" (Matt. 9:37-38; Luke 16:2). With John the Baptist the biblical period came to an end and a new era — that of the kingdom of God — began. Or as Jesus declared at the conclusion of his testimony about the Baptist, "All the prophets and the law prophesied until John" (Matt. 11:13).[39]

It was (and is) a common Jewish opinion that the kingship of God is both present and future, and that it has existed from the creation of the world, or at least from Abraham's time. This was not the position of Jesus. According to him the concept of the kingdom of heaven was not static but dynamic. It was a movement which began with John the Baptist. There are a number of reasons why Jesus' concept on this point differs. One is that Jesus understood the kingdom of heaven as not only God's kingship, but as we have noted a kind of intermediary period between the historical time and the end of history. In the messianic timetable of Jesus it occupied the same place that is represented in other Jewish tripartite systems as "the days of the Messiah." The fact that Jesus has spoken about the period of the kingdom of heaven, instead of the days of the Messiah, hints to his own messianic self-awareness.

We have indicated that the coming of an eschatological Redeemer and the kingdom of heaven are in Judaism two different structures. [40] So it was in Jesus' mind. This explains why Jesus did not try to bring these two independent systems into a complete harmony. It is true he recognized that the kingdom of heaven is a dynamic power with an imminent tendency to spread on earth, but he did not say (nor did he probably believe) that the final realization of the kingdom of heaven would culminate with the coming of the Son of Man[41] and the Last Judgment. Evidently he could not claim — as I believed before — that the Son of Man would arrive in the moment when, so to say, the invisible church would become identical with the visible church simply. This would mean that the end of the period of the kingdom would come in the fullness of time (Eph. 1:10), when all the

39. Flusser, *Gleichnisse*, 270-273.

40. Vielhauer, op. cit.

41. In one of my studies ("Jesus and the Sign of the Son of Man," *JOC*, 526-534), I have tried to show that Jesus evidently identified himself with the future Son of Man. If I am correct, this would be his second coming.

14. **Sunset, looking west from the Arbel, in Lower Galilee.** Photo by J. H. Charlesworth.

potential elect of God will take the kingdom of heaven in possession. However, such an "ecclesiastic" notion of a separate unity of elect did not fit the open-mindedness of the "historical" Jesus.[42] According to Jesus, the hour of the coming of the Son of Man is known only to his heavenly Father (see Mark 13:32; Matt. 24:36; Acts 1:7). "The Son of Man[43] will be like the lightning, which flashes and lights up the sky from one end to another" (Luke 17:24).[44] One should remember that the Jewish Sages also warned those who tried to discover the hidden date of redemption.

The older Jewish redemptive timetable was bipartite. Accordingly, at the end of history there would be judgment, and the post-historical future would be the eschatological "age to come." This is the eschatology of the earlier apocalyptic literature of the Dead Sea Sect[45] and that of John the

42. About the elect in the Synoptic Gospels, see chapter ten, 126-129 below.

43. The words "in his days" are not attested in the best manuscripts.

44. Luke 17:22-24, 26-32, 34-37. The preceding passage (Luke 17:21-22) seems to be a Lukan invention, a kind of doublet to the following Luke 17:23. In any case, the futuristic "kingdom of God" is surely Lukan terminology. See also the Last Supper in Luke 22:16 and 18!

45. See chapter ten, n. 12. There is, however, an analogy between the common Jewish di-

Baptist. When the centrality of the Messiah increased, however, the conception of the messianic era emerged. It created a tendency to insert this era into the current eschatological scheme. The solutions were not simply a compromise, as it is often thought today. The only possibility was to let the messianic era follow our historical period, placing the Days of the Messiah prior to the post-historical era, "the age to come" (עולם הבא). In so doing, a clear division between history and "post-history" was finally achieved. "The Days of the Messiah" belong, strictly speaking, to the history of mankind, while the "age to come" is considered beyond current history.[46] The final epoch contains the Last Judgment, a new heaven and earth, the resurrection and eternal life.[47]

Today, it is impossible to know exactly when this tripartite eschatology was formulated. In rabbinical Judaism a precise distinction between the messianic age and the "age to come" was very quickly forgotten, and the pertinent early rabbinical sayings are too short to indicate fully their thinking. In any event, this kind of eschatology was without doubt already firmly established in the second half of the first century A.D. This can be

---

vision into three periods and the timetable of the Dead Sea Sect; there the three periods are: the biblical past (evidently more or less the period until the destruction of the first Temple), the present wicked period (the "days of the rule of Belial" in 1QS 2:19), and the purely eschatological time: in the time of a (new) creation God "will create My temple and establish it for Myself (God) for all times" (11QT 29:7-10). In any case this tripartite division is by no means identical with that of Jesus and the parallel Jewish sources.

46. See P. Volz, *Die Eschatologie der jüdischen Gemeinde im neutestamentlichen Zeitalter, nach den Quellen der rabbinischen, apokalyptischen und apokryphen Literatur dargestellt* (Tübingen: Mohr, 1934), 64-67 and especially 71-77; M. Zobel, *Gottes gesalbter; der Messias und die messianische zeit in Talmad und Midrasch* (Berlin: Schocken Verlag, 1938), 69-74, 125-129. See also Schürer, op. cit., 2:537-547; Billerbeck, op. cit., 4b:799-976. See also *b. Sanh.* 91b, especially the words of Rabbi Samuel, and *Sipre* on Deut. 6:6 (Finkelstein ed.), 62 and the note there. For Nachmanides, see *Kitve Rabenu Mosheh ben Nahman: yotsim la-or 'al-pi kitve yad u-defusim rishonim 'im mare mekomot, he'arot u-mevoot* (2 vols.; ed. C. B. Chavel; Jerusalem: Mosad ha-Rav Kuk, 1963), 300-303 [Hebrew]: "One calls the age after the resurrection of the dead 'the age to come.'" See also Flusser, *Gleichnisse*, 270-272, 280-281. According to the rabbinical sources, Moses and the prophets referred to the future and until the messianic age, but the age to come was outside of their scope. Jesus, however, put the limit before the days of the Messiah (see Matt. 11:13). By the way, the term "the age to come" is attested in 1 Enoch 71:15.

47. Already Paul knew this eschatological scheme and modified it according to his outlook. See 1 Cor. 15:23-28; Conzelmann, *Die erste Brief an die Korinther* (Göttingen: Vanderhoeck & Ruprecht, 1989), 315-320.

recognized also from rabbinical literature. Almost all the Jewish Sages who tried to calculate the duration of the messianic period lived in the second half of the first century or in the second century A.D.[48] They evidently thought that after this period the "age to come" would begin. It could even be that the teaching of Jesus is the earliest unequivocal evidence for this messianic timetable.

While the tripartite division of time was not an invention of Jesus, he accepted it[49] and adapted it with his own personal inspiration. While its roots lay in contemporary rabbinism, if one wants to understand it more clearly, one has to ask for help from three apocalyptic texts, all of which were written at the very end of the first century A.D. One of them is the book of Revelation, the last book of the New Testament. The Last Days are there described in chapters 20-21. According to this book the messianic reign will endure a thousand years.[50] After the end of this period the Last Judgment and the resurrection of the dead will take place (20:11-15). After this (21:1), says the author (22:1), "Then I saw a new heaven and a new earth, for the first heaven and the first earth had passed away, and there was no longer any sea." Then the Holy City, the new Jerusalem will come out of heaven from God (21:2).

The two other apocalyptic texts from the same period resemble one another. One is the Syriac Apocalypse of Baruch,[51] and the other is Fourth Ezra.[52] The eschatological material in the Apocalypse of Baruch is contained in chapters 29–30, 39–42, and 72–74. The author describes there mostly the messianic era, and he hints only to the "age to come." The end of the messianic era is described in 30:1: "And it will happen after these

48. *B. Sanh.* 99a; *Midr. Ps.* 90:15 and parallels. See Volz, op. cit., 226-228; Zobel, op. cit., 72-73.

49. See Luke 18:29-30 (and Mark 10:29-30; Matt. 19:20): "No one who has left his home . . . for the sake of *the kingdom of God*, will fail to receive many times as much *in this age* and, in the *age to come,* eternal life." See also the "eternal life" in Matt. 25:46.

50. This opinion was accepted by some Jewish Sages (see Volz, op. cit., 226-228) and is also attested in one of the variants in 4 Ezra 7:28. See also *Seder Eliyahu raba ve-seder Eliyahu zuta ha-muvaim be-shem Tana de-ve Eliyahu* (ed. M. Friedmann; Wien, 1902), 6-7, and Friedmann's comments there. The text is quoted in *b. Sanh.* 97a/b; *b. 'Abodah Zar.* 9a. About the number 2000 years, see Volz, op. cit., 227.

51. See *Apocalypse de Baruch* (ed. P. Bogaert; Paris: Éditions du Cerf, 1969), especially 415-420.

52. M. Stone, *Fourth Ezra: A Commentary on the Book of Fourth Ezra* (Minneapolis: Fortress Press, 1990), especially 92-93 and 112-118.

things when the time of the appearance of the Anointed One has been fulfilled and he returns with glory, that then all who sleep in hope of him will rise."[53] After the resurrection, judgment will follow. Especially interesting is the content of 32:1-6, where the author speaks about the destruction of the First Temple, the rebuilding of the Zion (32:102), and the second destruction (32:3). Finally, the temple will be renewed again "in glory and will be perfected into eternity" (32:4). It will happen "when the Mighty One will renew his creation." This description of the eschatological Temple resembles very much the Temple Scroll from Qumran (11QT 29:7-10).[54] In the time of a new creation God "will create My temple and establish it for Myself (God) for all times." By the way, also according to Revelation 21:1-2 the Holy City, the new Jerusalem, will come down out of heaven after the creation of a new heaven and a new earth. Thus, this will happen in the "age to come."[55]

Even more instructive for our study is Fourth Ezra (chapters 7 and 12:32-36).[56] There the different content of the messianic age and the age to come is clearly indicated. The Messiah "will deliver in mercy the remnant of my people . . . and he will make them joyful *until the end comes,* the day of judgment" (12:34). The author is more explicit in 7:29-31:

> For my Messiah shall be revealed with those who are with him, and he shall make rejoice those who remain for four hundred years.[57] And after these things my servant the Messiah shall die, and all who draw human breath. And the world shall be turned back to the primeval silence for seven days, as it was at the first beginnings; so that no one shall be left. And after seven days the world which is not awake shall be raised and that which is corruptible shall perish . . . and the treasuries shall give up the souls which have been committed to them. And the Most High shall be revealed upon the seat of judgment.

53. The temporal limitations of the messianic period are also hinted at in 40:7.
54. See above, n. 45.
55. But see 4 Ezra 7:26.
56. See Stone, op. cit., 92-93, 112-113 and 367-370. In a vision in 4 Ezra 13, the Davidic Son of Man is described (see 4 Ezra 13:3, "something like a figure of a man flew with the clouds of heaven," a hint to Dan. 7:13!), but in 4 Ezra he becomes a supernatural messianic savior, and his appearance there does not form a part of any eschatological system. He is *not* the eschatological judge.
57. Other variants: "thirty" and "a thousand."

We see that according to this passage at the end of the messianic days the Messiah and the whole of mankind shall die, and then the new creation and the Last Judgment will take place. It may be helpful for the reader at this point to outline the main points in the two eschatological systems and the specific position Jesus' own opinion holds.

Bipartite System	Jesus	Tripartite System
a. The present wicked age.	a. The present "biblical" age until John the Baptist.	a. The present age.
		b. The messianic era.
	b. The realization of the	
b. The Last Judgment	kingdom of heaven.	c. Last Judgment.
(usually with the Son of	c. The Last Judgment: the	d. End of this world. In the
Man as judge).	Son of Man as judge,	post-historical age to
c. End of this world and	resurrection, beginning of	come a new creation,
a new creation.	the age to come, and	resurrection, and eternal
	eternal life.	life.

It belongs to Jesus' personal eschatological perspective that for him the second stage of redemption, the messianic era, is to be identified with the realization of the kingdom of heaven. "No one who has left his house . . . for the sake of *the kingdom of God* will fail to receive many times as much *in this age* and, in the *age to come,* eternal life" (Luke 18:29-30; Mark 10:19-30; Matt. 19:20). This will happen after the Last Judgment, performed by the Son of Man. Then the wicked "will go away to eternal punishment, but the righteous to *eternal life*" (Matt. 25:46). Luke 20:33-35 furnishes a further confirmation for this concept of Jesus: "The people *of this age* marry and are given in marriage. But those who are considered worthy of taking part *in that age* and in the *resurrection from the dead* will neither marry, nor be given in marriage." Thus, according to Jesus, the period of the kingdom of heaven will precede the coming of the Son of Man and his Last Judgment. This will be the time of the resurrection of the dead. In that post-historical age to come, also the resurrected will be a kind of new creation — they will be like angels (see also 1 Cor. 15:42-54).

There are only a few scholars who have paid due attention to the nature and history of the two eschatological ages both in Judaism and in Jesus' eschatology. One cannot blame them, because the differences between the messianic age and the age to come, both in rabbinism and in early Christianity, are not well documented. In both, this messianic timetable became almost forgotten. In the Gospels it is better preserved than in rabbinism, but already in the Gospels the critical moment of history became the Cross, and so the messianic chronology of the "historical" Jesus was only of second importance. In rabbinism, although the terms "the days of the Messiah" and "the age to come" coexist until now, the difference between these two ages became almost instantly meaningless. Thus, the best witnesses for the Jewish tripartite chronology are the three apocalyptic texts from the end of the first century A.D. Through the book of Revelation, it has been often partially renewed by chiliastic movements until today.

We do not know when in Jewish thought the messianic age was harmonized with the former two-fold concept of the unredeemed world and the time of salvation. As I have already said, Jesus seems to be the earliest witness for this new system. His creative spirit and his high, messianic self-awareness have changed its structure. Jesus has adopted from apocalyptic expectations the sublime figure, who executes divine judgment. This was evidently also the hope of the Baptist. According to the rabbinical system — and also according to Jesus — the Last Judgment will take place after the messianic period. While in rabbinism the Son of Man as the eschatological judge is not present, according to the apocalyptic trend he figures as the eschatological judge. So it will happen also in the view of Jesus. Therefore in his eschatological system, the coming of the Son of Man is postponed together with the Last Judgment into a distant future. This change lies at the center of the conflict between the Baptist and Jesus. Moreover, I believe that Jesus came to the conclusion that he himself would be revealed as the divine Son of Man.[58]

The most important innovation by Jesus was that he identified the messianic age with the rabbinical kingdom of heaven. He has borrowed the kingdom from another, independent system, and incorporated it in the other rabbinical system, namely, the tripartite redemptive timetable. The identification by Jesus between the messianic age and the kingdom of heaven in which Jesus will have the central task is, by the way, an additional proof that Jesus was sure that he is the Messiah. Moreover, in his answer to John the Baptist he has claimed that his own blessed activities show that the time of salvation is here (Matt. 11:4-6; Luke 7:22-23). There were many at that time who believed that John was Elijah. Jesus described him as the man who opened the way for the realization of the kingdom (Matt. 11:12-

---

58. See Flusser, "Jesus and the Sign of the Son of Man," *JOC*, 515-534.

15). He finished his words by saying, "and if you are willing to accept it, he is Elijah to come." According to the common opinion, Elijah would announce the coming of the Messiah.[59] "He who has ears to hear, let him hear!"[60] Jesus was not wrong when he asserted that before the "day of the Son of Man" the age of the kingdom of heaven will *still* come. Those who are shown to be wrong are the modern adherents to the "acute eschatology" of John, and not Jesus.

Our study has important consequences for the evaluation of the messianic self-awareness of Jesus. He adopted contemporary Jewish interpretations that divided history, and he identified the Days of the Messiah with the period of the kingdom of heaven. For Jesus the messianic period no longer lay as a hope in the future. It had already begun with John the Baptist, and Jesus was now the Messiah. It is also possible to understand how Jesus modified the structure of the concept of the kingdom of heaven. In the understanding of Jesus, the kingdom of heaven became more dynamic than in rabbinical thinking. Since according to Jesus, the kingdom of heaven was identical with the messianic period, it was no longer, as in rabbinic thought, an eternal suprahistorical entity. It became a dynamic force that broke through into the world at an identifiable point in history. The kingdom of heaven began to break through with John, and Jesus — the Messiah — was in the center of the movement.[61] "He who is not *with me* is against me, and he who does not gather *with me* scatters" (Matt. 12:30).

---

59. About the future coming of Elijah, see Zobel, op. cit., 58-68; Billerbeck, op. cit., 4b:779-798; Volz, op. cit., 195-197.

60. It is astonishing to discover that Jesus' messianic timetable is not far from the tripartite eschatological scheme of the medieval eccentric thinker, Joachim of Fiore (ca. 1132-1202). He divided history into: the history of the Old Testament, the present period of the New Testament grace, and the future period of Spirit. But the differences in content are not small.

61. "If I drive out demons *by the finger of God,* then the kingdom of God has come upon you" (Luke 11:20). As already mentioned above, the "finger of God" is taken from Exodus 8:19 [HMT 8:15]. By this quotation Jesus hints at the understanding that through himself God's redemption had already begun. See the chronological prayer of Sir. 36:1-22, especially verses 6-7:

> Show signs anew and work further wonders,
> make Thy hand and Thy right arm glorious.

Through Jesus' healings God repeats the "signs" and "wonders" of the liberation from bondage in Egypt.

CHAPTER 8

The Son

Jesus is portrayed in the Gospels as a miracle-worker. Rabbinic literature tells us of four other such men who flourished before the destruction of the Second Temple. Two[1] of these were Galileans. The rabbinic literature describes them as extremely poor men, and one of the two, Abba Hilkia, was a day laborer.[2] On one occasion when two scribes[3] had been sent to ask Abba Hilkia to pray for rain, he responded to them in a rather peculiar manner. The reason for this, in part, was undoubtedly the tension that existed between miracle-workers and scribes. The second Galilean, Rabbi Hanina ben Dosa,[4] lived a generation after Jesus and was famous for his miracles of healing.[5] A heavenly voice said of him, "The whole world will be nourished because of my son Hanina — and a morsel of carob-bean will satisfy my son Hanina for a week."[6]

It is no accident that the heavenly voice addressed Hanina as "My son." The miracle-worker is closer to God than other men. When Hanina healed

---

1. Abba Hilkia and Rabbi Hanina ben Dosa.

2. See *b. Ta'an.* 23a; Schlesinger, op. cit., 71-77.

3. On the Jewish and early Christian custom of sending men out in pairs, see chapter three, n. 19.

4. See G. Vermes, "Hanina ben Dosa," *JJS* 23 (1972), 28-50; idem, 24 (1973), 51-64; *Post-Biblical Jewish Studies* (Leiden: Brill, 1975), 118-214. See also A. Büchler, *Types of Jewish-Palestinian Piety from 70 B.C.E. to 70 C.E.: The Ancient Pious Men* (New York: Ktav Publishing House, 1968); S. Safrai, "The Teaching of the Pietists in Mishnaic Literature," *JJS* 16 (1965), 15-33.

5. *M. Ber.* 5:5.

6. *B. Ta'an.* 24b.

the son of Rabbi Yohanan ben Zakkai by prayer,[7] the scribe's wife said, "Is Hanina greater, then, than you?" and he answered, "No, but he is like a slave before a king, and I am like a higher official before a king."[8]

Something similar is said about Honi the "circle-drawer,"[9] who died in the spring of 65 B.C. Once, when he was asked to pray for rain, he drew a circle round himself and prayed. "Ruler of the world, Your children have turned to me, because I am in Your presence like one of Your household. I swear by Your great name that I will not move from this place until You have pity upon Your children." Then, when rain came, the chief of the Pharisees at that time, Simeon ben Shatah, complained of his audacious behavior, "Were you not Honi I would excommunicate you. What can I do with you?[10] You ingratiate yourself to God and He does what you ask, as when a son curries favor with his father, who then does what the son wants." The miracle-worker is close to God — like a household companion, like a son.

Honi was killed in the civil war between the two Maccabean brothers, Aristobulos and Hyrcanus. Josephus[11] reports how he went into hiding because of the war, but was fetched to the camp of Hyrcanus and asked to curse Aristobulos who was besieged in the city of Jerusalem. Refusing Hyrcanus' demand to curse his brother, he was executed. A medieval Hebrew author[12] was perceptive enough to detect that Josephus had misunderstood and expanded the oral tradition concerning Honi's death. In his redaction of the story, he left out the alleged reason for Honi's concealment. Honi hid not from fear of the war, but because such was the habit of this pious miracle-worker. He was a hidden saint, like Hanan "the hidden"

---

7. B. Ber. 34b.

8. The official, though possessing a more elevated status, nevertheless does not enjoy the intimacy with the king that the king's personal servant does.

9. M. Ta'an. 3:8; Ant. 14:22; Schlesinger, op. cit., 62-65.

10. The Hebrew words of Simeon ben Shatah are precisely the same as the reaction of the bystanders when Jesus healed the man with the withered hand. They became baffled (not "furious") and said one to another: "What can we do with Jesus?" (Luke 6:11), because he has done nothing to violate the Sabbath. Luke understood well his source, as one can see from Acts 4:16, but the other two Synoptic Gospels interpreted the original reaction wrongly (Mark 3:4 and Matt 12:14). See my discussion in JOC, xxv-xxvi. See chapter four, n. 16.

11. Ant. 14:22-24.

12. The so-called Josephus Gorionides (Josippon). The Josippon: Edited with an Introduction, Commentary and Notes (2 vols.; ed. D. Flusser; Jerusalem: Bialik Institute, 1980-1981), 1:149 (35:99ff.).

of a later date. "When rain was needed the scribes used to send school children to Hanan to grasp the hem of his cloak and say, 'Abba, Abba,[13] give us rain!' Then he would address God, 'Ruler of the universe, do this for the sake of those who cannot distinguish between a father (Abba) who can give rain and a father who cannot.' And why did they call him Hanan the Hidden? Because he used to hide himself."[14]

The story about Hanan has some points of contact with Jesus' activity. The holy man addresses God as "Abba" — father. The motif of sonship is typical for this kind of Jewish holy man. Even more important is that Hanan used to hide himself, as Honi the Circle Drawer probably did. All who read the Gospels know that Jesus also hid himself from the multitudes and commanded the person who was cured to say nothing about his cure.[15]

The most important contact, however, between the two is in Jesus' teaching about little children (Luke 18:15; Mark 10:13-16). Hanan is the only ancient pious man about whom we are certain that children had easier access to than the rabbis did. When the children were brought for Jesus to touch them,[16] he said, "the kingdom of God belongs to such as these. I tell you that whoever does not accept the kingdom of God like a child will never enter it." This sublime saying naturally means that one has to accept the kingdom of God simply and without mental reservation. This was also the essence of Hanan's prayer. "Ruler of the universe, do this for the sake of those (the children) who cannot distinguish between the father who can give rain and a father who cannot."

We see, then, that in those days there was an understandable tension

13. As is evident from Abba Hilkia whom we have cited, and from Matthew 23:7-9, as well as other sources, in those days "Abba," like "Rabbi," was a title of honor. The Aramaic *abba* as a designation or as a sign of affection is used also in Hebrew texts. See chapter two, n. 27.

14. *B. Ta'an.* 23b.

15. Thus the behavior of Jesus in these points has nothing to do with his assumed "messianic secret," as Mark developed it. The Evangelist describes Jesus as a lonely, holy man who was not understood by others and died on the cross abandoned. This is evidently far from the truth. As for Jesus' last hours, see Flusser, "The Crucified One and the Jews," *JOC*, 575-587. Nevertheless, it is true that Jesus did not say in so many words that he was the Messiah, because he had not yet fulfilled his messianic task. See Flusser, "Two Notes on the Midrash on 2 Samuel VII," *JOC*, 93-98.

16. It was a custom in Jerusalem and in other cities to bring small children to respected men to be blessed by them. See *Masekhet Soferim: ve-nilvu 'aleha midrash Masekhet Soferim II* (ed. M. Higger; New York: Deve Rabanan, 1937), 318-319 (18:7); Billerbeck, op. cit., 1:807-808.

between the charismatic holy man and the Pharisaic establishment. Nor is it strange that such holy men would practice poverty, whether by compulsion or freely. Because of the scarcity of information about such pious men, it is impossible to know how far the way of life of Jesus and of his disciples, and Jesus' positive evaluation of the religious value of poverty, reflect the attitude of the whole group. One point is certain, namely that sociologically Jesus belonged with them. We have already seen (chapter six) that regarding the issue of poverty and wealth, Jesus accepted some Essene views. It is likely that these motifs were transmitted to him via John the Baptist.[17]

It was also in character for these people to perform their miracles in secret. Historically speaking, this applies to Jesus. For example, Jesus commanded the person who had been cured to say nothing about his cure (Mark 5:43; Luke 8:56). This apparently was also one of the reasons that he did not want to reveal completely the secret of his divine election.

We have seen how the relationship to God of three of the miracle-workers belonging to the period of the Second Temple was described as that of a son to his father. The earliest, Honi, prayed to God as a member of his household, and he was likened to a son who was accustomed to ingratiate himself with his father. Hanina stood before God as his personal servant, and was addressed by a heavenly voice as "My son!" Hanan the Hidden took up the children's word "Father," and in prayer described God as "the father who can give rain." How could it have been otherwise that such men, who were like sons to God, should have addressed God as "Father"? Jesus spoke in the same way.[18]

The charismatic pious men believed that their ties with God were stronger than those of other men, although they certainly did not exclude the possibility that others were able to attain a similar position. By comparison, however, the self-awareness of Jesus was even higher. This can be seen from the first three Gospels. Evidently according to the existing texts, Jesus distin-

---

17. See Flusser, "Jesus' Opinion about the Essenes," *JOC*, 150-168, especially 162-163.

18. J. Jeremias, *Abba. Studien zur neutestamentlichen Theologie und Zeitgeschichte* (Göttingen: Vandenhoeck & Ruprecht, 1966), 15-67. B. M. F. Van Iersel correctly perceived that, among the rabbis, addressing God as "our Father" did not have the same weight as "my Father," or "Abba" as used by Jesus. Considering the scarcity of rabbinic material on charismatic prayer, however, this does not tell us very much. *'Der Sohn' in den synoptischen Jesusworten; Christusbezeichnung der Gemeinde oder Selbstbezeichnung Jesu? Der Sohn*, NovTSup 3 (Leiden: Brill, 1961).

guishes between God as the common father of the believer and God as *his* father. He names God "*your* father," but on the other hand he speaks about "*my* father." The Lord's prayer is not an exception, because "our Father who art in Heaven" (Matt 6:9) is the opening of a prayer prescribed for others.

This way of speaking surely betrays Jesus' own high self-awareness, because there is no evidence of a later hand introducing utterances about "our Father." This is remarkable when we remember that the church's Christology includes an understanding that Christ had given to the believer the Spirit of his sonship (Rom. 8:15). We read, "To all who received him, who believed in his name, he gave power to become children of God" (John 1:17). Nevertheless, even John's Gospel, which bears signs of these later christological developments, is able to retain the distinctive sonship of Jesus in the statement of the resurrected Lord, "I am ascending to my Father and your Father, to my God and your God" (John 20:17). As we have seen, the "historical" Jesus did not speak in quite this way, but he evidently did distinguish between his unique sonship and the common fatherhood of God. This indication is described in a somewhat distorted manner in the Johannine Jews expression of hatred of Jesus, "because he called God his *own* father, making himself equal with God" (John 5:18).[19] Unfortunately this is not the place to show that the whole accusation is historically unrealistic. Nonetheless, Jesus evidently did understand his divine sonship as unique and decisive.

If Jesus was like a son to God, this denoted more than the mere sonship of the miracle-workers. For him, sonship was also the consequence of his election through the heavenly voice at his baptism. As the son he knew his Father in heaven. "I thank thee, Father, Lord of heaven and earth, that Thou hast hidden these things from the wise and understanding and revealed them to the simple; yea, Father, for such things have been delivered to me by my Father; and no one knows the son[20] except the father, and no one knows the father except the son and any one to whom the son chooses to reveal it" (Matt 11:25-27).[21] Not until the discovery of the Essene writings at the Dead Sea did we know about any such high degree of self-

---

19. Nor did Jesus "break the Sabbath," as he is accused of in the same passage.

20. So, according to Luke 10:22. On the meaning, see G. Dalman, *Die Worte Jesu: mit berücksichtigung des nachkanonischen jüdischen Schrifttums und der aramäischen Sprache* (Leipzig: J. C. Hinrichs, 1930), 231-233. See Flusser, *Gleichnisse*, 265-268. This is not a christological utterance, but simply an observation about the relation between a father and son.

21. The continuation of the saying (Matt. 11:28-30) also seems to be original.

15. Mount Tabor, traditionally thought to be the site of the Transfiguration.
Photo by J. H. Charlesworth.

awareness in ancient Judaism. Now we recognize that this jubilation of Jesus is in line with Essene hymn writing.[22] Jesus' hymn begins with the same word as do most of the prayers in the Essene hymnbook, and even the rhythmic structure is similar. The Essene author, like Jesus, says that "his message will be prudence to the simple";[23] and like Jesus, the revelation consists in knowledge of the mysteries of God.

> Through me Thou has illuminated the face of many,
> and hast shown Thy infinite power.
> For Thou has given me knowledge
> of Thy marvelous mysteries,
> and hast shown Thyself mighty with me
> through the secret of Thy marvels.

22. Meyer, op. cit., 1:280-291, correctly guessed that there were such hymns in ancient Judaism. See also the excellent analysis of Matt 11:25-27 in E. Sjöberg, *Der verborgene Menschensohn in den Evangelien* (Lund: C. W. K. Gleerup, 1955), 190-195.

23. 1QH^a 2:9-10.

Thou hast done wonders before many
for the sake of Thy glory,
that they may make known Thy mighty deeds
to all the living.[24]

This is the mentality of the charismatic apocalyptist who has access to the mysteries of God, through which he is able to "illuminate the face of many."

According to the Gospels, Jesus was addressed by the heavenly voice as "Son" as early as his baptism. The assumption is justified, however, that at that time he was simply being addressed as the chosen servant. Not until the voice at the Transfiguration was he truly named "Son." Jesus took Peter, John, and James, and climbed with them up a mountain. His face became different, and his clothes turned shining white; and Moses and Elijah spoke to him. As they were departing, Peter said to Jesus, "Master, it is good for us to be here; let us make three huts, one for you, one for Moses, and one for Elijah." Then a cloud came and overshadowed them and a voice out of the cloud said, "This is my only[25] Son, hear him." After the two departed, Jesus was alone (Luke 9:28-36).

Even Meyer[26] regarded this vision as authentic. The heavenly voice is significant. The words "hear him" are made intelligible by the prophecy of Moses. "The Lord your God will raise up for you a prophet like me from among you, from your brethren — *listen to him*" (Deut. 18:15). The appearance of two great prophets of old, Moses and Elijah, underlined the significance of the voice. Jesus is the prophetic preacher to whom the Old Testament had pointed. The voice designated Jesus as the "only Son," as God had said to Abraham, "Take your son, your only son Isaac, whom you love . . . and offer him there as a burnt offering . . ." (Gen 22:2). This designation of Jesus thus hints to his coming martyrdom. Luke 9:31 says, in fact, that on the occasion of the Transfiguration, Moses and Elijah spoke with Jesus about his imminent death (lit. *his exodus:* τὴν ἔξοδον αὐτοῦ) in Jerusalem.

Jesus linked his sense of sonship, his predestination as prophetic preacher, and his knowledge of his tragic end in the parable of the tenants of the vineyard (cf. Luke 20:9-19 and par.). Jesus told this parable in the Temple in the presence of the high priests shortly before his death: "The

24. 1QH[a] 4:27-29.
25. "Beloved" is the Greek translation of "only." See chapter three, n. 11.
26. Meyer, op. cit., 1:151-157.

16. Sacrifice of Isaac. Mosaic from Beth Alpha Synagogue. Photo by D. Harris.

master of the vineyard sent a servant to the tenants of the vineyard to collect his dues. The tenants beat him and sent him back. Again he sent another servant whom they beat and mocked. He sent yet another whom
they wounded and threw out. At last he sent his son, thinking that they
would respect him. But when the tenants of the vineyard saw him they said
to one another, 'This is the heir, let us kill him and the inheritance will be
ours.' They took him out of the vineyard and killed him. What will the
master of the vineyard do to them? He will come and destroy these tenants
and give the vineyard to others." Observing that the parable was aimed at
them, the priests considered how they might apprehend Jesus, but they
feared the crowd.

Here we are at the epicenter of Jesus' clash with the Sadducees, the
Temple aristocracy — the clash that was to lead to his death. The high
priests interpreted the parable correctly. They were the wicked tenants of
the vineyard, who on account of their office, held a monopoly over the

people of God — for the vineyard was the people of Israel.[27] The high priests would be destroyed, and God would give his vineyard to others. This did indeed happen after the destruction of the Temple, when the priestly caste was destroyed and disappeared. The servants who had been sent to the vineyard were God's prophetic messengers who had been persecuted and slain. Included in their number was Jesus, the Son.

Yet, at the same time, Jesus was sure that the murder of the Son would not be the end of the tragedy. He closed the parable (Luke 20:17) by quoting Psalm 118:22: "The very stone which the builders rejected has become the head."[28] Jesus was sure that even if the Son were to be killed, his cause would be victorious.[29] This is Jesus' unequivocal "christological" utterance.

There is a Jewish parable[30] of a proprietor and his wicked, thieving tenants. The proprietor took the estate away from them and gave it to their sons, but these were even worse than their fathers. Then a son was born to the proprietor. He drove out the tenants, and put his son on the estate. Jesus apparently knew a similar parable, but he adapted it to become a tragedy. In his version the son is killed.

Jesus' sonship therefore leads, not to life, but to the death that other prophets before him had suffered. After the Transfiguration, his awareness of the sonship of God was linked with the premonition that he had to die. Even before his entry into Jerusalem he sensed his tragic end, but for Jesus this knowledge of divine sonship was scarcely identical with his consciousness of being the Messiah. The Jews of those days were, it is true, acquainted with the image of martyrdom as an atoning sacrifice.[31] Nevertheless, a careful philological analysis of the relevant texts shows that in the first three Gospels there is no completely reliable utterance of Jesus in

27. Isa. 5:1-7.

28. The following verse in Luke 20:18 is, "Every one who falls on that stone will be broken to pieces, but when it falls on any one it will crush him." These words appear only in Luke and its Jewish parallels. See Young, *Parables*, 293-316; idem, *Jesus the Jewish Theologian*, 215-224. Concerning Matt. 21:44, see B. M. Metzger, *A Textual Commentary on the Greek New Testament: A Companion Volume to the United Bible Societies' Greek New Testament* (New York: United Bible Societies, 1971) 58. See also below chapter eleven, n. 26.

29. Did Jesus even see in the stone a metaphor for himself? In any case, the stone in Ps. 118:22 was identified in Jewish sources with David. See the Aramaic Targum of Ps. 118:22 and Young, *Parables*, 293-294.

30. *Sipre* on Deut. 32:9. See Billerbeck, op. cit., 1:874.

31. Beginning with the cases of martyrdom in the persecutions by the Seleucid Antiochus Epiphanes (167 B.C.). See 2 Macc. 6–7.

which he unequivocally expresses that he is to die in order to expiate the sins of his believers.[32] Nor is it likely that he saw himself as the suffering, atoning servant of God described by the prophet Isaiah. This idea is heard retrospectively in the early church — but not until after the crucifixion.[33] Jesus had neither subtly nor mythically worked out the idea[34] of his own death from the ancient writings, let alone did he carry it out. He was no "Christ of the festival," of a medieval sacred drama, for he wrestled with death to the very end.

32. For example, compare Mark 10:45 with its parallel in Luke 22:27. See Flusser, "Salvation Present and Future," *JOC*, 233, n. 4.

33. See Hooker, op. cit., 151-157.

34. The two cardinal verses in which it is reported that Jesus expressly proclaims that he will die to expiate are Mark 10:45 (and Matt. 20:28) and in the Markan report about the Last Supper (Mark 14:24 and Matt. 20:28). As to the second item, it is known to many that the parallel in Luke 22:20 is not original, as it is lacking in an important old manuscript, and that the whole passage (Luke 22:19b-20) is a secondary addition to the original Lukan text, taken from 1 Cor. 11:23-25. See Flusser, "The Last Supper and the Essenes," *JOC*, 202-206. The parallel in Mark 14:24 (and Matt. 26:28) depends on the same tradition as is represented by 1 Cor. 11:23-24. See now R. S. Notley, "The Eschatological Thinking of the Dead Sea Sect and the Order of Blessing in the Christian Eucharist," in *Jesus' Last Week: Jerusalem Studies in the Synoptic Gospels, Volume One* (ed. R. S. Notley, M. Turnage, and B. Becker; Leiden: Brill, 2006) 123-127. Regarding the other saying, namely Mark 10:45 (and Matt. 20:28), it is evident that Jesus' words in Luke 22:28 are authentic, and there Jesus' vicarious offering is not mentioned. About the authenticity of Luke 22:24-27, see above, chapter four, 50-51.

CHAPTER 9

The Son of Man

"Now it happened that as he was praying alone the disciples were with him; and he asked them, 'Who do the people say that I am?' And they answered, 'John the Baptist; but others say, Elijah; and others, that one of the ancient prophets has risen.' And he said to them, 'But who do you say that I am?' And Peter answered, 'The Christ of God'" (Luke 9:18-20). According to Matthew (16:17-19) on this occasion he said to Peter, "Blessed are you, Simon Bar Jona! For flesh and blood has not revealed this to you, but my Father who is in heaven."[1]

According to this report, the people regarded Jesus as a prophet. They had identified John the Baptist with Elijah[2] who was to return. The belief in the return of Elijah was only one aspect of a hope in the renewal of prophecy that would be initiated by a prophet at the end of time.[3] This expectation also lies behind Luke's account that there were people who believed that Jesus was one of "the ancient prophets who had arisen" (Luke

---

1. I also regard the continuation (Matt. 16:18-19) as fundamentally genuine. See Flusser, "Qumran und die Zwölf," in *Initiation; contributions to the theme of the study-conference of the International Association for the History of Religions held at Strasburg, September 17th to 22nd 1964* (ed. C. J. Bleeker; Leiden: Brill, 1965), 138-139; idem, *JOC*, 177-178; Young "Messianic Blessings in Jewish and Christian Texts," *JOC*, 280-300.

2. See Matt. 14:1-2; Mark 6:14-16; Luke 9:7-9.

3. The belief concerning Elijah was based upon Mal. 4:5 [HMT 3:23] and that concerning Moses was based on Deut. 18:18; Hahn, op. cit., 351-404. On the subject of the prophet of the last days, see P. Volz, *Die Eschatologie der jüdischen Gemeinde im neutestamentlichen Zeitalter, nach den Quellen der rabbinischen, apokalyptischen und apokryphen Literatur dargestellt* (Tübingen: Mohr, 1934), 191-197.

9:19). The words are drawn from Deuteronomy 18:18, "I will raise up for them a prophet. . . ."

All of these opinions (i.e., the Baptist, Elijah, and the risen prophet) represent a *single* idea; namely, that Jesus is the prophet of the last days. The hope in an eschatological prophet was one held by many, and it originated in the fact that classical (biblical) prophecy had ceased. So thought rabbinic Judaism as well as other streams of Jewish thought in the period, e.g., the Essenes from Qumran. Throughout the New Testament we find unmistakable indications that many believed that Jesus was the eschatological prophet. One poignant passage is Acts 3:17-22. In this specific case it is possible that a tradition about John the Baptist has been shifted to Jesus.[4]

The opinion that Jesus is the eschatological, "true prophet," was one of the central doctrines of the Jewish Christian sect of the Ebionites.[5] Indeed, Jesus saw himself as a prophet. His remark, "for it cannot be that a prophet should perish away from Jerusalem" (Luke 13:33), confirms this. His words reflect the notion that Jerusalem "kills the prophets and stones those who are sent to it" (Luke 13:34; Matt. 23:38).[6] Furthermore, Jesus speaks in the parable of the wicked husbandmen (Luke 20:9-19) about himself as a prophet — and at the same time as the Son of God — who would be killed, just like the prophets before him.

The impression given by this parable is that the prophetic chain to which Jesus and others belonged had not been interrupted after the prophet Zechariah. This position does not fit the doctrine of either the Pharisees or the Essenes. One should note that Jesus never identifies himself as the prophet of the last days. Perhaps he did not accept the popular notion that prophecy ceased after the days of the Old Testament, and he may not have been the only person who declined to accept uncritically the

4. O. Bauernfeind in *Abraham unser Vater; Juden und Christen im Gespräch über die Bibel. Festschrift für Otto Michel zum 60. Geburtstag* (ed. O. Michel, O. Betz, M. Hengel, and P. Schmidt; Leiden: Brill, 1963), 13-23; reprinted in Bauernfeind's *Kommentar und Studien zur Apostelgeschichte* (Tübingen: Mohr, 1980), 473-483.

5. G. Strecker, *Das Judenchristentum in den Pseudoklementinen* (Berlin: Akademie-Verlag, 1981), 145-153; H. J. Schoeps, *Das Judenchristentum: Untersuchungen über Gruppen-bildungen und Parteikämpfe in der frühen Christenheit* (Bern: Francke, 1964), 56-62.

6. About the killing of the prophets, see E. E. Urbach, *The Sages* (2 vols.; Jerusalem: Magnes Press, 1979), 1:548-563; Schoeps, *Aus frühchristlicher Vorzeit, religionsgeschichtliche Untersuchungen* (Tübingen: Mohr, 1950), 126-143.

prevailing opinion. In any event, these considerations do not have much bearing on the question of Jesus' messianic self-awareness, which certainly existed. We have heard that many recognized him only as the eschatological prophet, but there were obviously others who thought that he was (or aspired to be) the Messiah. This we learn indirectly from the inscription on the cross ("the King of the Jews").

Matthew's version of Jesus' address to Peter has an authentic ring about it. Can one, following the belief of the Church, think that Jesus regarded himself as the Messiah, or must one agree with those who suggest that Jesus' life was "non-messianic"?[7] The latter opinion is based upon the fact that Jesus apparently never used the title "Messiah" to speak of himself. Moreover, he always spoke of the Son of Man in the third person, as though he himself were not identical with that person. The Gospel sayings about the Son of Man fall into three groups: (1) those referring to the coming Son of Man, (2) those referring to his suffering and resurrection, and (3) those in which the son of man is at work in the present. "Foxes have holes, and birds of the air have nests; but the son of man[8] has nowhere to lay his head" (Matt. 8:19-20). In this and other sayings from the third group, the Aramaic or Hebrew term "son of man" means simply "man." This group of sayings, therefore, has nothing to do with Jesus' eschatological hope.[9] The second group is that in which the title, "son of man," is used in connection with the passion, death and resurrection of the Lord. In the past I was sure — as many still are — that this group was a product of early Christianity. The three so-called "passion predictions" (Luke 9:22; 9:43b-45; 18:31-34 and par.) are evidently, in their present form, shaped by the early church. Only the second prediction was seen by a prominent New Testament scholar[10] as original. According to it (Luke 9:44) Jesus said to

---

7. R. K. Bultmann, *Theology of the New Testament* (2 vols.; New York: Scribner, 1951-1955), 1:30f. On the question of Jesus' awareness of his Messiahship, see Bultmann, op. cit., 1:26-32. Concerning the messianic self-awareness of Jesus, see especially Hengel, "Jesus, der Messias Israels," in the collected papers *Messiah and Christos: Studies in the Jewish Origins of Christianity: Presented to David Flusser on the Occasion of His Seventy-fifth Birthday* (ed. I. Gruenwald, S. Shaked, and G. A. G. Stroumsa; Tübingen: Mohr, 1992), 155-176.

8. See chapter six, n. 2.

9. About the notion of the Son of Man in Judaism and in the New Testament, see Flusser, "The Reflection of Jewish Messianic Figures in Early Christianity," in *Messianism and Eschatology: A Collection of Essays* (ed. Z. Baras; Jerusalem: Zalman Shazar Center, 1983), 105-112 [Hebrew]. See below, n. 17.

10. J. Jeremias, *New Testament Theology* (London: SCM Press, 1971), 281-282. Regarding

his disciples, "Listen carefully to what I am about to tell you. The son of man is going to be delivered into the hands of men." This is reminiscent of another authentic saying of Jesus. During the Last Supper he said, "The hand of him who is going to hand me over is on the table. The son of man will go as it has been decreed, but woe to that man who hands him over" (Luke 22:21). These two sayings are similar even in their form, and both are based on a play on words in Hebrew.

In both sayings Jesus speaks about the handing over of the "son of man," and in both he speaks about his tragic end at the hands of men (in Hebrew also: "sons of men"). In the first case (Luke 9:44) Jesus ("the son of man") will be delivered into the hands of men ("sons of men"), while in the second case (Luke 22:21-22) he speaks about the man (Hebrew: "son of man") who shall hand him over. Nevertheless, the formal side of these two authentic sayings is less important than the fact that Jesus speaks about himself as the "suffering son of man." This way of speaking about himself as "the son of man," either out of modesty or in a statement with an unwelcome content, can be seen elsewhere, and seems to fit the manner of Jewish expression in antiquity. Vermes has already drawn attention to the fact[11] that in Aramaic one can designate oneself in such a situation as "that man" (ההוא גברא). Often an unpleasant, frightening, or fateful statement employs this circumlocution.[12] Nevertheless, Jeremias rightly observed[13] that while it is the meaning of the term "that man" to which Jesus alludes, there exists no clear example in which our title, "son of man," is used in the known sources in such a purely euphemistic meaning. While Jeremias' objections are not out of place, they are not decisive, because much of the Hebrew and Aramaic material from the days of Jesus no longer exists.

We have noted that according to the Gospels, Jesus used the title "the son of man" with three meanings. The third type was used by Jesus, as it is in Hebrew discourse today, simply as a term for "man." In the second type,

---

the whole question, see also R. E. Brown, *The Death of the Messiah: From Gethsemane to the Grave: A Commentary on the Passion Narratives in the Four Gospels* (2 vols.; New York: Doubleday, 1994), 2:1468-1491.

11. G. Vermes, *Jesus the Jew: A Historian's Reading of the Gospels* (Philadelphia: Fortress Press, 1981), 160-191, especially 163-168 and 188-191.

12. Such a kind of euphemism was then (and even today) also used on other occasions. When one said something unpleasant about Jews, one used to speak about the "enemies of Israel"!

13. Jeremias, op. cit., 261 n. 1.

he evidently referred to himself as the "son of man" as a euphemistic circumlocution. We have yet to consider the first meaning of the expression, in which he announced the coming of the Son of Man as an eschatological figure. In the second and third groups it is clearly a self-designation, but in the case of the eschatological Son of Man, it is not easy to demonstrate decisively that Jesus believed he would eventually be revealed as the heavenly Son of Man. I once[14] tried to show that he indeed had such an aspiration. If I am right, then the threefold meaning of the designation "son of man" in the mouth of Jesus betrays his manner of sometimes creating a kind of fourth dimension behind his utterances.[15] He is in solidarity with other human beings and is subject to the same humanity, but he personally has to suffer a cruel death, and he will also be revealed as an eschatological figure. All this is speculative. In any event, we do not recommend trying to harmonize and to seek for a consistency among the three meanings of the "son of man." Our task is far more restricted. We need now to speak only about the coming of the future "Son of Man," as this concept is relevant to Jesus' doctrine of the Savior.

Before treating this subject more fully, allow me to make a linguistic remark. I belong to those scholars who believe that Jesus' teaching was *in Hebrew* and that the Semitic language behind the first three Gospels was Hebrew. On the other hand, the *bar anosh* or Son of Man in Daniel 7:9-14 is an Aramaic expression. Why? Because the *whole* of Daniel 7 is written in Aramaic. Are we obliged to believe that even if his teaching was in Hebrew, when Jesus was speaking about the "son of man" he used the Aramaic term? Surely not! As we will see momentarily,[16] in the *Testament of Abraham*, the eschatological Son of Man is identified with Abel, the son of the first Adam. This is proof that the Son of Man was so called *in Hebrew: ben adam.*

The phrase "son of man" appears in the Old Testament. In a vision, Daniel describes the coming judgment of God upon all the kingdoms of the world.

> As I looked, thrones were placed and one that was the Ancient of Days took his seat . . . the court sat in judgment, and the books were opened. . . . I saw in the night visions, and behold, with clouds from heaven there came one like a son of man, and he came to the An-

14. Flusser, "Jesus and the Sign of the Son of Man," *JOC*, 526-534.
15. For example, Jesus defines this side of his character and preaching in Matt. 10:16.
16. See n. 20 below.

cient of Days and was presented before him. And to him was given dominion and glory and kingdom, and all peoples, nations, and languages should serve him; his dominion is an everlasting dominion, which shall not pass away, and his kingdom one that shall not be destroyed. (Dan. 7:9-14)

For Daniel, the son of man was a symbol of the "saints of the Most High." Yet, as we learn from other writings, notably the Ethiopian Book of Enoch, this identification is secondary.[17] Originally the Son of Man was the man-like eschatological judge. Jesus spoke of him:

> When the Son of Man comes in his glory, and all the angels with him, then he will sit on his glorious throne. Before him will be gathered all the nations, and he will separate them one from another as a shepherd separates the sheep from the goats, and he will place the sheep at his right hand, but the goats at the left. Then the King will say to those at his right hand, "Come, O blessed of my Father, inherit the kingdom prepared for you from the foundation of the world. . . ." Then he will say to those at his left hand, "Depart from me, you cursed, into the eternal fire prepared for the devil and his angels. . . ." And they will go away into eternal punishment, but the righteous into eternal life. (Matt. 25:31-36)

In all of the sources, the one resembling a man is portrayed in a consistent manner. The Son of Man has a superhuman, heavenly sublimity. He is the cosmic judge at the end of time. Sitting upon the throne of God, judging the entire human race with the aid of the heavenly hosts, he will consign the just to blessedness and the wicked to the pit of hell. Whatever sentence he metes out, he will execute. Frequently he is identified[18] with the Messiah, but he can also be identified with Enoch, who was taken up into heaven.[19] According to *The Testament of Abraham*,[20] the Son of Man is lit-

---

17. I follow the researchers: S. O. Mowinckel, *He That Cometh* (Oxford: B. Blackwell, 1956); E. Sjöberg, *Der Menschensohn im äthiopischen Henochbuch* (Lund: C. W. K. Gleerup, 1946); idem, *Der verborgene Menschensohn in den Evangelien* (Lund: C. W. K. Gleerup, 1955).

18. For example, *1 En.* 48:10; 52:4. Sparks, op. cit., 230, 232; and *4 Ezra* 13, where the cosmic "Man" is unmistakenly the Messiah.

19. *1 En.* 71; Sparks, op. cit., 255-256.

20. *T. Ab.*, chapters 12-13; *The Testament of Abraham: The Greek Text Now First Edited with an Introduction and Notes* (ed. M. R. James and W. E. Barnes; Cambridge: Cambridge

erally the son of Adam — *ben Adam* — Abel, who was killed by the wicked Cain. God appointed Abel to be the eschatological judge, because he desired that every man would be judged by his peer. At the second judgment the twelve tribes of Israel will judge the whole of creation. Not until the third judgment will God himself judge. This apocalyptic tradition explains why Jesus said to the twelve, "You, who have persevered with me in my tribulations, when the Son of Man sits upon his glorious throne will also sit upon thrones, judging the twelve tribes of Israel" (cf. Matt. 19:28; Luke 22:28-30).

In one of the Essene fragments[21] Melchizedek, the Old Testament priest-king of Jerusalem in the time of Abraham, figures as the eschatological heavenly priest at the end of times.[22] In company with the angels, from on high he will judge men and the wicked spirits of Belial. It is of him the psalmist speaks, "God has taken His place in the divine council; in the midst of the gods He holds judgment" (Ps. 82:1). Elsewhere, too, in the Bible, Jewish tradition understands the word "god" as simply "judge,"[23] but the Essene identification gives us a remarkable glimpse of what majesty could be attributed to the "manlike" judge at the end of time.

The view that the executor of the last judgment would be the biblical Melchizedek was based upon Psalm 110. "The Lord says to my lord, 'Sit at My right hand. . . . You are a priest for ever *after the order* of Melchizedek. . . .'" The Hebrew phrase "after the order of" could be understood to mean "I (God) have said to you (Melchizedek)." In this sense God is addressing Melchizedek himself in the psalm. Thus it was understood by the Essene author. According to the usual interpretation, he who will sit at God's right hand is not Melchizedek himself, but merely one who is the same kind of person as Melchizedek. That is how Jesus understood this psalm. On one occasion, reported in Luke 20:41-43, he quoted the beginning of Psalm 110 with reference to the Messiah. On another occasion, be-

---

University Press, 1892), 90, 92; F. Schmidt, *Le testament grec d'Abraham* (Tübingen: J. C. B. Mohr, 1986), 132-139.

21. M. de Jonge and A. S. Van der Woude, "11Q Melchizedek and the New Testament," *NTS* 12 (1966), 301-321; Flusser, "Melchizedek and the Son of Man," *JOC*, 186-192. See now an edition of 11Qmelch. with commentary by E. Puech, *RevQ* 12 (1987), 483-513. Obviously this Essene fragment is important in connection with the Epistle to Hebrews.

22. Together with him "the Anointed by Spirit" (i.e., the eschatological Prophet) will appear.

23. For example, *Midr. Pss.* on Ps. 82:1.

17. Van Eyck, The Son of Man
Photo credit: Scala/Art Resource, NY

fore being handed over to the Romans, he alluded to the words of this psalm when the high priest asked him if he were the Messiah. He said, "But from now on the Son of Man shall be seated at the right hand of the power of God" (Luke 22:69). Those present correctly understood this as Jesus' indirect admission of his messianic dignity.[24]

It is quite certain that in his own lifetime Jesus became accepted by many — not just by Peter — as the Messiah. Had it not been so, Pilate would not have written above the cross of Jesus, "King of the Jews."[25] On the other hand, one cannot rule out the possibility that Jesus sometimes referred to the coming Son of Man in the third person simply because he wanted to preserve his *incognito*. At first he was possibly awaiting another. In the end, however, the conviction prevailed that he himself was the coming Son of Man. Otherwise, Jesus' answer to the high priest makes no sense. According to Luke 22:67-70, Jesus was asked, "If you are the Messiah, tell us!" Jesus answered, "If I tell you, you will not believe me, and if I asked you, you would not answer. But from now on, the Son of Man will be seated at the right of the power of God."[26] This saying in particular can hardly be an invention of the Church, because the evangelists, thinking that it was not a sufficiently unequivocal confession of his Messiahship, enhanced it.[27]

The one like a man who sits upon the throne of God's glory, the sublime eschatological judge, is the highest conception of the Redeemer ever developed by ancient Judaism. Only one artist has captured it, Van Eyck. He depicted, above the altar at Ghent, the Son of Man as a human being who is divine.[28] Could Jesus of Nazareth have understood himself thus? Let us not forget that he felt he was God's chosen one, his servant, the only Son to whom the secrets of the heavenly Father were open. This very sense

24. See Flusser, "11Q Melchizedek," 192 "additional note." From there one can see that the difficult — and probably corrupted — verse in Ps. 110:3 likely meant that the hero of the Psalm was already born to his high task by God, while in Psalm 2 God says to the hero of the Psalm, "You are My son, *today* I have begotten you." There is not a great difference between the two biblical verses.

25. Mark 15:26.

26. For a parallel to these words in the Dead Sea Scrolls, see Flusser, "At the Right Hand of Power," *JOC*, 301-305.

27. Matt. 26:64 adds, "you have said"; Mark 14:62 adds "I am"; Luke 22:67-70 adds, among other things, "you say that I am."

28. L. van Puyvelde, *L'Agneau mystique d'Hubert et Jean van Eyck* (Brussels: Meddens, 1964), 30.

of sublime dignity could have led him finally to dare that he would be revealed as the Son of Man; and in Judaism the Son of Man was frequently understood as the Messiah.

The New Testament links Jesus' death with his Messiahship, but it seems that Jesus himself connected his tragedy on the cross with his own divine sonship. Moreover, both ideas of his sonship and his death were in his mind connected with his prophetic task. These links were evidently expressed by the heavenly voice at the Transfiguration: "This is my *only* (or: *beloved*) son, listen to him!" (Matt. 17:5; Mark 9:7; Luke 9:35 with variants). The first part alludes to the sacrifice of Isaac, the *only beloved* son of Abraham (Gen. 22:2), and in the second half the heavenly voice hints at the eschatological prophet (Deut. 18:15). Also, in the parable of the wicked husbandmen (Luke 20:9-19 and par.), Jesus speaks about the prophet, the son of the proprietor (i.e., God), who will be killed. I believe that this connection between Jesus' prophetic task, his sacrifice, and the final tragedy originated in Jesus' own intuition. He who had commanded us not to resist evildoers went to his death without a fight. At the end, did he realize that his execution was the crown of his transvaluation of all the usual values? By it the highest was indeed made lowest and the lowest, highest. "For Christ also died for sins once for all, the righteous for the unrighteous, that he might bring us to God" (1 Pet. 3:18).

CHAPTER 10

Jerusalem

"At that very hour some Pharisees came, and said to him, 'Get away from here, for Herod wants to kill you.' And he said to them, 'Go and tell that fox, Behold, I cast out demons and perform cures today and tomorrow, and the third day I finish my course. Nevertheless I must go on my way to-day and tomorrow and the day following; for it cannot be that a prophet should perish away from Jerusalem'" (Luke 13:31-33).

Herod Antipas believed that Jesus was the Baptist, whom he had be-headed, raised from the dead, and he was prepared to kill him "again." Jesus knew that his life was in danger — a heavenly voice never comes out of the clear blue — but he did not want to die in Galilee, where he had been preaching the kingdom of heaven. He would die in Jerusalem, reputed for "killing the prophets and stoning those who are sent to you" (Luke 13:34). The ostensible reason for his pilgrimage was something else, however. The Passover was approaching. Jews were accustomed to making a pilgrimage to Jerusalem to sacrifice the paschal lamb and cele-brate their deliverance from slavery in Egypt. Jesus, too, longed ear-nestly to eat this festive meal with his disciples.[1] So his way of the cross began.

According to Luke, Jesus was accompanied along his last way by the sympathy of his own people. By contrast, according to Mark — who is ac-cepted by Matthew — he was abandoned by all, with the exception of those who formed the kernel of the future Church. Mark is also palpable in his virtual elimination of Jesus' expression of his strong ties with Jerusalem

---

1. Luke 22:15.

18. Jerusalem from the Church of Dominus Flavit that remembers Jesus
weeping over Jerusalem (Luke 19:41-44).

and its tragic future. While Luke's passion narrative often speaks (Luke 13:34-35;[2] 19:41-44; 21:28; 23:27-31) about Jesus' attachment to the "city of the great king" (Matt. 5:35), only his prediction of the destruction of the Temple (Luke 21:5-7) is paralleled by Mark 13:2-4 (and Matt. 24:1-3).

Jesus lamented over Jerusalem for the first time when he began his last journey (Luke 13:34-35): "O Jerusalem, Jerusalem, you who kills the prophets and stones those sent to you, how often have I longed to gather your children together, as a hen gathers her brood under her wings, but you were not willing! Look, your house is left to you desolate."[3] Jesus uttered his lament soon after having been warned by some Pharisees that Herod Antipas sought to kill him. In Luke, Jesus' lament over Jerusalem is a good continuation of the preceding sentence. Matthew (23:37-39) preserves the lament more or less identically with the Lukan parallel. Nevertheless, in Matthew the lament over Jerusalem is misplaced — not unintentionally. While Luke (13:34-35) places the lament following the Pharisees' warning, in Matthew (23:37-39) the lament is presented — before the announce-

2. We will address below the parallel text in Matt. 23:37-39.
3. I have omitted here the following verse (Luke 13:35b; Matt. 23:39).

ment of the destruction of the Temple of Jerusalem (Matt. 24:1-2) — as a final conclusion of Jesus' invectives against the Pharisees! Matthew's transposition of the setting implies that the Pharisees themselves are those "who kill the prophets." In Jesus' day it is certain that they neither killed nor persecuted the visionaries (Matt. 23:29-31).

The pathos in Jesus' lament over Jerusalem is the same as his prediction about the destruction of the city in Luke 19:41-44.[4] As Jesus approached Jerusalem and saw the city, he wept over it and said, "If you, even you, had only known on this day what would bring you peace — but now it is hidden from your eyes. The days will come upon you when your enemies will build an embankment against you and encircle you and hem you in on every side. They will dash you to the ground, you and your children within your walls. They will not leave one stone on another, because you did not recognize the time of your visitation." The "visitation" is intended to be the occasion of salvation as proclaimed by Jesus. Unrecognized as such, this same visitation becomes the basis for a judgment that is yet to come.[5] The city could have learned the way of peace from his teaching; before (Luke 13:1-9), Jesus made it completely clear what he meant: "Unless you repent, you will all perish" (see Luke 13:3 and 5).[6] He presents the people with a deadline in his story of the fig tree — "if the fig tree does not bring fruit, it will be cut down." Jesus wept over Jerusalem, because he feared that it would reject his message. Nevertheless, Jerusalem was given its chance (Luke 19:41-44).[7] Jesus bore the intentions that he stated when he began his way to Jerusalem (Luke 13:34-35). How often he had longed to save Jerusalem, but the people were not willing. "Look, your house is left to you desolate."

As Jesus approached the city he sent two disciples to fetch an ass. When they returned, Jesus mounted the animal and rode it into Jerusalem. Entering the city, he was greeted with "Hosanna!" and a verse of a psalm (118:26), "Blessed be he who enters in the name of the Lord!" On pilgrimage festivals these words were sung and were used to greet pilgrims as they

---

4. About the authenticity of the passage, see especially the study of Dodd in n. 17 and Marshall, op. cit., 717-719.

5. Marshall, op. cit., 719.

6. About this parable and its rabbinic parallels, see Flusser, *Gleichnisse*, 80-85; C. Thoma, S. Lauer, and E. Hanspeter, *Die Gleichnisse der Rabbinen* (Bern: Peter Lang, 1986), 237-239, 321-323.

7. Marshall, op. cit., 717.

19. "Steps of Ascent" leading to and from the Temple along the southern wall.
Photo: Joseph Frankovic; Courtesy of Jerusalem Perspective.

20. Huge stones, each weighing
several tons, resting on the
Herodian street where they fell
in A.D. 70 during the destruction
of Jerusalem and its temple by
the Roman army (Luke 21:6).
Photo by R. Steven Notley; Courtesy of
JerusalemPerspective.com.

arrived in Jerusalem.[8] Strewing garments[9] in his path may have been the people's way of showing honor to the prophet from Galilee (Matt. 21:11). He entered Jerusalem, visited the Temple, and then went to Bethany, a village on the outskirts of the city. There, among friends, he spent his last nights.[10] By day he went to Jerusalem and taught in the Temple. The Temple officials asked him, indeed, by what authority he did this, but he replied, "Let me ask you a question. John's baptism, was it of God or of men?" This answer sent his interrogators into disarray. The Sadducean Temple authorities had no love for the Baptist, so they could not say that John's baptism was of God. However, to say that it was of men was too dangerous, for they feared the crowd who believed John the Baptist to have been a prophet of God. Therefore they merely said. "We do not know." Jesus said to them, "Nor do I tell you by whose authority I do this." There the matter rested (Luke 20:1-8).

This skirmish set off a series of clashes between Jesus and the Temple hierarchy in which he consciously took the initiative, and won over to himself the crowd who hated the Sadducean high priests. His prophetic anger was perfectly genuine; but what did he mean to accomplish, the victory of his cause, with the help of God and man — and without having to die — or the death of a prophet? According to Luke, Jesus' first attack followed immediately upon the conversation concerning John's baptism. In the parable of the tenants in the vineyard (Luke 20:9-18), Jesus spoke of his death at the hands of the high priests, and announced to them their own overthrow. "The scribes and the chief priests tried to lay hands on him at that very hour, but they feared the people; for they perceived that he had told this parable against them" (Luke 20:19).

Thus he taught daily in the Temple. The high priests sought to destroy him, but they were afraid, for the crowd hung upon his words.[11] On one occasion, when some people said of the Temple, "What stones, what a

---

8. See Safrai, *Wallfahrt*, 158. He quotes *Midr. Ps.* 118 (Buber ed., 488): The people of Jerusalem used to say: "Save us O Lord! (Hosanna!),", and the pilgrims replied: "So be it, Lord!" The people of Jerusalem used to say: "Blessed is he who comes in his name!" and the pilgrims replied: "We bless you from the house of the Lord."

9. According to John 12:13, Jesus was also welcomed with palm branches. Matthew 21:8 and Mark 11:8 are different. Luke omits this.

10. See Safrai, op. cit., 135, 159, 162.

11. Mark 11:18-19; Luke 19:47-48. The "scribes" may have been the Temple scribes (Matt. 21:15-16).

building!" Jesus announced, "As for what you see here, the time will come when not one stone will be left on another; every one of them will be thrown down" (Luke 21:5-6). Forty years later, the Temple went up in flames at the hands of the Romans. The unbearable Roman oppression provoked insurrection and terrorism by fanatics, and the sanctuary in Jerusalem was the bulwark of the hated Sadducees who had made a pact with the Romans. Indignation sharpens vision, and many foresaw the destruction of the Temple. Thus, for example, in A.D. 62 on the Feast of Tabernacles, it happened that Joshua the son of Ananias, a simple peasant, was seized by the Spirit in the Temple, and suddenly poured forth a prophetic malediction in which he foretold its destruction. Like one possessed, he kept up his cry day and night in the streets of Jerusalem. The authorities dragged him before the Roman governor, Albinus, who had him scourged to the bone. Yet, the man only went on repeating his gruesome prophecy. The governor then let him go free, considering him to be out of his mind.[12]

Much has already been written about the so-called "Synoptic apocalypse" (Matt. 24; Mark 13; Luke 21). Lindsey[13] rightly assumed that the whole text is a composite work. The fruit of our philological collaboration on this subject was included in one of my Hebrew studies.[14] The inquiry concluded that although all the sources of this "apocalypse" spoke about the future, only a small part of the speech in Luke describes the last days.[15] Luke knew very well that he was speaking about various periods of the future after the crucifixion. He himself indicates explicitly the several points of time when he writes, "This must first take place, but the end will not be at once (21:9). . . . But before all this (21:12). . . . But when you see (21:20) . . . then (21:21) . . . until the times of the Gentiles are fulfilled (21:24). . . . Now when these things begin to take place (21:28)." Luke presents the following distinct periods of time: the destruction of the Temple (21:5-6); the future appearance of false chiliastic prophets (21:7-8); catastrophes of the last days (21:9-11); persecutions of the disciples after the crucifixion (21:12-19); the Roman conquest of Jerusalem,

12. *J.W.* 6:300-305.

13. R. L. Lindsey, "A Modified Two-Document Theory of the Synoptic Dependence and Interdependence," *NovT* 6 (1963), 239-263, and see especially 243-244.

14. Flusser, "A Prophecy about Jerusalem in the New Testament," in *Jewish Sources in Early Christianity* (Jerusalem: Bialik, 1979) 253-274 [Hebrew].

15. The indisputable "eschatological" elements are, strictly speaking, only Luke 21:10-11 and 25-27. About the second passage, see below, n. 19.

the tribulation of Israel, and the period of its dispersion (21:20-24); the eschatological coming of the Son of Man (21:25-33); "your liberation" (21:28).

The description of future persecutions of Jesus' disciples (Luke 21:12-19 and Mark 13:9-13a) is lacking in Matthew because he has already provided it (Matt. 10:15-23). The future lot of the disciples is included in Matthew at the end of Jesus' exhortation to the twelve when he sends them out (Matt. 10:5-15). I believe that Matthew has preserved the original *Sitz im Leben* of this saying, because the Matthean form of the saying is preferable to its parallels in Luke (21:12-19) and Mark (13:9-13a).[16] There is also another question that should be asked. Was the prophecy of the destruction of Jerusalem in Luke 21:20-23 written after the real catastrophe, or can it be that these were Jesus' own words? An eminent classical scholar[17] has shown that Luke's words about the tragic future of Jerusalem could have been uttered before the final catastrophe. Thus Luke 21:20-23 may have been a prophecy of doom by the "historical" Jesus, especially since it is well known that he was not alone among those in his day who foresaw what would happen.

Now the way is free for a correct appreciation of the sketch regarding the future history of the Jewish people (Luke 21:20-24, 28).[18] "But when you see Jerusalem encircled by armies, then know that her desolation is near. Then let those who are in Judaea flee to the mountains, and let those in the city get out, and let those in the country not enter the city; for these are days of retribution to fulfill all that is written. Woe to those who are with child and to those who give suck in those days! For great distress shall come upon the earth and wrath upon this people; they will fall by the edge of the sword, and be led captive among all nations; and Jerusalem will be trampled on by Gentiles, until the times of the Gentiles are fulfilled . . . .[19]

16. An instructive example for understanding the Synoptic problem is the evolution of Jesus' words in Matt. 10:17-18 about the future persecutions of the disciples, "they will be delivered both to Jewish and Gentile authorities to bear testimony before them (the Jews) and the Gentiles" (cf. Acts 9:15). This is repeated in the "Synoptic apocalypse" — in a worse version — in Mark 13:9. The following verse 10 ("And the gospel must first be preached to all nations") is an addition. Mark 13:10 was then taken over and enlarged by Matt. 24:14.

17. C. H. Dodd, "The Fall of Jerusalem and the 'Abomination of Desolation,'" *JRS* 37 (1947), 47-54. See also Marshall, op. cit., 771.

18. Flusser, op. cit., 253-274.

19. According to the apocryphal *Psalms of Solomon* (17:21-22) the Son of David will "purge Jerusalem from Gentiles who trample her." This was written shortly after the conquest of Jerusalem by Pompey (cf. *OTP* 2:667). I have omitted here the apocalyptic description of the future coming of the Son of Man, although it is present in all the three Synoptic Gospels (Matt. 24:29-

21. Arch of Titus. Notice the menorah from the Temple,
destroyed by Titus's troops in A.D. 70   Photo by J. H. Charlesworth.

When all this begins to happen, stand up and lift up your heads because your liberation is drawing near."

After having said that the liberation of his people *is drawing near,* Jesus concluded (in Matt. 24:32-33; Mark 13:28-29; Luke 21:29-31) his vision of the future by saying, "Now learn the lesson from the fig tree. As soon as it puts forth fruit, you can see for yourselves and know that summer *is near.* Even so, when you see these things happening, you know that *it is near,*

31; Mark 13:24-27; Luke 21:25-26), and it cannot be excluded that the passage belonged to the original discourse, but this is not sure (see Taylor, *Mark,* 517, 519 and Marshall, op. cit., 774). What is sure is that Luke 21:25-26 constitutes an interruption between 21:24 and 21:28; moreover, the passage about the Son of Man is purely Greek and does not betray any traces of Hebraisms (or even pseudo-Hebraisms). It is more natural to see that the words, "When all this begins to happen" (v. 28), are a continuation of verse 24, "When the times of the Gentiles will begin to be completed, then your liberation will draw near." One should also note the disagreement between the detailed description of the coming of the Son of Man in the "Synoptic apocalypse," and Jesus' view that the day of the Son of Man will come like a thief in the night (cf. 1 Thess. 4:2). Jesus himself clearly expressed his position in Luke 17:22-37 (vv. 25 and 33 are evidently interpolated, and possibly also v. 31). Matthew saw the identity of the theme between the two passages, but did not recognize that they are contradictory (cf. Matt. 24:26-28)!

right at the door." Jesus alludes here to the fig tree in Song of Songs 2:13, in accordance with the common Jewish opinion that the whole passage (2:11-13) speaks about the redemption of Israel.[20] The intricate relationship of the motif of redemption with Jesus' allusion to the Song of Songs 2:13 is disrupted by Mark's omission of the parallel to Luke 21:28, "lift up your heads, because your liberation is drawing near." Once again, we see that the original structure of Jesus' sayings is better preserved in Luke.

The passage in Luke is a product of a basic scriptural prophetic scheme.[21] It usually begins with destruction. It then follows a consequence of tribulations and suffering in the dispersion, concluding happily with the return to the homeland when the times are ripe. The oldest example of this paradigm is found in God's words to Abraham (Gen. 15:13-16). There the destruction is lacking, but Abraham's descendants will be strangers in a foreign country and will be enslaved and ill-treated; afterwards, however, they will come back. This will happen only in the fourth generation, "for the sin of the Amorites has not yet reached its full measure." The ancient scheme reappears later in the book of Tobit (14:4-5). There the elder Tobit describes the future to his family. Jerusalem will be desolate and the (First) Temple burned down, but at the end the Jews will return to their home and they will rebuild the Temple. This (Second) Temple will not be "like the former" Solomonic Temple, "until the times of the age are completed," i.e., in the time of full redemption. Here the prophetic scheme is more complex, but its main structure is preserved: destruction, dispersion, and a glorious return to the homeland. The similarity between these two examples and Luke 21:24 is striking. From the comparison with the two other texts there can be no doubt that Luke's "Jerusalem will be trampled down by Gentiles, until the times of the Gentiles are fulfilled" can only mean that Jerusalem will no longer be trampled on by the Gentiles when finally their (i.e., the Gentiles') times will come to an end.[22] I am personally fascinated

---

20. See, for example, the very ancient Aramaic translation of the whole passage and *Cant. Rab.* on Cant. 2:13. These sources reflect the time after the destruction of the Temple, while Jesus' interpretation of Cant. 2:13, "The fig tree forms its early fruit" because "the winter is past" (Cant. 2:11), is earlier. Jesus explains, "as soon as it puts forth fruit, you can see for yourselves and know that *it is near*, right at the door." By the way, Jesus' parable of the fig tree (Luke 13:6-9) is also dependent upon Luke 21:28. See now R. S. Notley, "Learn the Lesson of the Fig Tree," *Jesus' Last Week*, 107-120.

21. Flusser, "A Prophecy about Jerusalem," 258-259.

22. For the convenience of the reader I will cite the similar phrases in the three

22. Judaea Capta coin, struck in Rome in A.D. 71, after the Roman conquest of Jerusalem in 70.

by the way this literary scheme recurs, not only in texts but in the concrete long history of the Jewish people.[23]

I see no serious obstacle in accepting the passage about the future liberation of Israel as an authentic utterance of the "historical" Jesus. Why should we doubt his solidarity with his people? Should he not feel the same grief and hopes as his compatriots? Who would have blamed a Dutch pastor — or priest — when he longed for the liberation of the Netherlands under the yoke of foreign occupation? According to Luke, Jesus' disciples also shared this sentiment. "We had been hoping that he was the man to liberate Israel" (Luke 24:21). Again, according to Acts 1:6-7, the apostles asked the resurrected Jesus, "Lord, is this the time when you are to establish once again the sovereignty of Israel?" He responded to them, "It is not for you to know about dates or times, which the Father has set within His own authority."

The same desire for Israel's liberation is attested in the events of the

---

sources. Gen. 19:16, "For the sin of the Amorites has not yet reached its full measure"; Tob. 14:5, "until the times of the age are completed"; Luke 21:24, "until the times of the Gentiles are fulfilled."

23. There can be a reciprocal dependence between these two spheres.

infant Jesus in the Temple of Jerusalem (Luke 2).[24] When he was brought there, both the aged Simeon, who "was looking for the consolation of Israel" (Luke 2:25), and the prophetess Anna (Luke 2:36-38) met the child. The prophetess "spoke of him to all who were looking for the redemption[25] of Jerusalem." "The freedom of Zion" and "the redemption of Zion" are slogans imprinted upon the coins of the First Revolt against Rome, and the motto "freedom of Jerusalem" was inscribed upon Bar Kokhba's coins.[26] The views of the circles to which both Simeon and Anna belonged are reflected in one of the extracanonical psalms from a Qumran scroll (vv. 3-4 and 9): "Generation after generation will dwell in thee (Jerusalem) and generations of pious will be thy splendor: those who yearn for the day of thy salvation, may they rejoice in the greatness of thy glory. . . . How they have hoped for thy salvation, thy pure ones have mourned for thee."[27]

Even during Jesus' agonizing final steps to his violent death, he was weighted down by the future tragedy of Jerusalem. A large number of people followed him, many women among them who mourned and wailed for him. Jesus turned and said, "Daughters of Jerusalem, do not weep for me; weep for yourselves and for your children. For the time will come when you will say, 'Happy are the barren, the wombs that never bore and that never nursed!' Then they will start saying to the mountains, 'Fall on us,' and to the hills, 'Cover us.' For if these things are done with the green wood, what will happen to the dry?" (Luke 23:27-31).[28] The green wood is difficult to kindle, while the dry is easy to burn. If the life of the pious Jesus ends with a tragedy, what will happen to a sinful Jerusalem? The disaster becomes inevitable, but there is hope for Jerusalem in a distant future, when the times of the Gentiles will be completed (Luke 21:24).

---

24. See Flusser, *JOC*, 127.

25. The Greek substantive in Luke 2:38, λύτρωσις, has the same root and meaning as ἀπολύτρωσις (liberation) in Luke 21:28. The latter occurs in the Gospels only in Luke 21:28; λύτρωσις also appears in Luke 1:68. Both substantives are the equivalent for the Hebrew גאולה, which appears on Hebrew coins from both the First Revolt and the Bar Kokhba rebellion. See Schürer, op. cit., 1:605-606.

26. See Schürer, ibid.

27. *The Psalms Scroll of Qumran Cave 11 (11QPsᵃ), Discoveries in the Judaean Desert, Vol. 4* (ed. J. A. Sanders; Oxford: Clarendon Press, 1965), 86-87.

28. For Jewish parallels to the proverbial verse 31, see Billerbeck, op. cit., 2:262-263 and Brown, *The Death of the Messiah*, 2:924-927.

We have seen that the Lukan picture of Jesus' strong ties with Jerusalem is historically reliable and consistent, but it is more or less absent in Mark — the only exception is Mark 13:2, in the introduction to the "Synoptic apocalypse!"[29] Does it mean that the "Lukan" Jesus is too Jewish, or that Mark has purposely changed the picture? Happily enough, it can be easily shown that the reworking of the tradition comes from Mark. Where in the "Synoptic apocalypse" Jesus speaks about the future tragedy of Jerusalem, Mark omits it or supplants Jerusalem and the Jewish people with the *"elect ones,"*[30] i.e., the Christian believers, the kernel of the future early church. Mark 13:19b-20 (and Matt. 24:21-22) probably constitutes the best example of this technique. While in Luke 21:23-24 Jesus speaks about imminent destruction as "the wrath against this people" and the tragedy of the Jewish nation "until the times of the Gentiles are fulfilled," Mark (13:19b-20) employs the more common apocalyptic phrase "the abbreviation of times,"[31] and he says that God will shorten the days "for the sake of *the elect,* whom he has chosen." Two verses later, Mark 13:22 (and Matt. 24:24), in a passage that has no parallel in Luke, we read, "False christs and false prophets will appear and perform signs and miracles to deceive the elect — if that were possible."

29. Matthew follows Mark, with the exception of Matt. 23:37-39, which is identical to Luke 13:34-35. According to the classical "two source" Synoptic solution, this passage is taken from Q.

30. In addition to the "Synoptic apocalypse" in Mark (13:20, 22, and 27) and its parallels in Matthew (24:22, 24, and 31), the term "the elect ones" appears only twice at the end of a parable: once in Matthew (22:14) and once in Luke (18:7). In both cases the term does not have the specific meaning it has in Mark and appears not to stem from Jesus. It seems to me that the designation "the elect ones" is derived from a dualistic worldview that does not fit the theology of Jesus. About the Essene root of this concept, see Flusser, *JOC,* 30-31. An important observation — before the discovery of the Scrolls — was made by E. Meyer in a chapter about the Essenes in his *Ursprung und Aufänge des Christentums* (3 vols.; Stuttgart: J. G. Cotta, 1921-1923), 2:402.

31. See, for example, the War Scroll from Qumran (1QM) 1:11-12, "that is the time of mighty trouble for the people to be redeemed by God. In all their troubles there was none like it, being hastened to its completion to the eternal redemption." See Yadin's note in *The Scroll of the War of the Sons of Light against the Sons of Darkness* (Oxford: Oxford University Press, 1962), 260. The whole complex is based upon Dan. 12:1 and an exegesis of Isa. 60:12, "In its time, I will hasten it." Ben Sira (36:10) prays, "Hasten the ending, appoint the time!" See also Billerbeck, op. cit., 1:599-600 and 953. See especially *b. Sanh.* 98a, "If Israel will merit it, 'I will hasten it,' but if they will not merit it, 'In its time.'" See also *3 Bar.* 4:3 and *Pss. Sol.* 17:45.

The third — and most interesting — appearance of the elect is in Mark 13:24 (and Matt. 24:31) at the end of the passage about the coming of the Son of Man, who "will send the angels and gather the elect from the four winds, from the ends of the earth to the end of heaven." The gathering of the Gentile church is a basic concept of earliest Christianity,[32] but it very quickly lost its importance. Originally the two concepts of gathering were linked together,[33] but almost immediately the situation changed. The extant sources betray various grades of connection or tension between the hope of the gathering of the Old Israel and the gathering of Gentile believers. One sometimes gets the impression of a kind of rivalry between the old and new concepts of the gathering of the dispersed. The whole early Christian complex is fluid.

There exists no visible contrast in John 11:52 and 12:32 between the historical Israel and the gathering of Gentile Christianity. Jesus died not only for the Jewish nation, but also "to gather into one the children of God who are scattered abroad" (John 11:52). And according to this Gospel Jesus is supposed to have said, "I, when I am lifted, will draw *all* men to myself" (John 12:32). This reminds us of the strange description in 1 Thessalonians 4:15-17, when Paul describes "the coming of our Lord Jesus Christ and his gathering of us to himself" (cf. 2 Thess. 2:1). In the same way, "The Lord himself will descend from heaven and the dead in Christ will rise first, then we who are still alive and are left shall be caught up together with them in the clouds to meet the Lord in the air. And so we will be with the Lord forever." In the early Christian document, the *Didache* (ca. A.D. 100), the gathering of Christians is twice mentioned, without the apocalyptic lifting up into the clouds — namely, in the eucharistic prayers in chapters 9 and 10: "As this fragment (of bread) lay scattered upon the mountains and became a single (fragment) when it had been gathered, may your church be gath-

---

32. About the idea, see L. Clerici, *Einsammlung der Zerstreuten; liturgiegeschichtliche Untersuchung zur Vor- und Nachgeschichte der Fürbitte für die Kirche in Didache 9,4 und 10,5* (Münster: Aschendorffsche Verlagsbuchhandlung, 1966); K. Niederwimmer, *Die Didache* (Göttingen: Vandenhoeck & Ruprecht, 1989), 187-191; Flusser, "Matthew's 'Verus Israel,'" *JOC*, 561-574. See also the composite biblical quotation by Justin Martyr in *1 Apol.* 52:10; cf. O. Skarsaune, *The Proof from Prophecy: A Study in Justin Martyr's Proof-text Tradition: Text-type, Provenance, Theological Profile*, Supplements to Novum Testamentum, vol. 56 (Leiden: Brill, 1987), 76-78.

33. See especially Acts 1:6-8 and my forthcoming contribution about Paul in the *Theologische Real-Encyclopädie*.

ered into your kingdom from the ends of the earth" (*Did.* 9:4). "Be mindful, Lord, of our church and, once it is sanctified, gather it from the four winds, into the kingdom which you have prepared for it" (*Did.* 10:5).

In John 11:52 the gathering of the Gentile believers is mentioned together with the Jewish nation; in both the two Epistles to the Thessalonians and in the *Didache,* we read about the gathering of the Church without any connection to the gathering of Israel. The situation worsens in the so-called Fifth Esdras,[34] and in the concept represented in the *Dialogue* with the Jew Tryphon by Justin Martyr (ca. A.D. 100-105) where it appears in 26:1; 80:1; 113:3-4; 139:4-5.[35] In Fifth Esdras and Justin Martyr, the Christian gathering comes instead of the gathering of the "historical" Israel. It is not the Jews, but Gentile Christians who will inherit the Holy Land and Jerusalem. Justin Martyr insists that the Gentile Christians will be gathered then, but the Jews who oppose Christianity "shall not inherit anything in the Holy Mountain, but the Gentiles who have believed in Him . . . shall receive the inheritance . . ." (26:1). Similarly in Fifth Esdras (2:10-13), this is what the Lord says to Ezra: "Inform my people that I will give them the kingdom of Jerusalem which I have given to Israel . . . the kingdom is already prepared for you" (see also 1:24-27, 30-40).

Elsewhere[36] I have tried to show that the final redactor of the Gospel of Matthew embraced the same opinions as Fifth Esdras and the eschatology contained in Justin Martyr's *Dialogue,* and that there are even literary motifs common to the three sources. Here it must suffice to bring two Matthean passages. "Therefore I tell you that the kingdom of God will be taken from you and given to a people who will produce its fruit" (Matt. 21:43). "Many, I tell you, will come to feast with Abraham, Isaac and Jacob in the kingdom of Heaven. But those who were *born to the kingdom* will be driven out into the dark, the place of wailing and gnashing of teeth" (Matt. 8:11-12).[37]

---

34. These are the first two chapters of Fourth (or Second Book of) Esdras. They are preserved only in Latin and do not belong to the book itself. The small booklet was originally written in Greek; it is of Christian provenance and was evidently written in the second century A.D. The English translation used here is that of J. M. Myers, *I and II Esdras* (AB 42; Garden City, N.Y.: Doubleday, 1974), 140-158. Another translation is found in *OTP,* 1:525-532. See also Flusser, "Verus Israel," *JOC,* 568-571. About the transfer of the election of Israel to the Gentile Church, see Skarsaune, op. cit., 326-374.

35. Flusser, "Verus Israel," 568-571.

36. Flusser, "Verus Israel," 558-574.

37. Justin Martyr has certainly understood Matthew's final redactor correctly when he

How far was Mark related to such a dangerous position? It is clear that he saw the Christian believers as a body separate from the non-Christian Jews. He mentions only the eschatological gathering of the Christian believers. Yet, there is no sign that he also believed that God's election was transferred to Gentile Christianity, and that "those who were born to the kingdom" would be condemned to hell. Even though Mark was not prone to accept the extreme position of the final redactor of Matthew, the redactor did not feel it necessary to oppose Mark.

Mark deliberately omits — with one exception (Mark 13:2)[38] — from his "apocalypse" any mention of the future tragedy of Jerusalem. Instead, he places three times on the lips of Jesus (Mark 13:20, 22, 27) statements about the future of the elect, i.e., the Christian kernel of the coming Church. In the end, Jesus is not only a Kafkaesque, lonely, holy man, abandoned in his death and despised by his own people, but his teaching is not even considered to be like that of the Jewish Sages. According to Mark, Jesus' ties with his people and with Jerusalem are practically non-existent. Mark preserves almost nothing about the future of the children of Israel and their holy city. Their mention is replaced by the "elect ones," the Christian believers. Thus, Mark already shows symptoms of an exclusivist ecclesiology.[39] I personally admire his ingenuity in creating, compelled by his sectarian impulse, the imposing figure of a lonely, holy giant! It would be irresponsible to blame Mark for the subsequent developments — we must be cautious in our judgment. Yet, we can be grateful to Luke that he has preserved the true historical picture of Jesus' solidarity with his people.

Jesus' pilgrimage to Jerusalem is the first act of his tragedy. He went there not to heal, but as a prophet of doom. He desired to prevent the inevitable. As we have heard, he even predicted that he would die there as other prophets had before him (Luke 13:33). Jesus expressed his opposition to the abuses in the Temple, not only by words but by deeds. As it often happens at shrines, a brisk trade went on at the Temple in Jerusalem in those days. Jesus was not the only one whose displeasure had been aroused by the ta-

---

quotes three times (*Dial.* 76:4; 120:5-6; 140:4) the passage in Matt. 8:11-12 as a scriptural proof for the view that the election of guilty Israel was abolished and transferred to the Christian Church.

38. Mark needs his mention of the future destruction of the Temple, in order to bring the following "Synoptic apocalypse."

39. Nothing of this kind can be found in Paul! For example, see the famous passage in Romans 11.

bles of the moneychangers, and the stalls of the dove-sellers at the place of sanctification.[40] Nevertheless, it was not until after Jesus' death that the scribes adopted practical measures to keep the trade necessary for the Temple sacrifices out of the Temple precincts. When Jesus visited there, however, these measures were not yet in effect. Having entered the Temple area, he began removing[41] those who were selling, by saying, "Scripture says, 'My house will be a house of prayer';[42] but you have made it a den of robbers'"[43] (Luke 19:45-6).[44]

John reports that at this point Jesus also said, "I will destroy this Temple that is made with hands, and in three days I will build another, not made with hands" (John 2:19; cf. Matt. 26:61). In Mark (14:57-59), however, this is the testimony of a false witness.[45] If it was true that Jesus re-

40. See Safrai, op. cit., 185-188.

41. The Greek verb means in Luke 19:45-46, as elsewhere in the New Testament, "to take out, remove" *without any connotation of force*. Nevertheless, it is true that the main meaning of this Greek verb is "to drive out, expel, literally to throw out" more or less forcibly. See Bauer and Danker, op. cit., 299. According to Luke, Jesus evidently used no force. He persuaded the merchants to leave only by quoting the pertinent words from the Bible. Mark (11:15) — and following him Matthew (21:12) — understood the Greek ἐκβάλλειν in his source according to its main meaning, and he thus believed that Jesus "began to drive out" the merchants from the Temple using force. See below, n. 44.

42. Isa. 56:7.

43. Jer. 7:11.

44. That which certainly belonged to the original account can be read in Luke. Mark 11:15-17 expands the account on the basis of the physical reality of the Temple. We cannot tell, therefore, whether or not Jesus succeeded by his words in persuading the merchants to leave. Matthew 21:12-13 follows Mark, but turns Jesus' attempt to drive out the merchants into an accomplished deed. John 2:13-17 transposes the incident to the beginning of Jesus' public life, and he underscores and exaggerates the episode. For example, he reports that Jesus drove out bulls from the Temple (John 2:15), something that surely was never present in the Temple area. However, John does preserve the connection between the cleansing of the Temple and the prophecy about the Temple (John 2:19).

45. According to the original text of Matt. 26:60, the two who inform the high priest of the saying are not false witnesses. The episode is missing entirely from Luke. According to John 2:19, it really was the utterance of Jesus. The nearest parallel to the eschatological Temple "not made with hands" is found in the Temple Scroll (11QT 29:9-10) from Qumran. In the passage, God says: "And I will consecrate My [T]emple by My glory, (the Temple) on which I will settle My glory, until the day of (a new) creation on which I will create My Temple and establish it for Myself for all times, according to the covenant which I have made with Jacob at Bethel." See the additional note in Flusser, *JOC*, 98; and the newly published, *The Temple Scroll: A Critical Edition with Extensive Reconstruction* (ed. E. Qimron; Beer

ally said that he would rebuild the Temple, then Caiaphas, the Sadducee, was not listening to rabbinic fantasies. There is a biblical verse that was understood by all to speak about the Messiah, who would build the Temple. "The man whose name is Branch . . . he shall build the Temple of God" (Zech. 6:12). The Branch was generally understood to be a designation for the Messiah. It is therefore logical to suppose that *if* Jesus said that he would build the Temple, he confessed that he was the Messiah. Likewise, it would be logical for the high priest to respond and ask him, "Are you then the Christ?"[46]

It would seem that we do not have the saying in its original form. The three days are connected with the belief that Jesus rose on the third day. Nevertheless, the saying was expressed originally in the first person. Jesus evidently spoke in the name of God,[47] in the spirit of Jewish apocalyptism.[48] The present Temple would be destroyed, and another would be raised up by the hand of God. The saying is, then, another prophecy about the destruction of the Temple. As he was leaving Galilee, Jesus said, "Behold, your house is forsaken" (Luke 13:35), and he was sent to Jerusalem to announce this. Seen from this angle, his removal of the traders and the

---

Sheva-Jerusalem: Ben Gurion University Press/IES, 1996), 44. The Temple, described in the Temple Scroll, on which God settles his glory is the interim Temple. The Temple that God builds will be erected by himself in the day of the new creation. This threefold division between the (biblical) past, the present period (i.e., "the days of the rule of Belial" — 1QS 2:19) in which the sect lived, and the purely eschatological future, is evidently central to the timetable of the Qumran sect. It resembles in some ways the threefold partition of time by Jesus: the "biblical" period until John the Baptist (Matt. 11:13; Luke 16:16), the period of the realization of the kingdom of Heaven, and the coming of the Son of Man. See Flusser, "Die jüdische Messiaserwartung Jesu," 37-52; idem, *Gleichnisse*, 270-273. The similarity between the two concepts is only external, because Jesus' messianic system depends on rabbinic premises. The best explanation for the affinity between the timetable of the Essenes, the rabbinic system, and the view of Jesus seems to be the existence of an *earlier* division into three periods: the biblical period, our time, and the purely post-historical eschaton.

46. Luke 22:67; Matt. 26:63; Mark 14:61. Luke has apparently abbreviated the report of the interrogation and removed the issue concerning the building of the Temple, which led to the high priest's question.

47. As in Matt. 23:24 and, perhaps, Matt. 23:37.

48. Bultmann, *Synoptic Tradition*, 125f.; Flusser, "The Temple Not Made with Hands in the Qumran Doctrine," *JOC*, 88-93. See now especially D. Dimant, "The Apocalyptic Interpretation of Ezekiel at Qumran," in *Messiah and Christos: Studies in the Jewish Origins of Christianity: Presented to David Flusser on the Occasion of His Seventy-fifth Birthday* (ed. I. Gruenwald, S. Shaked, and G. A. G. Stroumsa; Tübingen: Mohr, 1992), 38. See above, n. 45.

connected saying about the Temple, provide the climax of his prophetic mission to Jerusalem.

Jesus' words and actions in Jerusalem precipitated the catastrophe. The Sadducean priesthood, despised by everyone, found its sole support in the Temple. This prophet from Galilee, in front of the crowd assembled for the festival in the Temple, had foretold not only its destruction, but the end of their priestly caste. Moreover, capitalizing on the bitter feelings about the trade that went on in the sanctuary, he struck a painful blow against the Temple authorities. As we have seen, thirty years later, the authorities handed over Joshua ben Ananias to the Romans, because he too prophesied the Temple's ruin. Throughout their whole empire, the Romans diligently protected all religious sanctuaries. They also evidently made it their business to protect the high priests from importune agitators.

Luke states that Jesus merely began to remove the traders from the Temple. Apparently he was not able to carry out his intention, and we do not know how many obeyed his directions, nor have we any report of the reaction of the crowd of pilgrims who were present. It is almost certain that the Temple guard eventually intervened. We may also presume that the cleansing of the Temple took place shortly before the arrest of Jesus — something he had been able to avoid on the first occasion.

According to the first three Gospels, the Last Supper was a paschal meal. Jesus had, therefore, already offered the paschal lamb. As it was prescribed that the roasted lamb be eaten within the walls of the holy city,[49] on the last evening Jesus did not return to Bethany, but remained in Jerusalem.[50] We have no record of the host's name, for in those days pilgrims were gladly received everywhere and anywhere. When night had fallen he reclined at the table with the twelve and said,

> "With all my heart I have longed to eat this paschal lamb with you before I die;[51] for I tell you, I will never eat it again until a new one will be eaten[52] in the kingdom of God." And he took a cup of wine, recited a benediction over it and said, "Take it and share it among you; for I tell you, I will not again drink of the fruit of the vine until

49. M. Zebah. 5:7-8; cf. m. Pesah. 7:9.
50. Matt. 26:17-20. See Safrai, op. cit., 220-223.
51. Luke 22:15 reads, "before I suffer."
52. Thus it reads in Codex Bezae.

23. Garden of Gethsemane.

I drink it new in the kingdom of God."[53] And he took bread, recited a benediction over it, broke it and gave it to them, saying, "This is my body."[54]

Catastrophe was imminent. Jesus made no secret about it to his disciples.[55] He evidently hinted to his future martyrdom when he said over the broken bread: "This is my body." He told Peter that before the cock crowed he would deny him thrice.[56] As they were eating the feast, begun under the shadow of death, he said, "Behold the hand of him who hands me over is[57]

---

53. It is more likely that in both sayings Jesus said, "in the world to come."

54. Cf. Luke 22:15-19. In the important manuscript mentioned in n. 52, this is where the text ends. On this point, see R. Otto, *Sünde und urschuld, und andere aufsätze zur theologie* (Munich: Beck, 1932), 96-122; Flusser, "The Last Supper and the Essenes," *JOC*, 203; Notley, "Eucharist," 123 n. 13; Metzger, op. cit., 173-177.

55. Luke 22:21-22.

56. Luke 22:34.

57. The words "with me" are missing in some manuscripts of Luke 22:21. See Fitzmyer, op. cit., 2:1410. The prepositional phrase probably crept into the text from Matt. 26:23 (cf. Mark 14:20), where the phrase "with me" is indispensable.

on the table" (Luke 22:11). Had he discovered the betrayer? Earlier, probably after the clash in the Temple, Judas Iscariot, one of the twelve, had gone to the high priests to deliver Jesus over to them. They had promised to pay him handsomely for his deed (Luke 22:3-6 and par.). We do not know why he did this, and the accounts of his death are contradictory. Most likely he disappeared after the betrayal, for there were plenty of people at that time who would have repaid him in blood for handing a Jew over to the Romans.

After the meal, the hymn of praise having been sung,[58] Jesus left the city along with his disciples and went to the nearby Mount of Olives, to a place known as Gethsemane.[59] There he bade the disciples to wait and watch. He walked on a little farther, prostrated himself, and prayed, "Father, if You will, let this cup pass me by; but not as I will, but as You will." Then he went back and found the disciples asleep, and said to them, "Why do you sleep? Get up and pray that I do not fall into temptation.[60] The spirit is willing, but the flesh is weak"[61] (cf. Luke 22:39-46). He was tempted to betray the voices that had proclaimed to him his election and divine sonship, but he overcame the impulse to flee into the darkness of that night from Gethsemane, and to eke out an anonymous, secret existence somewhere. He submitted to the will of his Father in heaven to drink the cup, which he had already guessed was predestined for him.

The Temple guard approached, accompanied — according to John 18:3 — by a Roman cohort[62] and Judas Iscariot. Judas greeted Jesus in the customary manner as a way of identifying him for the officers in the darkness. The treachery of Judas' actions and the irony of his greeting were ex-

---

58. The so-called Hallel, i.e., Psalms 113–118.

59. Safrai has brought to my attention that according to a tradition known in the days of the Second Temple, there was a specified location on the Mount of Olives where King David had prayed over Jerusalem, and it became a focal point of prayer. It seems likely that if Jesus customarily retreated to the Mount of Olives to pray as Luke 22:31 records, it is to this location that Jesus and his disciples came after the Passover meal. See *y. Ber.* 4:8b.

60. In the sources: "that you do not fall into temptation." See Jean Hering, "Zwei exegetische Probleme in der Perikope von Jesus in Gethsemane," in *Neotestamentica et Patristica. Eine Freundesgabe, Herrn Professor Dr. Oscar Cullmann zu seinem 60. Geburtstag überreicht.* Supplements to Novum Testamentum, vol. 6 (Leiden: Brill, 1962), 64-69.

61. The last sentence, "The spirit . . . weak" (Matt. 26:41b and Mark 14:32b), does not appear in Luke.

62. I believe that it is a tendentious invention by John's source. See Flusser, "What Was the Original Meaning of *Ecce Homo?*" *JOC*, 593-603.

24. The Caiaphas Ossuary. Courtesy of Israel Antiquities Authority.

posed by Jesus' response, "Judas, are you delivering the son of man (or: a person) with a kiss?" (Luke 22:48). Suddenly, one of Jesus' followers struck the servant of the high priest and cut off his ear, but Jesus said, "Stop! no more of this." "Then Jesus said to the chief priests and officers of the Temple and elders, who had come out to arrest him, 'Have you come out as against a brigand, with swords and clubs? When I was with you day after day in the Temple, you did not lay hands on me'" (Luke 22:52-53).[63] Then Jesus was taken off and brought in custody to the high priest's house.

63. Joseph Frankovic has reminded me in a private communication that Xenophon (*Mem.* I.1, 10) stresses that Socrates also spoke about his philosophy openly.

CHAPTER 11

Death

In A.D. 62, the Sadducean high priest, Annas, convened a session of the Sanhedrin at which the Lord's brother James and other Christians were indicted before the judges and condemned to be stoned. The Pharisees engineered the deposition of Annas, because in their opinion, the session had been illegal — called without their knowledge.[1] The Sanhedrin was the Jewish supreme court and numbered seventy-one members. To pass a sentence of death, the presence of twenty-three judges was needed.[2] If the Sanhedrin was in session at Jesus' inquiry, one must assume that the high priest had assembled a sufficient number of judges who were from among his Sadducean friends. We have noted earlier, that in the first three Gospels, the Pharisees are not mentioned in connection with the trial of Jesus. And according to all that is reported about the Pharisees, they could not have acquiesced in the surrender of Jesus to the Romans. If, then, there was a session of the Sanhedrin before the crucifixion of Jesus, it must have resembled the arbitrary assembly of distinguished Sadducees who later condemned James, the Lord's brother, to death.

Was it an official assembly of the Sanhedrin that condemned Jesus to death? John knew nothing about it, and in the whole of Luke — not just in his description of the Passion — a verdict of the supreme court is not even mentioned.[3] Mark was the first to alter the ancient report. He attempted to portray a session of the judiciary passing judgment. Matthew subsequently

---

1. *Ant.* 20:200-203.
2. *M. Sanh.* 4:1.
3. See P. Winter, *On the Trial of Jesus* (Berlin: De Gruyter, 1961), 28.

based his account upon Mark. The time and place of the inquiry, however, vary in each of the different Gospel accounts.

According to Luke (22:66) the proceedings took place after that anguished night. In the morning Jesus was taken "to their Sanhedrin."[4] According to Mark (14:53-65) and Matthew (26:57-68), the proceedings took place during the night itself, in the high priest's house, where "all the chief priests and the elders and the scribes were assembled" (Mark 14:53; cf. Matt. 26:57). Later in the accounts (Mark 14:55; Matt. 26:59), the assembly is suddenly transformed into "the chief priests and the whole Sanhedrin."

On the following morning — so writes Mark (15:1) — "the chief priests, with the elders and scribes, and the whole Sanhedrin held a consultation. They bound Jesus and led him away and delivered him to Pilate." Matthew (27:1-2) omits "and the whole Sanhedrin," which he apparently thought superfluous. Thus, Luke (22:26) and Matthew (26:59) explicitly mention the Sanhedrin only once, while Mark mentions it twice (14:55; 15:1). All this demonstrates that something disturbing has happened — not in reality, but in Mark and Matthew. There was not a double session of the Sanhedrin. To be blunt, the night session in the high priest's house is a product of Mark's literary creativity, as is his notion of Jesus' condemnation to death by the Jewish supreme court.[5] By contrast, Luke is free from the assertion that Jesus was formally condemned to death by the Jewish authorities. This presentation is consistent with his versions of the "passion predictions" (Luke 9:22, 44; 18:31-34). Luke also lacks mention of any *night* session by the high council. Thus, it is more reasonable to follow here the Lukan report.

One final additional piece of evidence allows us to deduce that it was not the Sanhedrin who condemned Jesus to death. This is indicated by the fact that he was buried in neither of the two graves reserved for those executed by order of the supreme council.[6] Joseph of Arimathea begged Pilate to let him have the corpse. He took it down, wrapped it in linen, and laid it in a tomb cut out of the rock where no one had yet been laid (Luke 23:50-

---

4. The Greek term, συνέδριον, can refer to the "council" or the "room where the council met." Bauer and Danker, op. cit., 967.

5. I hope that I have succeeded in proving the unreality of these inventions by my literary analysis of the Gospels in my study: Flusser, "Who Is It That Struck You?" *JOC*, 604-609.

6. *M. Sanh.* 6:5; Billerbeck, op. cit., 1:1049.

56). Matthew alone includes the questionable detail that the tomb in which Jesus was laid belonged to Joseph (Matt. 27:60). Nevertheless, this was a profound act of love, for one can find scarcely any ancient Jewish graves from that time in which there were not several occupants. Joseph of Arimathea was a member of the city council of Jerusalem — a rich man — and as such was expected to dispense charity. This duty he fulfilled in the burial of Jesus.

According to John (19:39), Nicodemus, whom Jesus had met some time earlier (John 3:1-15), came too, bringing a mixture of myrrh and aloes, and together Joseph and Nicodemus buried Jesus. Nicodemus, like Jesus, originated from the Galilee (John 7:52). We know from rabbinic sources that this Nicodemus, the son of Gorion, was also one of the Jerusalem councilors and one of the three richest patricians in the city. Later, during the Jewish-Roman war, the fanatical rebels burned down his granary.[7] Nicodemus probably died in the war, and his daughter then lived in dire poverty. Her marriage contract was signed by the peace-loving pupil of Hillel, Rabbi Yohanan ben Zakkai.[8] Nicodemus' son was most likely the Gorion who, at the beginning of the uprising, took part in negotiations that led to the surrender of the Roman garrison in Jerusalem.[9] Then, when the insurgents had forced all to take part in the war, a certain Joseph — son of Gorion — and Annas the Sadducean high priest, who previously had had James the Lord's brother executed, and who was an opponent of the fanatics, were elected to supreme power in Jerusalem.[10] The father of this

---

7. *B. Git.* 56a. "The man of the Pharisees named Nicodemus, a member of the Jewish ruling council" (John 3:1), appears not only in John (chapter 3 and 7:50-52; 19:39-40), but he is also known from rabbinic sources (see, e.g., "Nakdimon ben Guriyon," in *EJ*, 12:801-802). It is said in John 7:52 that he was from Galilee. This is confirmed by *t. 'Erub.* 3(4):17, where one reads that the estates of the family were in Ruma, Lower Galilee. According to John 19:39-40, Nicodemus together with Joseph of Arimathea took part in the burial of Jesus. He brought "a mixture of myrrh and aloes, about a hundred pounds." This "extraordinary amount" (R. E. Brown, *The Death of the Messiah: From Gethsemane to the Grave: A Commentary on the Passion Narratives in the Four Gospels* [2 vols.; New York: Doubleday], 1260) fits the proverbial charity of the "rabbinic" Nicodemus. This outstandingly wealthy man was at the same time a saintly man, and he had good connections with the Roman administration (see *b. Ta'an.* 19b). Thus, rabbinic sources complement John's picture of Nicodemus.

8. *T. Ketub.* 5:9-10; *b. Ketub.* 66b; *Mek. R. Ishmael* (Rabin and Horovitz ed.), 203-204.

9. *J.W.* 2:451.

10. *J.W.* 2:563.

25. The so-called Herod's Family Tomb. Photo by J. H. Charlesworth.

Joseph was almost certainly Gorion, a man of outstanding respectability and nobility, who was later executed in Jerusalem under the reign of terror by the fanatics.[11]

In an earlier report, a man named Gorion, son of Joseph, and the Pharisee Simeon, son of the famous Gamaliel who came to the apostles' defense and was Paul's teacher, had tried in vain to oppose the fanatics.[12] It would seem that all of these men belonged to the same propertied patrician families of Jerusalem. They distinguished themselves by their resistance to the extreme militant party of the fanatics, and they were close in outlook to the moderate Pharisees. The fact that two Jerusalem councilors performed the final act of charity for Jesus appears to contradict the conclusion that the Sanhedrin, functioning in its official capacity, had delivered Jesus up to the Romans.[13]

11. *J.W.* 4:358.
12. *J.W.* 4:159.
13. See above, n. 6.

According to John (18:12-14, 24) Jesus was brought first from Geth-semane "to Annas," who was the father-in-law of Caiaphas, "the present high priest." Annas, even if he was no longer the high priest, was still a kind of very influential "gray eminence." On this point, John is to be trusted. In any case, Jesus spent his last night in custody, in the house of the presiding high priest, Caiaphas.[14] In order to pass the time and amuse themselves, "the men who were guarding Jesus mocked him. They beat him, they blindfolded him, and they asked him, 'Prophesy, who is it that struck you?'" (Luke 22:63-64 and par.). The soldiers were playing a brutal, ancient, game that is still played even today.[15] In Jesus' case the behavior of the bodyguards was particularly offensive. The Sadducees did not believe in angels or in the spirit of prophecy. The bodyguards of the Sadducean high priest Caiaphas apparently thought as their master did — a modern-day prophet was a superstitious absurdity.

When day broke, the elders of the people, the chief priests, and the scribes met together and brought him into their *sanhedrin* (Luke 22:66), in other words, into the room where the Sanhedrin used to sit.[16] Although the term "sanhedrin" likely designates here the chamber rather than the "council," does this exclude the possibility that on that morning the San-hedrin actually met? Earlier (Luke 20:1) the "Jewish troika" of the elders, chief priests, and scribes appeared in the Temple and asked Jesus about his authority to teach. The phrase reads as a formal designation for the Temple committee; the elders were the elders of the Temple and the scribes were the Temple secretaries.[17]

Thus, on that fateful morning, Jesus was brought from the custody of the high priest's house into the Temple before the Temple committee — the same individuals who had previously decided to arrest him (see Luke 22:2 and par.). The aim of their session was not to reach a verdict. They merely functioned as a fact-finding committee. They wanted to collect

14. I have included more about Caiaphas in two additional studies. See Flusser, op. cit., 604-609; idem, ". . . To Bury Caiaphas, Not to Praise Him," *Jerusalem Perspective* 33-34 (1991), 23-28.

15. See more about the history of this game in the article, "Who Is It That Struck You?" above n. 5.

16. See above n. 4; Winter, op. cit., 20-21.

17. An edict of Antiochus III to the Jews in 198 B.C. said, "Let the senate and the priests, and the scribes of the Temple, and the Temple-singers be relieved from the poll-tax and the crown-tax and the salt-tax which they pay" (*Ant.* 12:142).

from the mouth of Jesus sufficient evidence to justify their next move —
his extradition to the Roman prefect.[18] They had attempted this before but
were unsuccessful. On that occasion, hoping to ensnare Jesus in something
he might say in order to hand him over to the Roman authorities, they had
sent agents. The spies had asked him, "Are we or are we not permitted to
pay taxes to the emperor?" Jesus saw through their trick and foiled their attempt to catch him in public (Luke 20:20-26). This failure did not, however, prevent them later, when they brought him before Pilate, from accusing him, "We have found this man subverting our nation. He opposes the
payment of taxes to the emperor and claims to be Messiah, a king" (Luke
23:1-2). In the fact-finding session of the committee, they tried to discover
only whether Jesus claimed to be the Messiah, and they did not ask him
about the payment of tributes to the Roman government. They already
knew that he would decline to confirm such an accusation (Luke 22:67-71
and par.).

At first they tried to find credible corroboration that Jesus had, in fact,
uttered the dangerous saying about the destruction of the Temple. At last
they found two men who gave reliable evidence that such a statement had
been made (Matt. 26:57-61).[19] Then the high priest rose to his feet and said
to Jesus, "You answer nothing?" But Jesus remained silent.[20] The public announcement of the destruction of the Temple, which Jesus probably had
made when he confronted the traders within the sanctuary, might well
have seemed to the high priest sufficient reason for handing Jesus over to
the Romans. It was in the Romans' interest to protect holy places. Nevertheless, of more interest to the Romans would be rumors that this Jesus

18. Although from the reports of the Gospels it is clear that Pilate was a Roman magistrate and that Roman soldiers erected Jesus' cross, the Romans are never named as such in
this connection — in the entire New Testament! Only once, in John 11:48, are the Romans
mentioned as a possible danger, if Jesus is not put to death.

19. This is the messianic allusion to the rebuilding of the Temple. See above, chapter
ten, n. 15.

20. Luke (23:6-12) reports that later on, Pilate sent Jesus to Herod Antipas who ruled in
Galilee but at the time was also in Jerusalem. Apparently, Jesus also answered nothing to
Antipas. At least the kernel of Herod's (Antipas) connection in Jesus' death is historical, because in Acts 4:25-28 a very early Christian "pesher" is quoted according to which both
Herod Antipas and Pontius Pilate caused Jesus' death. See Flusser, *JOC,* 376 and 382-383. The
apocryphal *Gospel of Peter* 1:1-2 also connects Herod Antipas with Pilate. The participation
of Herod Antipas in Jesus' trial can also be recognized from the Jewish-Christian texts published by Pinés, op. cit., 377-378.

was regarded as a Messiah.[21] The Romans suppressed messianic movements, because the Messiah was believed to be the king of the Jews. To make even more certain of getting rid of this troublesome incendiary, the high priest said to Jesus, "If you are the Christ, tell us." Jesus replied, "From now on the Son of Man shall be seated at the right hand of the power of God" (Luke 22:69).[22]

How could Jesus speak in this manner? He must have known that he had come to the end of his life. The Old Testament had recounted how both the prophet Elijah and Enoch never died, but were taken up into heaven. In Jesus' day this had captured popular imagination. People believed the same about Moses, although the Bible did speak of his death. It was also said of Melchizedek that not only had he neither father nor mother, but that he would appear as judge at the end of time.[23] People likewise believed that the prophet Jeremiah had never died.[24] We also have seen that there were men who were convinced that the beheaded John the Baptist had risen from the dead (Mark 8:28 and par.).

According to the book of Revelation (11:3-12), two prophets would come, but "the beast that ascends from the bottomless pit will make war upon them and conquer them and kill them." Their bodies would lie in the streets of Jerusalem for three-and-a-half days. Then they would rise again and go up to heaven upon a cloud. Some twenty years after the death of Jesus, an Egyptian Jew appeared and asserted that he intended to liberate Jerusalem from the Romans. The governor Felix marched against him with an army, and dispersed his band of supporters. The prophet himself disappeared, but people believed that God was keeping him in hiding, and they awaited his return. When Paul came to Jerusalem he was asked if he were the Egyptian.[25]

I am convinced that there are reliable reports that the Crucified One "appeared to Peter, then to the twelve. Then he appeared to more than five hundred brethren at one time. . . . Then he appeared to James, then to all

21. Note, for example, the inscription, "king of the Jews," on the cross.

22. See above, chapter nine, n. 26.

23. Flusser, "Melchizedek," *JOC*, 186-192. About Moses, see *Ant.* 4:326 and L. Ginzberg, *The Legends of the Jews* (7 vols.; Philadelphia: Jewish Publication Society, 1946), 6:161-162 n. 951.

24. Matt. 16:14. See J. R. Harris, *The Rest of the Words of Baruch: A Christian Apocalypse of the Year 136 A.D.: The Text Revised with an Introduction* (London: Clay, 1889).

25. *J.W.* 2:261-263; *Ant.* 20:169-172; Acts 21:38. See Hengel, op. cit., 236-237.

the apostles." Last of all, he appeared to Paul on the road to Damascus (1 Cor. 15:3-8). When Jesus answered the high priest's question about his Messiahship with the words, "From now on the Son of Man shall be seated at the right hand of the power of God," did he believe that he would escape the fate that threatened him? Or, as is more likely, did he believe that he would rise from the dead?[26] In any event, the high priest correctly understood that by Jesus' words he was confessing that he was the Messiah. Therefore they said, "What need have we of further witnesses? You have heard it from his own mouth" (Luke 22:71). Jesus was taken straightway to Pilate.

At this point I will digress in order to draw a character sketch of the famous governor of Judea, Pontius Pilate.[27] It is no accident that he is named in the early Apostles' Creed in connection with the crucifixion of Jesus. In two Jewish sources Pilate is described in similar terms, namely as a cruel villain. Even Luke (13:1) mentions a horrible incident instigated by him. "Now there were some present at that time who told Jesus about the Galileans whose blood Pilate had mixed with their sacrifices." Philo, the Jewish philosopher from Alexandria, said that Pilate "was a man of an inflexible, stubborn, and cruel disposition."[28] Philo further enumerated[29] Pilate's seven mortal sins, "his venality, his violence, his thievery, his assaults, his abusive behavior, his frequent executions of untried prisoners, and his endless savage ferocity." This negative assessment of the governor does not differ much from what Josephus reported about

---

26. What is completely sure is that Jesus knew that his cause would not be extinguished by the cross — see Luke 20:17 and par. It is not by chance that Jesus here quotes Psalm 118:22. He indicates that he will be the "cornerstone." What is equally significant is that he alludes to the future, indicating that Jesus expected that the cross would not be an end. See also chapter eight, n. 28.

27. About Pilate see Schürer, op. cit., 1:358, 383-387; G. Winkler, "Pilate," *Der Kleine Pauly: Lexikon der Antike* (5 vols.; ed. K. Ziegler, W. Sontheimer, H. Gärtner, and A. F. von Pauly; Berlin: Deutscher Taschenbuch Verlag, 1979), 4:1050; *The Jewish People in the First Century: Historical Geography, Political History, Social, Cultural and Religious Life and Institutions* (2 vols.; ed. S. Safrai, M. Stern, D. Flusser, and W. C. van Unnik; Assen: Van Gorcum, 1974-1976), 1:316, 349-354; F. Millar, *Das Römische Reich und seine Nachbaren* (Frankfurt a. M., Hamburg: Fischer-Bücherei, 1966), 68-69; *Philonis Alexandrini: Legatio ad Gaium* (ed. E. M. Smallwood; Leiden: Brill, 1961), 128-131, 294-305; S. Mason, *Josephus and the New Testament* (Peabody, Mass.: Hendrickson, 1993), 103-105, 109, 114-117.

28. *Legat.* 38:301.

29. *Legat.* 318:299-305; cf. *J.W.* 2:169-177; *Ant.* 18:55-62, 85-90.

26. A Roman sarcophagus relief (second century) depicting
Christ before Pilate. Museo Pio Cristiano, Rome.

him. Once, in a private conversation with me, a New Testament scholar
aptly and succinctly described Pilate. He said that Pilate was "a butcher."

How are we to reconcile this dark picture with the Pilate of the Gospels? There he appears as a sensitive and just man, as a pawn in the hands
of the Jewish leaders.[30] Moreover, Matthew intensifies this positive ap-

30. Mason, op. cit., 116.

preciation of Pilate in his Gospel.[31] Matthew demonstrates elsewhere, however, a theological penchant to vilify the Jews as a whole.[32] Must we be drawn into the old polarity, according to which there are only two opposite solutions? One sees the Jews (or a major part of them) guilty of Jesus' death and believes that there existed "a good old Pilate."[33] Or must we accept the contrasting view in which not a single Jew (with the exception of Jewish quislings) was involved in the so-called "trial" of Jesus, and the only monstrous criminal was Pilate — with the backing of Rome? This apparent antinomy can be resolved by taking seriously the numerous and cutting accusations against Pilate reported by Philo and Josephus, while recognizing the understandable, tendentious efforts to whitewash Pilate's person in the Gospels. Furthermore, one needs to pay careful attention to the *actions* of Pilate as reported in the Christian sources.

What one discovers is that Pilate's behavior in the Gospels is not very different from what is reported about him in the other sources. This approach allows his true character to emerge. The results are not flattering for him, but among other important things, one learns that it is not sufficient to speak about the "banality of evil."[34] One must distinguish between the various specifics of such banality. Not all evil is banal, but Pilate's wickedness does belong to the banality of evil.

Before addressing the important issue of Pilate's involvement in the crucifixion of Jesus, I want to make some additional preliminary comments. The alleged report about Jesus in Josephus (*Ant.* 18:63-64), the so-called *Testimonium Flavianum,* is rightly regarded in its present form as inauthentic, or at least "Christianized."[35] Nevertheless, I believe that a form of this witness about Jesus by Josephus did exist, and has been discovered by Pinés.[36] In the tenth century, the Christian author Agapius

31. Ibid.

32. Today many believe that Matthew is a Jewish-Christian Gospel, but the situation is far more complex. See Flusser, "Two Anti-Jewish Montages in Matthew" and "Matthew's 'Verus Israel,'" *JOC,* 552-576.

33. So in "Jesus Christ Superstar."

34. This was what Hannah Arendt wrote about Adolf Eichmann in her report, *Eichmann in Jerusalem: A Report on the Banality of Evil* (New York: Viking Press, 1963).

35. Mason, op. cit., 163-175; W. Schneemelcher, *New Testament Apocrypha* (2 vols.; Louisville: Westminster/John Knox Press, 1991-1992), 1:489-491.

36. Pinés, "An Arabic Version of the Testimonium Flavianum," op. cit., 37-115.

wrote a history of the world in Arabic, in which he reproduced Josephus' statement about Jesus.[37]

> At this time there was a wise man who was called Jesus. And his conduct was good, and he was known to be virtuous. And many people from among the Jews and the other nations became his disciples. Pilate condemned him to be crucified and to die. And those who had become his disciples, did not abandon his discipleship. They reported that he had appeared to them three days after his crucifixion and that he was alive; accordingly, he was thought to be the Messiah (the Christ) concerning whom the prophets have recounted wonders. And the people of the Christians, named after him, have not disappeared till this day.

I tried to show elsewhere that this form of the *Testimonium Flavianum* is basically that of Josephus.[38] The fact that it was Pilate who condemned Jesus to be crucified is referred to even in the Greek text of Josephus. In the newly discovered Arabic version nothing is said about Jewish accusations against Jesus. Similarly, the Roman historian Cornelius Tacitus[39] reports that Pilate executed Jesus "in the reign of Tiberius." As did Josephus, Tacitus wanted to explain why the Christians received their name. "'Christus' was the name of the founder." In this connection Tacitus speaks about the "procurator" Pontius Pilate. In reality, Pilate, like the other governors of Judea before the time of Claudius, was officially called "praefectus Iudaeae," and not procurator.[40] This is certain because of an inscription that was found in Caesarea. The inscription runs as follows:[41]

> [Dis Augusti]s Tiberieum
> [-Po]ntius Pilatus
> [praef]ectus Iuda[ea]e
> [fecit, d]e[dicavit]

37. The last sentence was taken from the Greek Josephus. About all this see Pinés, op. cit., 70-71, n. 145.

38. Flusser, "Bericht des Josephus über Jesus," *Entdeckungen im Neuen Testament* (2 vols.; Vluyn: Neukirchen, 1987-1999), 1:216-225.

39. Tacitus, *Ann.* XV, 44:2-3.

40. Stern, *Greek and Latin Authors*, 2:92-93.

41. Safrai and Stern, *Jewish People in the First Century*, 1:316. The text of the inscription was restored by A. Degrassi, *Epigraphica* (4 vols.; Roma: Accademia Nazionale dei Lincei, 1963-1970), 59-65.

This inscription should lead to a reappraisal of Pilate's character and to a new understanding of what really happened in Jesus' condemnation. The new information obliges us to renew the analysis of Pilate's deeds according to both the Gospels and the Jewish reports about him.

A "Tiberieum" is a temple — in this case evidently a small one — dedicated to Tiberius. Pilate built this chapel in Caesarea where the inscription was found. Caesarea was then the principal site of the governor of Judea (see, e.g., Acts 23:23, 33). At the time of the temple's construction, Tiberius was the ruling Roman emperor. Roman rulers were normally deified only after their death, but the provincials and satellite rulers were permitted to erect sanctuaries even to a living emperor of Rome. Rome viewed such acts as an expression of devotion and fidelity to the emperor.[42] An outstanding example of this foreign adoration of the living emperor by his vassals is Herod the Great. The temples that Herod built for this purpose were named in Greek, *Kaisareia*.[43] Herod built one of his *Kaisareia* in Caesarea. It was erected in the center of the city on a hill and could be seen from afar by sailors on ships approaching the harbor. I suspect that later, in the vicinity of the temple of Augustus, Pilate erected the small sanctuary for Tiberius whose dedicatory inscription was discovered.

Certain Roman emperors placed limits on the cult directed at themselves. Augustus permitted his cult in the provinces, but did not allow it in Rome itself. Tiberius was more than skeptical about a cult of his own person, even though it is true that the city of Tiberias was named after him by the "oriental" ruler Herod Antipas. According to Suetonius (*Tiberius,* chapter 26) he even forbade the consecration of temples to himself. The erection of the "Tiberieum" in Caesarea surely would not have appealed to him. Even more distasteful was the fact that it had been erected by a Roman magistrate! Pontius Pilate is the only known Roman official who built then a temple to a living emperor. As we will see, this was not the only case of his exaggerated devotion to the emperor, and we will try to explain why he behaved in a manner that a twentieth-century "Stalinist" would have applauded.

---

42. Schürer, op. cit., 1:304-305 and 2:34-35, especially n. 27. In the 1995 season the foundations of the Temple of Augustus in Caesarea were excavated.

43. This form (*Caesareum* and in Greek, *Sabasteion*) corresponds completely with our "Tiberieum."

A short survey of Pilate's career[44] will show how his behavior in various situations was dictated by the interplay between his mental disposition and the structure of Roman administration of the provinces. As to Pilate's character, his brutality was evidently proverbial. He also apparently disliked Jews and Judaism. Minting their coins, other governors were careful not to offend Jewish religious feelings. Only Pilate may be regarded as exceptional on this point. Coins struck by him bore pagan symbols in the form of sacred vessels.[45] Yet, Pilate's brutality was a kind of overcompensation for his basic weakness; he attempted to demonstrate his strength by cruel acts, but because of his weakness one could influence him to abandon his designs. Unfortunately, the episode with Jesus merely seems to be one in a series of Pilate's tragic comedies, but in this case his weakness changed the course of history.

The first serious clash between Pilate and the Jewish people erupted when he introduced into Jerusalem military standards bearing the image of the emperor.[46] By this action Pilate betrayed both his Stalinistic devotion to the emperor and his intrinsic weakness in the face of strong opposition by the Jews. The multitudes streamed in protest to Caesarea, and for many days they implored him to take away the images. Initially, Pilate refused to yield, since to do so would have been an outrage to the emperor. Nevertheless, he soon recognized the people's readiness to die rather than suffer a profanation of their faith. Finally, he removed the images from Jerusalem and brought them back to Caesarea. Incidentally, we hear of other similar mass demonstrations before Pilate, one of them in connection with Jesus' "trial" (Matt. 27:11-23; Mark 15:6-12; Luke 23:18-21). The "natives" easily discovered Pilate's innate weakness. Sometimes the demonstration succeeded in breaking his will, and sometimes it did not.

In another case we find Pilate's tactics cruel and successful. He took money from the Temple treasury to finance the building of an aqueduct to supply water to Jerusalem. This step aroused resentment among the Jews, who demanded that he stop using Temple money. Tens of thousands of the Jewish populace assembled and protested against him. Pilate, however, interspersed among the crowd a troop of his soldiers in civilian dress, with orders to beat any rioters with the flat of their swords. He gave

---

44. See especially Safrai and Stern, op. cit., 1:349-353.
45. Ibid., 1:350.
46. *Ant.* 18:55-59.

his soldiers a prearranged signal and many of the unarmed participants of the demonstration perished. In this case the brutal strategies of Pilate were successful, and the "good old Pilate" again demonstrated that he could master the situation by being really clever. By the way, one sees that it was then impossible to discern between the Jewish "race" and the Roman soldiers![47]

Philo of Alexandria reports another clash between Pilate and the Jews.[48] The governor brought to Jerusalem gilded shields and set them up in Herod's palace. They bore an inscription with the name of the dedicator, namely Pilate, and the name of Tiberius to whom the shields were dedicated. The Jews sent an embassy to the prefect. Among the delegates were Herod's four sons, but Pilate refused to remove the shields from Jerusalem. Pilate was "in a serious dilemma; for he had neither the courage to remove what he had once set up, nor the desire to do anything which would please his subjects."[49] On the other hand, he feared that the Jews would send an embassy to the emperor, accusing him. "When the Jewish officials saw this, and realized that Pilate was regretting what he had done, although he did not wish to show it, they wrote a letter to Tiberius pleading their case as forcibly as they could."[50] Tiberius' reaction to the complaint was as the Jews hoped. Pilate removed the shields from Jerusalem to Caesarea, to be dedicated in the temple of Augustus. "In this way both the honor of the emperor and the traditional policy regarding Jerusalem were alike preserved."[51]

The two stories about Pilate and the Jews betray similar features, as also in the "trial" of Jesus. It is in all three cases the same Pilate.[52] Pilate's exaggerated dependence on the emperor in Rome was an important factor in his fatal decision about Jesus. According to John 19:12 — whom we may trust in this case — when Pilate thought to release Jesus, his Jewish opponents cried out, "If you release this man, you are not Caesar's friend; every one who makes himself a king is defying Caesar!" When Pilate heard this, he decided to execute Jesus.

---

47. *Ant.* 18:60-62; *J.W.* 2:175-177; Safrai and Stern, op. cit., 1:351-352.
48. *Legat.* 38.
49. *Legat.* 38:303.
50. *Legat.* 38:306.
51. *Legat.* 38:305.
52. According to John (19:12 and see 19:15) Pilate finally decided not to release Jesus because of the objection, "If you release this man, you are not Caesar's friend. . . ."

We have noted Pilate's "Stalinist" devotion to Tiberius, his attempt to portray strength through his stubbornness, his weakness and indecisive hesitation, and his cowardly withdrawal before massive demonstrations. These qualities of Pilate were accentuated by the external circumstances of his difficult task. A governor of a province depended on influential groups within the local population, especially the local aristocracy that was the link between the province and the empire. In the case of Jesus, this was the hierarchy of the Temple headed by the Jewish high priest. Such a governor, on the other hand, depended on the goodwill of the emperor who was the supreme judge when a complaint was sent to him. This configuration of forces, together with Pilate's character, eventually caused his downfall.[53]

Pilate's ruthless "strong-arm" policy against the Samaritans was answered by a complaint of the Samaritan council to Vitellius, governor of Syria, when he visited Jerusalem at the Passover Festival in A.D. 36. Pilate was dismissed and had to go to Rome to justify his policy before the emperor. His final end is not known. Through Pilate's deposition, Vitellius wanted to restore Jewish popular confidence in Roman rule. Thus, he not only caused the downfall of Pilate, but also the deposition of the high priest, Caiaphas, the loyal ally of Pilate.

We have recounted that Pilate gilded the shields in Herod's palace. This was also a fortress that was used as the governor's administrative headquarters when he went to Jerusalem, and soldiers were sometimes quartered there.[54] The location of the palace is in today's Armenian quarter of the Old City of Jerusalem. The question of where Jesus was brought by those who accused him still remains unanswered. Was he delivered to Pilate and imprisoned in the Antonia fortress that overlooked the Temple area? Or was he brought to Pilate in Herod's palace?

The whole question is decisive for those who seek to know the course of the famous *via dolorosa* (the way of suffering), because Jesus was led finally to his crucifixion from the praetorium as a prisoner of the Roman governor. According to the research and archeological discoveries of the last decade, the traditional path of Jesus cannot be authenticated. The ancient relics that mark the *via dolorosa* date from a later period, during the reign of the emperor Hadrian. As to the Antonia fortress, its location is im-

---

53. See Safrai and Stern, op. cit., 353; *Ant.* 18:85-89.
54. Smallwood, op. cit., 301.

possible to determine with certainty. Because of these and other considerations, today many scholars believe that Jesus was brought to Pilate while
he was residing in Herod's palace.[55]

The Roman governor asked Jesus, "Are you the king of the Jews?" The
sources tell us that Jesus answered, "You have said it." That is really all that
has been handed down to us. According to John (18:29-38), this ambiguous
saying signifies a denial. "You say that I am a king. Do you say this of your
own accord, or did others say it to you about me?" In fact, Jesus probably
made no answer at all to the Roman. Since Pilate had heard that Jesus was a
Galilean, and therefore a subject of Herod Antipas, he sent the prisoner to
Herod, who was also in Jerusalem for the Passover.

Evidently Herod Antipas stayed in the old Hasmonean palace, nearer
to the Temple than Herod's palace. This palace served as the residence of
the Herodian princes on their visits to the capital.[56] The tetrarch questioned him thoroughly, but Jesus remained silent, and Herod sent him
back to Pilate (Luke 23:6-12).[57] The "fox," who had sought to take Jesus' life
in Galilee, confidently left him in Jerusalem in the hands of the Roman
governor whose brutality was known far and wide.[58] The formalities of the
case were now over, but this courtesy on the part of Pilate led to the healing
of the previous estrangement between himself and Herod Antipas (Luke
23:12).

Jesus was incarcerated with at least three others. These were anti-
Roman guerrillas, and chief among them was Barabbas. He had taken part
in terrorism that had cost lives, and had been caught and imprisoned
along with the others. The governor regarded it as his duty to crucify these
terrorists — especially Barabbas. If this were done on the great festival of
the Jews, before the enormous pilgrim crowd, all would see the iron hand

---

55. See P. Benoit, "The Archeological Reconstruction of the Antonia Fortress," in *Jerusalem Revealed* (ed. Y. Yadin; Jerusalem: IES, 1976), 87-88. Pilate sent the gilded shields there.
See above n. 46.

56. See Smallwood, op. cit.

57. See above, n. 20.

58. Luke's report (23:6-12) is written in pure Greek without visible Semitic vestiges. It
seems that Luke (or his source) developed the whole incident in a free way. According to
Luke, Herod and his soldiers mock Jesus in a different way than in Mark (15:16-20) and Matthew (27:27-31), and the whole scene in Luke comes in place of the report in the two other
Synoptic Gospels. Even so, I believe that the other report is more trustworthy because of
other historical parallels to this Roman mockery. See also below, n. 67.

of Rome. However, the execution of a popular hero might lead to unrest. Indeed, the electric atmosphere of a pilgrim festival, especially the Passover, was always a potentially explosive time.[59] In all probability the Jewish "brigands" among the people would have wanted to avenge Barabbas' death, and if they had, scores of Jewish people would have fallen victim to a frenzy of Roman swords feeding off their flesh. The hated high priests for their part must have feared that such a scenario would indeed lead to a riot during the festival (Matt. 26:5). This could be avoided, only if Barabbas was kept alive.

An ideal opportunity presented itself. The Roman governor was in the habit of releasing a Jewish prisoner on the Passover.[60] From rabbinic literature[61] we know that this amnesty often went by default, or was granted only after long, weary entreaty. On this occasion, both the high priests and Pilate tried to manipulate the prisoner release to their own advantage. Before the hearing in front of Pilate, a select crowd — undoubtedly not the general masses of Jerusalem — had already gathered, and the people were clamoring for the customary clemency of a prisoner. We have seen that such mass demonstrations were usual in Pilate's time, because of his cruelty and his weakness. Pilate seized the opportunity and said to them, "Do you want me to release for you the King of the Jews?" (Mark 15:6-10).

In this "King of the Jews" Pilate saw little danger to the empire, and hoped that the Jews likewise would see that there was no sound reason for his execution. If he let this man free, he could have Barabbas crucified. But the high priests intervened; the crowd loved Barabbas, the freedom-fighter. Thus, it was easy on this occasion for the high priests to appear on the side of the populace. Finally, the proposal for the amnesty of Barabbas was accepted (Mark 15:11). Pilate asked, "Then what shall I do with the man whom you call the King of the Jews?" The answer he got

59. See Safrai, Wallfahrt, 204-205.

60. Young, Jewish Theologian, 225 and 239 n. 9, has shown that not only Mark (15:6), Matthew (27:15), and John (13:40), but also Luke 23:17 says, "For of necessity he (Pilate) must release one unto them at the feast." This Lukan verse is not embedded in many modern editions and translations, because it is omitted from some early witnesses. In Codex Bezae it appears after Luke 23:19. According to Metzger [op. cit., 179-180], Luke 23:17 "is a gloss." The textual situation is not too dissimilar to that which we find concerning the Codex Bezae reading of Luke 23:37. See below, n. 67.

61. Safrai, op. cit., 206.

was, "Crucify him." According to John (19:6) the cry came first of all from the high priests and their henchmen.[62] It can be that the cry was a historical reality. In any case the acclamation was superfluous, for Pilate knew that if Barabbas went free, Jesus would be crucified. Once again Pilate tried his luck to salvage the situation. He said that he could find no charge against Jesus serious enough to justify execution. He would scourge him and let him go (Luke 23:22), but even that was of no use. He had to let Barabbas go free, and Jesus was scourged and handed over to be crucified (Matt. 27:26).

Roman law prescribed that "instigators of a revolt, riot, or agitators of the people" were to be "either crucified, thrown to wild animals, or banished to an island." The punishment was determined by the perpetrator's position in Roman society.[63] Jesus' status earned him crucifixion.

Displaying a distorted sense of justice, Pilate freed Barabbas. This decision obliged him, for good or ill, to take the charge against Jesus much more seriously than before. Because of the incident at the Temple and Jesus' prophetic censure of the aristocratic priests, Pilate could easily crucify him as an agitator of the people. Furthermore, rumors were circulating that he was the Messiah.[64]

Apparently Jesus was handed over to Pilate without a verdict, and nowhere in the sources is a verdict by Pilate reported. In the catalogue of the crimes of Pilate, provided by the philosopher Philo of Alexandria,[65] among others we find "constant execution without passing judgment." It would seem, therefore, that Jesus' tragic end was preceded by no verdict of any earthly judiciary. It was the outcome of a grisly inter-

---

62. This important narrative of John is generally overlooked. The high priest and their servants were thus the organized popular mood of those days. According to the Gospels, the shout "Crucify!" rang out twice. This is intrinsically possible. That the various Gospels have intensified the shout can be seen in a reading of the individual accounts. The fact that the supposed deicide led to a concrete homicide belongs to a later period.

63. Paulus, *Sent.* 5, 22, 1 = dig. 48, 19, 38, par. 2. See O. Betz, *Was wissen wir von Jesus* (Stuttgart-Berlin: Kreuz, 1965), 56-57; Hengel, op. cit., 33-34; Brown, op. cit., 945-947.

64. Pilate had the words "King of the Jews" mockingly hung above Jesus. They are the same words with which Pilate had ironically played during his interrogation of Jesus. For further discussion about Roman law and the trial of Jesus, see A. N. Sherwin-White, *Roman Law and Roman Society in the New Testament* (Grand Rapids: Baker, 1994), 24-47. His discussion could have been strengthened by giving more attention to Roman policy and legal procedures in the newly acquired Eastern provinces during the time of Jesus.

65. See n. 27.

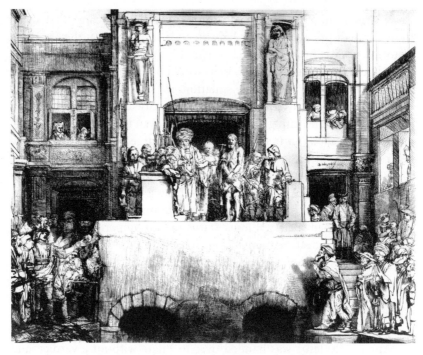

27. Rembrandt, Jesus with Pilate before the Jews (1655).
The Pierpont Morgan Library/Art Resource, NY.

play of naked spheres of interest in the shadow of brutal antagonisms. To outward appearance, it had no real connection with the man Jesus or his cause.

Only Rembrandt has captured the silent isolation of Jesus at his trial — which was no trial. In an etching, he depicts Jesus as he is brought from Pilate out to the people, and hardly anybody is actually looking at this strange spectacle. Jesus is quite passive as though waiting until this senseless pantomime is over. His depiction of Jesus is in strong contrast to the noisy hatred of the crowd described in the Gospels, but it is historically more correct. Apparently, Rembrandt was not satisfied with his portrayal, and so in a later version (1655) he removed the detached mob almost completely. Now an empty and hideous arch adorns the foreground of the scene. A single Jew remains on the right of the balcony, viewing the whole thing with pathetic and dream-like intensity. "Who is it? A friend? A good man? Someone who sympathized? Someone who wanted to help? Was it one person only? Or were they all there? Was help at hand? Where was the High Court to which he had never penetrated?"[66]

Now the Roman soldiers had their turn at degrading Jesus. They led him into the interior hall of the palace and assembled the entire cohort. They dressed him in a purple cloak, plaited a crown of thorns, and set it on his head. They also placed a reed in his right hand. When the "king" had received all his insignia, the soldiers genuflected, prostrated themselves before him, as before an oriental despot, and saluted him: "Hail! King of the Jews!" Then they spat on him, wrenched away his reed scepter, and struck him on the head with it (cf. Mark 15:16-20).[67]

The Roman soldiers made grisly sport of Jesus. As in the house of the high priest, when the high priest's bodyguards had played a brutal game with Jesus in order to ridicule the charisma of prophecy, the Roman soldiers used him to ridicule the Jewish hope of freedom.

This was neither the first nor the last time that Gentiles would deride the messianic hopes of the Jews. A few years after Jesus' death, when the Jewish King Agrippa visited Alexandria, the Alexandrians took a harmless lunatic called Karabas and

> drove him into the gymnasium and set him up on high to be seen of all and put on his head a sheet of byblus spread out wide for a diadem, clothed the rest of his body with a rug for a royal robe, while someone who had noticed a piece of the native papyrus thrown away in the road gave it to him for his scepter. And when as in some theatrical farce he had received the insignia of the kingship and had been tricked out as a king, young men carrying rods on their shoulders as spearmen stood on either side of him in imitation of a bodyguard. Then others approached him, some pretending to salute him, others to sue for justice, others to consult him on state affairs.

66. F. Kafka, *The Trial* (New York: Knopf, 1956), 248. However, see Flusser, "The Crucified One and the Jews," *JOC*, 575-587.

67. This incident (Matt. 27:27-31 and Mark 15:16-20) does not appear in Luke's Gospel. In its stead Luke describes a similar episode about Jesus before Herod (Luke 23:6-16). This Lukan passage has its own merits, especially when one considers the text of Luke 23:36-37 according to Codex Bezae and other Western witnesses. There it says: "And the soldiers approached (Jesus on the cross) and offered him vinegar and said, 'Hail! King of the Jews!' And they placed on him a crown of thorns." Steven Notley reminded me of this variant reading (private communication). If indeed this variant reading reflects the original narrative, then the crowning of Jesus with thorns belongs to the Passion in Luke's Gospel, too.

Then from the multitudes standing round him, there rang out a tremendous shout hailing him as Mari,[68] that is said to be the name for "lord" used by the Syrians.[69]

A badly preserved papyrus contains another account of a similar mocking of a "king of farce" that also took place in Alexandria, after the Jewish uprising of A.D. 115-117. Even the Roman governor himself seems to have participated on that occasion.[70]

After degrading Jesus, the soldiers led him away to be crucified. On the way to the execution site, the Romans compelled a passing Jew named Simon to carry the cross for Jesus (Mark 15:21). Simon originated from Cyrene in North Africa.[71] It was not uncommon for the Roman occupying forces to demand statutory labor of pilgrims during Jewish festivals.[72] Heading toward Golgotha (the place of the skull), the procession left the city. Compassionate Jews, as their custom, offered Jesus wine mixed with myrrh to help numb the agonizing death he faced; but he refused it (Mark 15:23).[73]

Three men were crucified together, two brigands, one on the right and one on the left, and Jesus in the middle. The soldiers placed Jesus in the position of distinction on purpose. It was their parting, cruel gesture of "honor" to "the King of the Jews."

Hanging upon the cross, Jesus said, "Father, forgive them, for they know not what they do."[74] As has been suggested already, Jesus was proba-

---

68. "Mari" (my Lord) was probably the Aramaic word. Compare 1 Cor. 16:22.

69. Philo, *Flacc.* 36-39. The similarity between the mocking of Jesus by the soldiers and the incident in Alexandria was noted by Grotius in his commentary on Matt. 27:28, op. cit., 2:356.

70. The text of this papyrus appears in *Corpus Papyrorum Judaicarum* (3 vols.; ed. V. A. Tcherikover and A. Fuks; Cambridge, Mass.: Harvard University Press, 1957-1964), 2:61-62 and *Acta Alexandrinorum: de mortibus Alexandriae nobilium fragmenta papyracea Graeca* (ed. H. Musurillo; Leipzig: Teubner, 1961), 37.

71. In those days, Cyrene was an important Jewish center. The name Simon and those of his sons, Alexander and Rufus, were very common among Jews everywhere. Simon is the equivalent of the biblical Simeon; Rufus is the equivalent of the biblical name Reuben. See *Corpus Papyrorum Judaicarum*, 1:29.

72. Safrai, op. cit., 205-206.

73. See Billerbeck, op. cit., 1:1037-1038.

74. Luke 23:34. See Flusser, "Sie wissen nicht, was sie tun," *Entdeckungen*, 1:179-196. I have noted that Luke 23:34 is lacking in important manuscripts. This verse was probably omitted by those who believed that Jesus had prayed for the Jews, and this seemed to them to be improbable. Luke 23:24 has a parallel in the last words of Stephen (Acts 7:60). See also Brown, op. cit., 971-981.

28. The crucifixion of Jesus and the suicide of Judas. HIP/Art Resource, NY.

bly not interceding on behalf of those Jews who were responsible for his execution by the Roman government, but for the ignorant, Gentile soldiers, who crucified him. The soldiers divided his clothing among themselves, and the people stood watching. The common folk pitied this most recent victim of Roman occupation;[75] however, those who were Jesus' enemies were surely content. The rulers, who were probably Jewish aristocrats, jeered at him and remarked sardonically, "If this man, who wants to save others, is the Messiah, may he first save himself!" The soldiers joined in the jeering. One even ran, and filling a sponge with vinegar, put it on a reed and gave it to Jesus to drink (Matt. 27:48; Mark 15:36; Luke 23:36).[76] The

75. See Flusser, "The Crucified One and the Jews," *JOC*, 575-587; Young, "The Cross, Jesus and the Jewish People," *Imm*, 24-25 (1990), 23-34; idem, "A Fresh Examination of the Cross, Jesus and the Jewish People," in *Jesus' Last Week: Jerusalem Studies in the Synoptic Gospels — Volume One* (ed. R. S. Notley, M. Turnage, and B. Becker; Leiden: Brill, 2006), 191-210.

76. Similar imagery is found in the Thanksgiving Hymns (1QHᵃ 4:11). There the sectarian author wrote about the opponents to his sect: "They withhold from the thirsty the drink of knowledge and assuage their thirst with vinegar."

high priests also mocked Jesus among themselves. Even the criminals, who were crucified next to him, added their own insults.[77] Finally, Jesus cried

77. According to Luke 23:39-43, only one of the two crucified criminals insulted Jesus.

"But the other rebuked him, saying, 'Have you no fear of God? You are under the same sentence as he. We are punished justly, for we are getting what our deeds deserve. But this man has done nothing wrong.' And he said, 'Jesus, remember me, when you come into your kingdom.' Jesus answered him, 'I tell you the truth, today you will be with me in Paradise.'"

This is indeed a moving and beautiful passage, which apparently is the earliest extant expression of an ancient, midrashic motif. In 1 Sam. 28:19, the spirit of Samuel told Saul that he would die in the approaching battle with the Philistines: "Tomorrow you and your sons will be with me." This is commented upon in a creative midrash preserved in *Leviticus Rabbah* 26:7 (Margulies ed., 605-606). According to the midrash, Saul asked Samuel's spirit: "Can I still save myself by flight?" Samuel replied, "Yes! If you flee, you are safe. But if you accept God's judgment, by tomorrow you will be united with me [i.e., in heaven]." See Ginsberg, op. cit., 4:71 and the gloss to *Leviticus Rabbah* 26:7 in Jastrow, op. cit., 760-761. Compare also Billerbeck, op. cit., 2:264-265. One wonders why *Pirqe de Rabbi Eliezer,* a much later midrashic work dating from the eighth or ninth century, is cited by Billerbeck rather than *Leviticus Rabbah.* In *Pirqe R. El.* 33 the midrash on 1 Sam. 28:19 is repeated. (Compare also *Midr. Sam.* 23:4.) Moreover, Billerbeck did not discuss satisfactorily the significance of this midrash in relation to Luke 23:39-43.

The midrash presents Saul's acceptance of his imminent death as an indication of repentance. In other words, by not fleeing, Saul accepted God's judgment and paid the penalty for his prior disobedience. The same sort of thinking is reflected in *m. Sanh.* 6:2:

When he was about ten cubits from the place of stoning they used to say to him, "Make thy confession," for such is the way of them that have been condemned to death to make confession, for every one that makes his confession has a share in the world to come. . . . If he knows not how to make his confession they say to him, "Say, May my death be an atonement for all my sins." (Danby ed., 390)

The one criminal's defense of Jesus is in essence a confession of guilt and acceptance of divine justice. Therefore, according to Jewish thinking, this criminal would merit a share in the world to come or Paradise. The motif is the same as that seen in *Leviticus Rabbah* 26:7. Of course, however, Jesus and the two criminals died on the very same day they were crucified, and therefore, the words "tomorrow you will be with me [in Paradise]" had to be changed to "Today you will be with me in Paradise."

Our opinion that this Lukan passage was spawned by midrashic impulses is supported by two further considerations. First, there is no parallel to the story in either Matthew or Mark. Second, this episode is not in harmony with the historically based tradition that Paul received (1 Cor. 15:4) and that was later absorbed into the Apostles' Creed: "He suffered under Pontius Pilate, was crucified, died, and was buried. He descended to the dead. On the third day he rose again." According to Christian tradition, Jesus was not in paradise on the same day of his death. Joseph Fitzmyer zeroes in on this tension when he says, "The joining

out loudly[78] — and died. "And all the multitudes who had gathered to see the sight, when they saw what had happened beat their breasts — as an expression of mourning — and returned home" (Luke 23:48).

---

of 'today' and 'in Paradise' in this verse creates a problem when one tries to relate it to the credal 'descent into Hell,' and even with 1 Pet. 3:19-20," Fitzmyer, op. cit., 2:1511.

78. In Mark 15:34 (followed by Matt. 27:46) the last cry of Jesus was Ps. 22:2 (see also the apocryphal *Gospel of Peter* 5:19). The Markan paradox is eliminated by Luke (23:46). In Luke's account, Jesus quoted Psalm 31:6 [HMT 31:5]. The same biblical verse (transliterated in Greek from the original Hebrew) appears in the apocryphal Acts of Pilate 11. Note that Psalm 31:6 is part of the standard confession said by a Jew on his deathbed. See *The Authorised Daily Prayer Book,* revised ed. (ed. J. H. Hertz; New York: Bloch, 1965), 1065. The easiest way to explain the discrepancy between Mark and Luke is to suggest that it was impossible to discern the meaning, if there were any, of Jesus' last, agonizing cry. Mark put in his mouth Ps. 22:2 in order to show that the lonely Jesus was apparently abandoned even by God himself. Luke, on the other hand, portrayed Jesus as uttering what one would expect a dying, observant Jew to say. See also above chapter one, n. 4.

CHAPTER 12

Epilogue

I will not speak here about Jesus after his death on the cross, except to address how, in the thinking of the early believing community, the high self-awareness of the "historical" Jesus began evolving into the Christology of the Christian faith.[1] In this book I have challenged the modern prejudice that sees little connection between Jesus' understanding of his task in the divine economy and the "kerygma" of the church. Facing imminent death, Jesus told the parable of the wicked husbandmen (Luke 20:9-16). At the end of the parable he added, "Have you never read in the scriptures, 'The stone the builders rejected has become the capstone'?" By quoting from Psalm 118:22, Jesus informed his hearers that the Cross would not hinder the triumph of his cause.[2] He was right.

Nevertheless, in the early history of the church two revolutionary trends brought about a change in the structure of the Christian faith. The first was the cognitive dissonance that arose in the wake of the tragedy of the crucifixion. Luke himself met some of the *dramatis personae* from this crisis and described their traumatic experience, especially in the Emmaus story (24:13-35) and the dialogue between the resurrected Lord and his apostles (Acts 1:1-9). If the fledgling community and its new faith were to overcome this crisis, they needed instinctively to find a solution. The compensation was found by stressing the divine character of Christ and the cosmic significance of his task. Thus, a metahistorical drama featuring the

---

1. See also Flusser, "Messianology and Christology in the Epistle to the Hebrews," *JOC*, 246-279.

2. Compare Dan. 2:34, where the stone motif also appears with similar implications.

29. Remains of the Roman road to Emmaus (Luke 24:13-35).
Photo by Richard and Lucinda Martin-Thomas; Courtesy of JerusalemPerspective.com.

incarnation of the pre-existent Christ, his death on the cross, resurrection, and return to his heavenly Father until the time of his awesome coming as the eschatological judge, came into existence. The subsequent second revolution occurred when Paul was still actively preaching and teaching about the new faith. During this time the Gentile church was born, and Christianity's formal ties to Judaism began unraveling. This second revolution fueled the christological development.

Yet it would be absolutely absurd to suppose that Christianity adopted an unambitious, unknown Jewish martyr and catapulted him against his will into the role of chief actor in a cosmic drama. I do not want to repeat here what has already been said about Jesus' high self-awareness and how it served as the germ from which the future Christology would sprout. I want only to mention the fact that Jesus himself was far from promoting a cult of his personality during his lifetime:[3] "Not everyone who calls me 'Lord, Lord' will enter the kingdom of heaven, but only those who do the will of my heavenly Father." Jesus' acute self-awareness cannot be denied, and I am convinced that he eventually embraced the conviction that he would be revealed as the Messiah of Israel. The inscription placed over Jesus on the cross, "This is the King of the Jews," suggests that others had reached the same conclusion. On the other hand, the first three Gospels show no clear indication of Jesus' demand that others accept his own high aspirations that grew out of his self-awareness. Nor can I find any clear sign in the first three Gospels that Jesus spoke about belief in himself. In the Synoptic Gospels Jesus speaks solely of belief in God. After the Resurrection, however, belief in Jesus became essential, as can be seen in numerous New Testament passages.

Despite the difficulty of obtaining an accurate portrayal of Jesus' life and message apart from the Gospels, these two revolutions in early Christianity did not efface the solid tradition of Jesus' teachings.[4] The core of the Gospels is the material that was preserved by Jesus' first disciples. Not long thereafter various individuals began making internal revisions to this precious nucleus of material,[5] and eventually the Evangelists themselves revised and augmented it.[6] Yet Jesus' message was never lost.[7] It can still be heard today — even if it has not been the focus of belief in Christianity

---

3. See Flusser, "Two Anti-Jewish Montages in Matthew," *JOC*, 554-556, where I have re-constructed a larger saying of Jesus against the void of his veneration.

4. I have already discussed this in "The Jewish-Christian Schism: Part 1," *JOC*, 621-625.

5. Compare Papias' statement that has been quoted in Eusebius' *Ecclesiastical History*, III, 39, 16.

6. Compare Luke's prologue to his Gospel (Luke 1:1-4).

7. The modern nostalgia for the early Jewish-Christian sects is not justified. When reading the extant fragments from the Jewish-Christian gospels, one finds there nothing new and important of Jesus' message. Even what we hear about his message in the Synoptic Gospels is nearly absent from the Jewish-Christian gospels — not a word about his message of all-embracing love!

throughout the ages. Over the long history of the Church, however, the religion of Jesus himself did become vital for small groups — to one of these dear groups the present book is dedicated. I hope that somehow in the future the situation will improve, and the Church will begin placing more stress upon Jesus' message.[8]

The last point of this Epilogue is the question of Jesus' Jewishness. I am personally interested in this question because the exegesis of the Gospels is far more determined by prejudices than I once thought. Some exegetical distortions are already reflected in the extant text of the Gospels themselves. Thus, they are quite old. Moreover, I think that many of the false interpretations that have persisted through history have become second nature to most modern scholars, whether they are willing to acknowledge it or not. What I set out to accomplish in this book was sound scholarship in the quest for the historical Jesus, and not simply in the points of his Jewishness.

---

8. See my Nachwort (epilogue) to Martin Buber's *Zwei Glaubensweisen* (Gerlingen: Lambert Schneider, 1994), 187-247. This epilogue has been reprinted in Flusser, *Das essenische Abenteuer* (Winterthur: Cardun Verlag, 1994), 121-153.

Chronological Table

330	Alexander the Great conquered the Persian Empire, which included Palestine.
3rd cent.	Palestine ruled by the Ptolemies of Egypt.
200	The Seleucid Antiochus III (Great) of Syria conquered Palestine.
after 200	The Jewish high priest Simeon the Just.
187-176	The Syrian King Seleucus IV, Philopator. Jesus ben Sira wrote Ecclesiasticus.
176	Antiochus IV, Epiphanes.
c. 175	The scribe Antigonos of Socho.
175	Hellenization of Jerusalem began under the high priests Jason and Menelaus.
168	Rome conquered Macedonia. Roman world-dominion founded.
166	Revolt of the priest Mattathias.
165	After his death, his son Judas Maccabeus continued the revolt. The Book of Daniel written.
164 (early)	Persecution of Jewish faith ended.
164 (late)	Judas took the Temple in Jerusalem. Consecration of the Temple.
161	Judas made an alliance with the Romans.
160	Judas Maccabeus slain, succeeded by his brother Jonathan.
152	Jonathan became high priest.
146	Jonathan died, succeeded by his brother Simon Maccabeus.

134	Simon died.
134-104	Simon succeeded by his son John Hyrcanus I. Toward the end of his reign he left the Pharisees and joined the Sadducees.
104-103	Aristobulus I succeeded John Hyrcanus and was named king. The Essene Judah.
103-76	Alexander Jannaeus, brother of Aristobulus, became high priest and king. He bloodily persecuted the Pharisees.
76-67	His widow, Salome Alexandra, became queen and made the Pharisees the ruling party. Sadducees oppressed. Alexandra's son Hyrcanus II became high priest.
67	Aristobulus II revolted against his brother Hyrcanus and made himself high priest and king after his mother's death. Start of the civil war. Hyrcanus was supported by the Pharisees, Aristobulus by the Sadducees.
65 (early)	Aristobulus besieged in the temple mount by Hyrcanus and his Arabian allies. Honi (Onias) the circle-drawer killed.
64	The Roman general Pompey brought the Syrian Empire of the Seleucids to an end.
63	Pompey in Damascus in early part of year. He arbitrated between the two brothers and decided in favor of Hyrcanus; he imprisoned Aristobulus and conquered Jerusalem in autumn. Judea became a vassal principality of Rome with Hyrcanus II as high priest. Catiline's conspiracy put down in Rome.
47	The Idumean Antipater, father of Herod, installed by Caesar as governor of Judea.
44	Caesar assassinated.
43	Antipater assassinated.
40	Hyrcanus II deposed by the Parthians, who were led by his nephew Antigonus; exiled to Babylon, and executed by Herod in 30 B.C.
37	Antigonus defeated by the Romans, and Herod installed by Anthony as king of Judea (37-4 B.C.).
31	Octavian (late Augustus) defeated Anthony at Actium.
31 B.C.–A.D. 14	Caesar Augustus.
C. 20 B.C.–A.D. 40	The Jewish philosopher Philo of Alexandria.
C. 20 B.C.	The two great Pharisee scribes, Hillel and Shammai.
4 B.C.	Death of Herod the Great. Division of the empire among his sons: Archelaus, ethnarch of Judea, Samaria and Idumea (4 B.C.–A.D. 6); Herod Antipas, tetrarch of Galilee and

	Perea (4 B.C.–A.D. 39); Philip, husband of Salome, tetrarch of the northeast (4 B.C.–A.D. 34)
c. 2	The probable birth of Jesus.

A.D.

6	Banishment of Archelaus. Judea under Roman governors. The Zealot (fanatics) movement founded by Judas the Galilean.
6-15	Annas (Ananos) the Sadducee, father-in-law of Caiaphas, high priest.
14-37	Tiberias Caesar.
c. 18-37	Caiaphas, son-in-law of Annas, high priest. He handed Jesus over to Pilate.
26-36	Pontius Pilate governor of Judea.
28/9	John the Baptist appeared. Baptism of Jesus and beginning of his ministry.
30 (Easter)	Crucifixion of Jesus.
c. 30	The scribe Gamaliel, teacher of St. Paul.
c. 35	Martyrdom of Stephen in Jerusalem.
37-41	Gaius Caligula Caesar.
c. 37-100	The Jewish historian Josephus Flavius.
39	Deposition of Herod Antipas.
41-44	Agrippa I, king of the Jews.
41-54	Claudius Caesar.
44	Judea again under Roman governors.
50-100	Agrippa II, ethnarch; from 53, king of part of northern Palestine.
54-68	Nero Caesar.
62	Annas (Ananos) II, son of Annas I and brother-in-law of Caiaphas, high priest. He had James the brother of the Lord executed.
64	Fire in Rome. Persecution of Christians. Paul and Peter executed in Rome.
66	Insurrection broke out in Palestine.
68	Caesars: Galba, Otto, Vitellius, and finally Vespasian (69-79).
70	Conquest of Jerusalem and destruction of the Temple by Titus, son of Vespasian.

Bibliography

G. Alon. *Jews, Judaism, and the Classical World: Studies in Jewish History in the Times of the Second Temple and Talmud* (Jerusalem: Magnes Press, 1977).

―――. *Studies in Jewish History in the Times of the Second Temple, the Mishna, and the Talmud* (Tel Aviv: ha-Kibuts ha-Me'uhad, 1958).

W. Bacher. *Die Agada der Tannaiten* (2 vols.; Strassburg: K. J. Trübner, 1890-1903).

―――. *Die Agada der Palästinensischen Amoräer* (3 vols.; Strassburg: K. J. Trübner, 1892-1899).

W. Bauer. *Das Leben Jesu im Zeitalter der neutestamentlichen Apokryphen* (Darmstadt: Wissenschaftliche Buchgesellschaft, 1967).

W. Bauer, F. W. Danker, and W. Arndt. *A Greek-English Lexicon of the New Testament and Other Early Christian Literature* (Chicago: University of Chicago Press, 2000).

O. Bauernfeind. *Kommentar und Studien zur Apostelgeschichte* (Tübingen: Mohr, 1980).

P. Benoit. *Jesus and the Gospel* (2 vols.; trans. B. Weatherhead; London: Darton, Longman & Todd, 1973-1974).

―――. "The Archaeological Reconstruction of the Antonia Fortress," in *Jerusalem Revealed* (ed. Y. Yadin; Jerusalem: IES, 1976), 87-89.

J. Blinzler. *Die Brüder und Schwestern Jesu* (Stuttgart: Verlag Katholisches Bibelwerk, 1967).

F. M. Brodie. *No Man Knows My History: The Life of Joseph Smith, the Mormon Prophet* (New York: Knopf, 1971).

M. Broshi. "Excavations in the House of Caiaphas, Mount Zion," in *Jerusalem Revealed: Archaeology in the Holy City, 1968-1974* (ed. Y. Yadin; Jerusalem: IEJ, 1975), 57-60.

M. Broshi and D. Bahat. "Excavations in the Armenian Garden," in *Jerusalem Re-*

vealed: Archaeology in the Holy City, 1968-1974 (ed. Y. Yadin; Jerusalem: IEJ, 1975), 55-56.

R. E. Brown. *The Gospel according to John* (AB 29-29a; 2 vols.; Garden City, N.Y.: Doubleday, 1966-1970).

―――. *The Death of the Messiah: From Gethsemane to the Grave: A Commentary on the Passion Narratives in the Four Gospels* (2 vols.; New York: Doubleday, 1994).

M. Buber. *Zwei Glaubensweisen* (Gerlingen: Lambert Schneider, 1994).

A. Büchler. *Types of Jewish-Palestinian Piety: From 70 B.C.E. to 70 C.E.; The Ancient Pious Men* (New York: Ktav Publishing House, 1968).

R. Bultmann. *History of the Synoptic Tradition* (New York: Harper & Row, 1963).

―――. *Theology of the New Testament* (2 vols.; New York: Scribner, 1951-1955).

J. H. Charlesworth, ed. *The Old Testament Pseudepigrapha* (2 vols.; Garden City, N.Y.: Doubleday, 1983-1985).

L. Clerici. *Einsammlung der Zerstreuten; liturgiegeschichtliche Untersuchung zur Vor- und Nachgeschichte der Fürbitte für die Kirche in Didache 9,4 und 10,5* (Münster: Aschendorffsche Verlagsbuchhandlung, 1966).

H. Conzelmann. *The Theology of St. Luke* (New York: Harper, 1961).

―――. *Die erste Brief an die Korinther* (Göttingen: Vanderhoeck & Ruprecht, 1989).

Ch. Couasnon. *The Church of the Holy Sepulchre in Jerusalem* (London: Oxford University Press for The British Academy, 1974).

J. D. Crossan. *The Historical Jesus: The Life of a Mediterranean Jewish Peasant* (San Francisco: Harper, 1991).

G. Dalman. *Sacred Sites and Ways: Studies in the Topography of the Gospels* (London: Society for Promoting Christian Knowledge, 1935).

―――. *The Words of Jesus Considered in the Light of Post-Biblical Jewish Writings and the Aramaic Language* (Edinburgh: T & T Clark, 1902).

Der Kleine Pauly: Lexikon der Antike (5 vols.; ed. K. Ziegler, W. Sontheimer, H. Gärtner, and A. F. von Pauly; Berlin: Deutscher Taschenbuch Verlag, 1979).

A. Dihle. *Die goldene Regel: eine Einführung in die Geschichte der antiken und frühchristlichen Vulgärethik* (Göttingen: Vandenhoeck & Ruprecht, 1962).

C. H. Dodd. *Historical Tradition in the Fourth Gospel* (New York: Cambridge University Press, 1963).

―――. *The Parables of the Kingdom* (London: Fontana Books, 1961).

Encyclopedia Judaica (ed. C. Roth; Jerusalem: Encyclopedia Judaica, 1972).

J. N. Epstein. *Introduction to Tannaitic Literature: Mishna, Tosephta and Halakhic Midrashim* (Tel Aviv: Devir, 1957).

J. A. Fitzmyer. *The Gospel according to Luke: Introduction, Translation and Notes* (AB 28-28a; 2 vols.; Garden City, N.Y.: Doubleday, 1981-1985).

D. Flusser. *Judaism and the Origins of Christianity: Collected Papers* (Jerusalem: Magnes Press, 1988).

―――. *Entdeckungen im Neuen Testament* (2 vols.; Neukirchen-Vluyn: Neukirchener Verlag, 1987-1999).

―――. *Das essenische Abenteuer: die jüdische Gemeinde vom Toten Meer: Auffälligkeiten bei Jesus, Paulus, Didache und Martin Buber* (Winterthur: Cardun, 1994).

―――. *Das Christentum — eine jüdische Religion* (München: Kösel-Verlag, 1990).

―――. *Bemerkungen eines Juden zur christlichen Theologie* (Munich: Chr. Kaiser, 1984).

―――. *Die rabbinischen Gleichnisse und der Gleichniserzähler Jesus* (Bern: Frankfurt am Main, 1981).

―――, ed. *The Josippon: Edited with an Introduction, Commentary and Notes* (2 vols.; Jerusalem: Bialik Institute, 1980-1981).

―――. "Pharisäer, Sadduzäer und Essener in Pescher Nahum," in *Qumran* (ed. K. E. Grözinger; Darmstadt: Wissenschaftlicher Buchgesellschaft, 1981), 121-166.

―――. "Die Versuchung Jesu und ihr jüdischer Hintergrund," *Judaica* 45 (1989), 111-128.

―――. "Jesus and Judaism," in *Eusebius, Christianity and Judaism* (ed. H. W. Attridge and G. Hata; Detroit: Wayne State University Press, 1992), 80-109.

―――. "'The House of David' on an Ossuary," *Israel Museum Journal* 5 (1986), 37-40.

―――. "Die Sünde gegen den heiligen Geist," *Wie gut Sind deine Zeite, Jaakow . . . : Festschrift zum 60. Geburtstag von Reinhold Mayer* (ed. E. L. Ehrlich, B. Klappert, and U. Ast; Gerlingen: Bleicher, 1986), 139-147.

―――. "Ein Sendschreiben aus Qumran (4QMMT) und der Ketzersegen," *Bulletin der Schweizerischen Gesellschaft für judaistische Forschung* 4 (Basel, 1995), 6-57.

―――. "Die Auslegung der Bibel im NT" and "Die Tora in der Bergpredikt," in *Juden und Christen lesen dieselbe Bibel* (ed. H. Kremers; Duisburg: Braun, 1973), 79-87, 102-113.

―――. "Das Aposteldekret und die Noachitischen Gebote (with Shmuel Safrai)," in *Wer Tora vermehrt, mehrt Leben: Festgabe für Heinz Kremers zum 60. Geburtstag* (eds. E. Brocke and H. J. Barkenings; Neukirchen-Vluyn: Neukirchener Verlag, 1986), 146-193.

―――. "Die Versuchung Jesu und ihr jüdischer Hintergrund," *Judaica* 45 (1989), 110-128.

―――. "'Den Alten ist gesagt' — Interpretation der sogenamuten Antithesen der Bergpredigt," *Judaica* 48 (1992), 35-39.

————. "Jesus and Judaism," in *Eusebius, Christianity and Judaism* (ed. H. W. Attridge and J. Hata; Detroit, 1992), 80-109.

R. T. Fortna. *The Gospel of Signs: A Reconstruction of the Narrative Source Underlying the Fourth Gospel* (London: Cambridge University Press, 1970).

————. *The Fourth Gospel and its Predecessor* (Edinburgh: T & T Clark, 1989).

H. Grotius. *Annotationes ad Novum Testamentum* (Groningen: Ex officina W. Zuidem, 1826-1834).

I. Gruenwald, S. Shaked, and G. A. G. Stroumsa, eds. *Messiah and Christos: Studies in the Jewish Origins of Christianity: Presented to David Flusser on the Occasion of His Seventy-fifth Birthday* (Tübingen: Mohr, 1992).

E. Haenchen. *Die Apostelgeschichte* (Göttingen: Vandenhoeck & Ruprecht, 1959).

E. Hahn. *Christologische Hoheitstitel; ihre Geschichte im frühen Christentum* (Göttingen: Vandenhoeck & Ruprecht, 1964).

A. von Harnack. *Die Mission und Ausbreitung des Christentums in den ersten drei Jahrhunderten* (2 vols.; Leipzig: Hinrichs'sche Buchhandlung 1924).

J. R. Harris. *The Rest of the Words of Baruch: A Christian Apocalypse of the Year 136 A.D.: The Text Revised with an Introduction* (London: Clay, 1889).

M. Hengel. *Die Zeloten: Untersuchungen zur jüdischen Freiheitsbewegung in der Zeit von Herodes I bis 70 n. Chr, Arbeiten zur Geschichte des Spätjudentums und Urchristentums* (2 vols.; Leiden: Brill, 1961).

————. "Jesus, der Messias Israels," in *Messiah and Christos: Studies in the Jewish Origins of Christianity: Presented to David Flusser on the Occasion of His Seventy-fifth Birthday* (ed. I. Gruenwald, S. Shaked, and G. A. G. Stroumsa; Tübingen: Mohr, 1992), 155-176.

E. Hennecke and W. Schneemelcher, eds. *New Testament Apocrypha* (2 vols.; Louisville: Westminster/John Knox Press, 1989-1991).

M. D. Hooker. *Jesus and the Servant: The Influence of the Servant Concept of Deutero-Isaiah in the New Testament* (London: S.P.C.K., 1959).

M. Jastrow. *A Dictionary of the Targumim, the Talmud Babli and Yerushalmi, and the Midrashic literature* (2 vols.; New York: Pardes, 1950).

A. Jaubert. *Épître aux Corinthiens,* Sources chrétiennes no. 167 (Paris: Éditions du Cerf, 1971).

J. Jeremias. *Jerusalem in the Time of Jesus: An Investigation into Economic and Social Conditions during the New Testament Period* (Philadelphia: Fortress Press, 1989).

————. *The Parables of Jesus* (New York: C. Scribner's Sons, 1963).

————. *Abba. Studien zur neutestamentlichen Theologie und Zeitgeschichte* (Göttingen: Vandenhoeck & Ruprecht, 1966).

————. *Unknown Sayings of Jesus* (London: S.P.C.K., 1957).

————. *New Testament Theology* (London: SCM Press, 1971).

W. Klassen. *Judas: Betrayer or Friend of Jesus?* (Minneapolis: Fortress Press, 1996).

Bibliography

C. H. Kraeling. *John the Baptist* (New York: Scribner, 1951).

J. Levy. *Wörterbuch über die Talmudim und Midraschim* (Berlin: B. Harz, 1924).

R. L. Lindsey. *A Hebrew Translation of the Gospel of Mark* (Jerusalem: Dugith Publishers, 1973).

————, ed. *Greek Concordance to the Synoptic Gospels* (3 vols.; Jerusalem: Dugith Publishers, 1985-1989).

E. Lohmeyer. *Das Urchristentum. Johannes der Täufer* (Göttingen: Vandenhoeck, 1932).

J. Maier. *Jesus von Nazareth in der talmudischen Überlieferung* (Darmstadt: Wissenschaftliche Buchgesellschaft, 1978).

I. H. Marshall. *Commentary on Luke: A Commentary on the Greek Text* (Grand Rapids: Eerdmans, 1978).

W. Marxsen. *Der Evangelist Markus* (Göttingen: Vandenhoeck & Ruprecht, 1959).

S. Mason. *Josephus and the New Testament* (Peabody, Mass.: Hendrickson, 1992).

B. M. Metzger, ed. *A Textual Commentary on the Greek New Testament* (London-New York, 1975).

E. Meyer. *Ursprung und Anfänge des Christentums* (Stuttgart-Berlin: J. G. Cotta, 1921-1923).

J. T. Milik. *The Books of Enoch* (Oxford: Clarendon Press, 1976).

F. Millar. "Reflections on the Trial of Jesus," in *A Tribute to Géza Vermès: Essays on Jewish and Christian Literature and History,* Journal for the Study of the Old Testament Supplement series, vol. 100 (ed. P. R. Davies and R. T. White; Sheffield, England: JSOT Press, 1990).

S. Mowinkel. *He That Cometh* (Oxford: Blackwell, 1956).

H. Musurillo, ed. *Acta Alexandrinorum: de mortibus Alexandriae nobilium fragmenta papyracea Graeca* (Leipzig: Teubner, 1961).

J. M. Myers. *I and II Esdras* (AB 42; Garden City, N.Y.: Doubleday, 1974).

K. Niederwimmer. *Die Didache* (Göttingen: Vandenhoeck & Ruprecht, 1989).

R. S. Notley. "The Kingdom of Heaven Forcefully Advances," in *The Interpretation of Scripture in Early Judaism and Christianity: Studies in Language and Tradition,* JSPSS 33 (ed. C. A. Evans; Sheffield: Sheffield Academic Press, 2000), 279-311.

R. S. Notley, M. Turnage, and B. Becker, eds. *Jesus' Last Week: Jerusalem Studies in the Synoptic Gospels — Volume One* (Leiden: Brill, 2006).

R. Otto. *Sünde und urschuld, und andere aufsätze zur theologie* (Munich: Beck, 1932).

S. Pinés. *The Collected Works of Shlomo Pinés: Studies in the History of Religion* (ed. G. G. Stroumsa; Jerusalem: Magnes Press, 1996).

B. Pixner. "Noch einmal das Praetorium, Versuch einer neuen Loesung," *Zeitschrift des Deutschen Palaestina-Vereins* 95 (1979), 57-86.

J. B. Pritchard, ed. *Ancient Near Eastern Texts Relating to the Old Testament* (Princeton: Princeton University Press, 1955).

E. Puech. "Une apocalypse messianique (4Q521)," *RevQ* 15/50 (1992), 475-519.

L. van Puyvelde. *L'Agneau mystique d'Hubert et Jean van Eyck* (Brussels: Meddens, 1964).

L. Ragaz. *Die Gleichnisse Jesu. Seine soziale Botschaft* (Hamburg: Furche-Verlag, 1971).

L. Y. Rahmani. "Jason's Tomb," *IEJ* 17 (1967), 61-100.

A. F. Rainey and R. S. Notley. *The Sacred Bridge: Carta's Atlas of the Biblical World* (Jerusalem: Carta Jerusalem, 2006).

H. M. Reimarus. *Apologie; oder, Schutzschrift für die vernünftigen Verehrer Gottes* (2 vols.; Frankfurt am Main: Insel Verlag, 1972).

R. Riesner. *Jesus als Lehrer: eine Untersuchung zum Ursprung der Evangelien-Uberlieferung* (Tübingen: Mohr, 1981).

S. Ruzer. "The Technique of Composite Citations in the Sermon on the Mount (Matt 5:21-22, 33-37)" *RB* 103 (1996), 65-75.

S. Safrai. "Teaching of Pietists in Mishnaic Literature," *JJS* 16 (1965), 15-33.

———. *Die Wallfahrt im Zeitalter des Zweiten Tempels* (Neukirchen-Vluyn: Neukirchener Verlag, 1981).

———. "Jesus and the Hasidim," *Jerusalem Perspective* 42-44 (January-June, 1994), 3-22.

———. "Jesus and the Hasidic Movement," in *The Jews in the Hellenistic-Roman World, Studies in Memory of Menachem Stern* (ed. A. Oppenheimer, I. Gafni, and D. R. Schwartz; Jerusalem: Zalman Shazar Center, 1996), 413-436 [Hebrew].

S. Safrai, M. Stern, D. Flusser, and W. C. van Unnik, eds. *The Jewish People in the First Century: Historical Geography, Political History, Social, Cultural and Religious Life and Institutions* (2 vols.; Assen: Van Gorcum, 1974-1976).

K. Schlesinger. *Die Gesetzeslehrer; von Schimon dem Wahrhaftigen bis zum Auftreten Hillels* (Berlin: Schocken Verlag, 1934).

K. L. Schmidt. *Der Rahmen der Geschichte Jesu: literarkritische Untersuchungen zur ältesten Jesusüberlieferung* (Darmstadt: Wissenschaftliche Buchgesellschaft, 1964).

H. J. Schoeps. *Das Judenchristentum: Untersuchungen über Gruppenbildungen und Parteikämpfe in der frühen Christenheit* (Bern: Francke, 1964).

———. *Aus früchristlicher Vorzeit, religionsgeschichtliche Untersuchungen* (Tübingen: Mohr, 1950).

E. Schürer. *History of the Jewish People in the Age of Jesus (175 B.C.–A.D. 135)* (4 vols.; ed. G. Vermes and F. Millar; Edinburgh: T & T Clark, 1973-1987).

A. Schweitzer. *In Quest of the Historical Jesus: A Critical Study of Its Progress from Reimarus to Wrede* (New York: Macmillan, 1968).

E. Sjöberg. *Der Menschensohn im äthiopischen Henochbuch* (Lund: C. W. K. Gleerup, 1946).

―――. *Der verborgene Menschensohn in den Evangelien* (Lund: C. W. K. Gleerup, 1955).

O. Skarsaune. *The Proof from Prophecy: A Study in Justin Martyr's Proof-Text Tradition: Text-type, Provenance, Theological Profile*, Supplements to Novum Testamentum, vol. 56 (Leiden: Brill, 1987).

M. Sokoloff. *A Dictionary of Jewish Palestinian Aramaic of the Byzantine Period* (Ramat Gan, Israel: Bar Ilan University Press, 1990).

H. F. D. Sparks, ed. *The Apoocryphal Old Testament* (Oxford: Clarendon Press, 1984).

J. Steinmann. *Johannes der Täufer* (Hamburg: Rowohlt, 1960).

M. Stern, ed. *Greek and Latin Authors on Jews and Judaism* (3 vols.; Jerusalem: Israel Academy of Sciences and Humanities, 1974-1984).

M. Stone. *Fourth Ezra: A Commentary on the Book of Fourth Ezra* (Minneapolis: Fortress Press, 1990).

H. L. Strack and P. Billerbeck. *Kommentar zum Neuen Testament aus Talmud und Midrasch* (München: Beck, 1922-1928).

G. Strecker. *Der Weg der Gerechtigkeit; Untersuchung zur Theologie des Matthäus* (Göttingen: Vandenhoeck & Ruprecht, 1966).

―――. *Das Judenchristentum in den Pseudoklementinen* (Berlin: Akademie-Verlag, 1981).

W. D. Stroker. *Extracanonical Sayings of Jesus* (Atlanta, Ga.: Scholars Press, 1989).

A. Suhl. *Die Funktion der alttestamentlichen Zitate und Anspielungen im Markusevangelium* (Gütersloh: Gütersloher Verlagshaus G. Mohn, 1965).

V. Taylor. *The Gospel according to St. Mark* (London: St. Martin's Press, 1957).

V. A. Tcherikover and A. Fuks, eds. *Corpus Papyrorum Judaicarum* (3 vols.; Cambridge, Mass.: Harvard University Press, 1957-1964).

C. Thoma, S. Lauer, and E. Hanspeter. *Die Gleichnisse der Rabbinen* (Bern: Peter Lang, 1986).

E. E. Urbach. *The Sages* (2 vols.; Jerusalem: Magnes Press, 1979).

W. Ustorf. *Afrikanische Initiative, Das aktive des Propheten Simon Kimbangu* (Bern: Herbert Lang, 1975).

B. M. F. Van Iersel. *'Der Sohn' in den synoptischen Jesusworten; Christusbezeichnung der Gemeinde oder Selbstbezeichnung Jesu? Der Sohn*, NovTSup 3 (Leiden: Brill, 1961).

G. Vermes. *The Complete Dead Sea Scrolls in English* (New York: Penguin Books, 1997).

―――. *Jesus the Jew: A Historian's Reading of the Gospels* (Philadelphia: Fortress Press, 1981).

―――. "Hanina ben Dosa," *JJS* 23 (1972), 28-50.

P. Vielhauer. *Aufsätze zum Neuen Testament* (2 vols.; Munich: Chr. Kaiser Verlag, 1965-1979).

P. Volz. *Eschatologie der jüdischen Gemeinde im neutestamentlichen Zeitalter, nach den Quellen der rabbinischen, apokalyptischen und apokryphen Literatur dargestellt* (Tübingen: Mohr, 1934).

————. *Der Geist Gottes und die verwandten Erscheinungen im Alten Testament und im anschliessenden Judentum* (Tübingen: Mohr, 1910).

J. Wilkinson. *Jerusalem as Jesus Knew It: Archaeology as Evidence* (London: Thames and Hudson, 1978).

P. Winter. *On the Trial of Jesus* (Berlin: De Gruyter, 1961).

Y. Yadin. *The Scroll of the War of the Sons of Light against the Sons of Darkness* (Oxford: Oxford University Press, 1962).

B. H. Young. *Jesus and His Jewish Parables: Rediscovering the Roots of Jesus' Teaching* (New York: Paulist Press, 1989).

————. *Jesus the Jewish Theologian* (Peabody, Mass.: Hendrickson, 1995).

J. Zias and E. Sekeles, "The Crucified Man from Givat ha-Mivtar: A Reappraisal," *IEJ* 35 (1985), 22-27.

M. Zobel. *Gottes Gesalbter der Messias und die messianische zeit in Talmud und Midrasch* (Berlin: Schocken Verlag, 1938).

Index of Subjects

Index of Scripture References